JPS GUIDE

AMERICAN JEWISH FICTION

JPS GUIDE

AMERICAN
JEWISH
FICTION

Josh Lambert

2009 • 5769
Philadelphia
The Jewish Publication Society

JPS is a nonprofit educational association and the oldest and foremost publisher of Judaica in English in North America. The mission of JPS is to enhance Jewish culture by promoting the dissemination of religious and secular works, in the United States and abroad, to all individuals and institutions interested in past and contemporary Jewish life.

The Jewish Publication Society
2100 Arch Street, 2nd floor
Philadelphia, PA 19103
www.jewishpub.org

Design and Composition by Masters Group Design

Manufactured in the United States of America

09 10 11 12   10 9 8 7 6 5 4 3 2 1

Library of Congress Cataloging-in-Publication Data:

Lambert, Joshua N.
  JPS guide : American Jewish fiction / Josh Lambert. — 1st ed.
     p. cm.
  Includes indexes.
  ISBN 978-0-8276-0883-2 (alk. paper)
  1. American fiction—Jewish authors—Stories, plots, etc. 2. American fiction—Jewish authors—History and criticism. I. Title. II. Title: Jewish Publication Society guide.
  PS153.J4L36 2009
  813.009'8924—dc22
                                        2008027299

JPS books are available at discounts for bulk purchases for reading groups, special sales, and fundraising purchases. Custom editions, including personalized covers, can be created in larger quantities for special needs. For more information, please contact us at marketing@jewishpub.org or at this address: 2100 Arch Street, Philadelphia, PA 19103.

CONTENTS

CONTENTS *(continued)*

CONTENTS *(continued)*

CONTENTS *(continued)*

CONTENTS *(continued)*

Appendixes

Indexes

To my parents and grandparents

ACKNOWLEDGMENTS

By exposing me to the vast and wonderful world of modern Jewish literature, my teachers—particularly Maxine Rodburg and Ruth Wisse at Harvard, and Anita Norich, Jonathan Freedman, and Julian Levinson at the University of Michigan—inspired this book. The financial support of the Frankel Center for Judaic Studies at the University of Michigan allowed me to undertake this project while researching and writing a doctoral dissertation. Carolyn Hessel of the Jewish Book Council graciously mentored me throughout the writing of this book, as she has guided me throughout my career as a reviewer of Jewish books and book review editor. The depth and breadth of my coverage of American Jewish fiction across its periods and languages would not have been possible without advice and suggestions from a generous group of scholars, writers, and journalists: Ken Gordon, Mikhail Krutikov, Dan Miron, Shachar Pinsker, Eileen Pollack, Derek P. Royal, Alan Wald, and Paul Zakrzewski. I'm grateful to them, and, of course, responsibility for any egregious omissions, eccentric choices, or errors of fact or interpretation rests solely with me. In my research, I relied on the collections of Harvard's Widener Library, the University of Michigan's Hatcher Library, and the extensive personal library of Susan and Stephen Kippur. Daniel Mintz and Benjamin Pollak read the manuscript and offered crucial feedback. Lisa Bankoff and Tina Dubois Wexler provided key practical advice. Norman H. Finkelstein, the series editor of the JPS Guides, shepherded this project into being, while the staff of The Jewish Publication Society in Philadelphia—Carol Hupping, Janet Liss, Julia Oestreich, Laurie Schlesinger, Robin Norman, and others—honor their organization's century-long history with their professionalism and passion for Jewish books. I am grateful that my parents and siblings exposed me to the texts and practices of a modern Jew and that they have supported this project as they have all my academic and professional undertakings. Finally, my astonishing wife, Sara Kippur, as per her usual, contributed to this book in ways too numerous to list; her willingness to proofread at any moment and the acuteness of her editorial eye will never cease to amaze me.

INTRODUCTION

If you've picked up this guide then you must already have some sense for what American Jewish fiction is or at least for what you'd like it to be. And so, rather than bogging you down with definitional quibbles, let me begin with some of the historical context for American Jewish fiction. Then I'll sketch a few of the fundamental themes you will encounter as you wander through the pages that follow (and through the literature itself), and I'll end by enumerating the sorts of books that have been left out for reasons of space or coherence. In the process, this introduction will endeavor to provide along the way a sense for what American Jewish fiction has meant, and could mean, to readers like you and me.

A Little History

According to the leading literary critics of the 20th century, American Jewish fiction did not begin in earnest until the 1950s, when books by Saul Bellow, Bernard Malamud, and Philip Roth won reviewer's plaudits and a spate of national prizes, while less sophisticated fictions by Leon Uris and Herman Wouk, among others, lit up the country's bestseller lists. This moment has often been referred to as the "breakthrough," when American Jewish writing exploded into the mainstream. These critics proclaimed that there had been a vibrant Yiddish literary culture anchored in Eastern Europe and perhaps a few gestures in the direction of American Jewish fiction in the late 19th century and the early 20th—maybe even a couple of lost American Jewish masterpieces that had never found the audiences they deserved—but nothing even worth comparing to the robust Jewish literary expression that flowered in English in the years following World War II.

The only problem with this story is that it is wrong. For one thing, Jewish novels began to be written in and about America by the final third of the 19th century. In 1918, when a rabbi in Cincinnati published a bibliography of English-language fiction about Jewish life in the United States, some 70 novels and short story collections already fit the bill. Then, instead of slowing down, Jewish literary production boomed in the 1920s, as Jews took on pivotal roles in the world of New York publishing. Dynamic entrepreneurs including Alfred Knopf, Ben Huebsch, Horace Liveright, Richard Simon, and Bennett Cerf, who founded the most important and prestigious American publishing houses of the 20th century, were ambivalent about their religious and ethnic backgrounds, but they printed and sold a flood of novels by and about Jews, many of which found favor with audiences and were even adapted, like Anzia Yezierska's early books, into the movies. In the 1930s, Jewish novelists influenced by Marxist and leftist politics produced a handful of stunning works of art as well as a veritable mountain of proletarian stories ranging from the mediocre to the execrable. In the 1940s a number of Jewish novels became blockbusters—as big or bigger than the bestsellers that would appear to much fanfare a decade later—including Sholem Asch's controversial take on the life of Jesus Christ and Norman Mailer's career-making debut, *The Naked and the Dead.* There can be no denying that the American Jewish fiction produced in the 1950s and early 1960s was extraordinary in its ambition and achievement—that it set new standards for the field that would be influential for decades to follow. But the same could be said of the work published in the 1920s, or the 1970s, or almost any decade of the 20th century. To deny the richness of American Jewish fiction before mid-century—as some astute critics, such as Lionel Trilling, have at times done—is simply to ignore the beginning of the story.

A similarly pervasive, similarly misguided perception has Yiddish literature predating American Jewish literature in English and then slowly dying out, as if Yiddish were English's doddering old country *zayde.* Again, facts belie this myth: the first American Jewish novel in English worth mentioning, Nathan Mayer's *Differences* (1867), appeared *before* the vast majority of modern literary works in Jewish languages, including the foundational texts in modern Hebrew and Yiddish through which S. Y. Abramovitch, also known as Mendele Mocher Sforim, more or less established the possibility for viable literatures in those languages. In the United States, English and Yiddish writing developed in rough parallel, with writers in both tongues experimenting during the same decades with the same techniques of naturalism and modernism. Sometimes the Yiddishists treated a topic first—as they did, for example, with representations of the Holocaust or, as they called it, *khurbn*—but sometimes English-language writers beat them to it, as with the immigration sagas. It's a tragic fact that Yiddish suffered a tremendous loss of readers in World War II, as so many of the world's Yiddish speakers were butchered by the Nazis. Still, it was during the postwar decades that several masterworks of American Yiddish fiction by the likes of Isaac Bashevis Singer and Chaim Grade were first published. The crucial point here is that Yiddish fiction thrived for many decades in the United States, and it constitutes a much larger portion of American Jewish fiction than critics and readers have acknowledged.

One could argue, in fact, that the two most salient requirements for the production of American Jewish fiction—a potential audience and creative motivation—emerged during the 1880s, at precisely the moment that the immigration of Yiddish-speaking Jews to the United States swung into high gear. In 1885, a non-Jewish writer named Henry Harland explained, in a letter to his godfather, why he took on the pseudonym Sidney Luska (which to him sounded Jewish) for the sake of marketing his new novel, *As It Was Written.* "With a Jewish name on the title page," Harland wrote, "the sale of the book would be vastly increased. I believe lots of Jews would buy it for that reason, if for no other—for the sake of seeing what New York can produce in the way of a truly Jewish story." He seems to have been right—*As It Was Written* sold some 50,000 copies—and what Harland's case makes clear is that well before the beginning of the 20th century enough folks wanted to read Jewish novels that marketing a book to them constituted a viable business plan. American publishers noticed, and they have been printing and selling books by and about Jews ever since.

Knowing a market exists is one thing, of course, and figuring out what that market wants or needs is quite another. The second suggestive development of the 1880s was the widespread establishment of Jewish libraries, literary societies, and cultural institutions in the United States. Resembling their counterparts in Europe, these organizations aimed to combat the fractiousness of the American Jewish community that seemed to be increasing as Portuguese, German, and Russian Jews found themselves more and more frequently bickering about matters of practice and propriety. (Sidney Nyburg's *The Chosen People* [1917] and Vera Caspary's *Thicker Than Water* [1934] both depict such intra-community tensions.) Of particular note among the resulting institutions was the Jewish Publication Society (JPS), which was founded in 1888 in Philadelphia. Today it is one of the oldest surviving nonprofit book firms in the country and also the publisher of this guide book.

Not unlike our contemporary Jewish Book Council, which assists in the administration of dozens of literary festivals across the country and awards annual prizes to Jewish books, the literary societies of the 1880s were established according to a belief that literary culture could, in the words of the JPS founders, "enlist the sympathy of all, even the most rigidly orthodox, and even the most wildly radical," and "form a meeting point of intellectual kinship to those who, on religious and doctrinal grounds, are most wildly and bitterly dissevered." In other words, the founders of JPS believed that Jews who wouldn't pray together, vote together, or even eat together might be able to read together. Or at least they could read and laugh at and be scandalized by the same shelf of books. In this sense the publishing of American Jewish fiction, and literature more broadly, has been a modern gloss on the ancient cultural practice in which Jews living very different lives in dissimilar locations have read and responded in diverse ways to the very same Torah and Talmud.

By a similar token, it should not be forgotten that beginning with what Christians refer to as the Old Testament, non-Jews have always found Jewish books an efficient way to learn about Jewish life and to enrich their perspectives on their own experiences. "Our career in the past and our activity in the present cannot be adequately set forth either to our own community or to our neighbors without a literature," the founders of JPS noted, and the goal of explaining Jewish life to other Americans had become especially pressing in the 1880s because of the rise of anti-Semitism in Germany and Russia. What better way to help non-Jews understand what the Jews are all about than presenting them with brilliant novelistic treatments of the Jewish experience in the United States?

Between overcoming Jewish infighting and combating anti-Semitism, the nascent American Jewish literary culture had its work cut out for it. One could debate, in retrospect, whether any publishing house or journal, no matter how well-funded or intelligently operated, could live up to such lofty goals—but more important for the purposes of this guide, these historical details indicate that in the United States, at least since the 1880s, there has been a general recognition of the potential readership for Jewish novels as well as compelling reasons to publish such books. The continued vitality of the field in the past century and a quarter suggests that while the demographics and motivations that make American Jewish fiction viable as an enterprise may have transformed dramatically over the years, they have never disappeared.

Immigration

The beginnings of American Jewish fiction matter, but the fictions discussed in this guide cannot be sensibly considered outside of their own specific historical contexts, whether those are the early 20th century or the early 21st. The novel as an art form has always been structured as much by political and historical concerns, and by the rhythms of common speech, as it is by aesthetic and symbolic investments and experiments. And despite reasonable claims to the contrary—in a fracas in the mid-1970s with the literary scholar Ruth Wisse, Cynthia Ozick objected that "fiction is *not* sociology, but *something else*"—American Jewish fiction has always reflected the patterns and movements of American Jewish life. How else could we explain the seemingly obsessive rewriting of stories on a scant handful of themes—immigration and intermarriage being the two most prominent examples—except as a reflection of the deep and pervasive importance those concerns have had in the lives and histories of American Jewish readers and writers?

Take immigration, for example. There's a classic plotline of American Jewish fiction: difficult childhood in Eastern Europe, voyage to the United States, obstacles along the way, and some sort of eventual success or failure to adjust to the new homeland. Among the earliest authors of stories on this model were a few heavyweight champions of the literary world: Abraham Cahan covered the topic in *Yekl* (1896) and *The Rise of David Levinsky* (1917), Sholem Aleichem described a plucky child's immigration in *Motl, the Cantor's Son* (1907–16), and Franz Kafka imagined a teenager's travels in *Amerika* (1927). Yet, as if those masters hadn't already done the immigrant journey justice, Ludwig Lewisohn included the same narrative in his capacious *The Island Within* (1928), and the poet Charles Reznikoff set coming to America as the elided center of his lyrical *By the Waters of Manhattan* (1930). Immigration serves only as a frame and subtext in Henry Roth's *Call It Sleep* (1934), but it takes center stage again in I. J. Singer's *The Family Carnofsky* (1943) and, in a historical treatment of the very first Jewish immigrants to America, in Louis Zara's *Blessed Is the Land* (1955). Raymond Federman leaps through formal hoops of his own making to avoid telling a straight immigration story in *Double or Nothing* (1971), while Lore Segal presents an immigrant's education as charming comedy in *Her First American* (1985), harking back at times to the language play of Leo Rosten's unintentional night school wits in *The Education of H*Y*M*A*N K*A*P*L*A*N* (1937). At the end of the 20th century, the immigrant story seemed more seductive than ever, reflecting recent waves of immigration from new Old Countries such as Cuba, as in Achy Obejas's *Days of Awe* (2000); Iran, as in Gina Nahai's *Moonlight on the Avenue of Faith* (1999); and, most prominently and repeatedly, post–Soviet Russia, as in Gary Shteyngart's hilarious *The Russian Debutante's Handbook* (2002) and Anya Ulinich's equally irreverent *Petropolis* (2007).

The focus on immigration is not, of course, difficult to explain. Everyone had to come to the United States from somewhere (except for aboriginals and Native Americans, who have for this reason been fetishized by European Americans, Jewish and non-Jewish alike). Any interest in an American's origins or history leads inevitably across an ocean, sooner or later, and American Jews have seized upon the search for origins—whether real, or imagined, as in Jonathan Safran Foer's *Everything Is Illuminated* (2002)—as a consistently compelling project.

Assimilation and Intermarriage

Meanwhile, as Jewish novelists sought out ancestors, they have also attempted to understand their relations with non-Jewish Americans. Indeed, the single most consistent topic in American Jewish fiction is exogamy—that is, marriage outside the faith. As Leslie Fiedler noticed back in the 1950s, it is not surprising that the American Jewish novel "must be a problem novel, and its essential problems must be identity and assimilation. . . . What is unexpected is that these problems be posed in terms of sexual symbols. . . . [I]t is in the role of passionate lover that the American-Jewish novelist sees himself . . . and the community with which he seeks to unite himself he sees as the *shikse* [non-Jewish girl]." There's just one necessary emendation to Fiedler's perspicacious insight: Jewish women novelists have been just as likely as their male counterparts to write stories of exogamy, and those books usually allegorize the Jewish community as a desirable Jewish woman and the American community as a pursuing *sheygets* [non-Jewish man]— which puts a different spin on what Fiedler calls "assimilation," one that helps to complicate his terms: when Jews and Americans come together to produce a new cultural hybrid, who's assimilating whom, exactly?

In fact, the first full-fledged example of this subgenre is Emma Wolf's *Other Things Being Equal* (1892), which features a French-born Jewess considering the attention of a gallant doctor, and Anzia Yezierska treats the subject with characteristic emotional intensity in *Salome of the Tenements* (1923). At least another half dozen or so novels from the first half of the century dramatize the conflicts of American Jewish life through the metaphor of an amorous relationship, such as Ezra Brudno's *The Tether* (1908), Lewisohn's *The Island Within* (1928), and Sholem Asch's *East River* (1948).

The apotheosis of this subgenre occurred in two novels that appeared in the late 1950s and the late 1960s: Myron S. Kaufmann's *Remember Me to God* (1957), a major bestseller, and Philip Roth's *Portnoy's Complaint* (1969), which was nothing less than a cultural phenomenon. Kaufmann's characters spin out their ideas about intermarriage at tremendous length, considering just about every possible angle on the question, while Portnoy—who, yes, spends much of his time talking about masturbation—must be understood as a character whose concern with his sexual opportunities functions as a wry and bombastic commentary on the possibilities and challenges of Jewish identity in the United States: "To me," Portnoy observes, after all, "America is a *shikse*."

Later novels—most often written by women—employ a similar approach to explore the relations, potential and actual, between Jews and other American minority groups. This is one reading of Erica Jong's *Fear of Flying* (1973), Susan Fromberg Schaeffer's *Mainland* (1985), Segal's *Her First American* (1985), Binnie Kirshenbaum's *A Disturbance in One Place* (1994), and Eileen Pollack's *Paradise, New York* (1998), all of which describe Jewish women attracted to Chinese American, Italian American, or African American beaux. The heroine of Allegra Goodman's *Paradise Park* (2001) samples from a vast assortment of American male types, including a military man, a biologist, and a Hawaiian Christian, before settling down—like so many of her predecessors—with a nice Jewish boy.

Of course, American Jewish identity can be explored in fiction without recourse to the representation of interethnic affairs. Occasionally a Jewish hero chooses between several Jewish partners, representing paths *within* the community: in Cahan's *Yekl*, between Old-Country values or immigrant mobility; in David Pinski's *Arnold Levenberg* (1928), between dissolute bourgeois indulgence and Yiddish political activism; in Isaac Bashevis Singer's *Shadows on the Hudson* (1957–58), between potential partners representing different sects or philosophies or idiosyncratic slices of Jewish experience. Not dispensing with romance but shifting it out of the spotlight, Gish Jen's *Mona in the Promised Land* (1996) explores the question of what it means to be an American Jew through the comic tale of a Chinese American convert, while Isaac Raboy's *Jewish Cowboy* (1942) dispatches its hero to a North Dakota ranch to discover if he can become American through manual labor. Tobias Wolff's *Old School* (2003), meanwhile, refracts the question of identity through the act of writing itself, as his teenage protagonist wonders what it would mean to write a story claiming his Jewishness.

Politics and Ideologies

For many of the writers discussed here, identity is more about what you do or what you profess than where you were born. From its beginnings, American Jewish fiction has been a vehicle for the expression of political programs and ideologies. In the late 19th and early 20th centuries, the ideology was most often socialism and, even more specifically, unionism: Edward King's *Joseph Zalmonah* (1893) is a non-Jewish journalist's glowing portrait of a Robin Hood–like labor leader, and though the organizer at the center of Beatrice Bisno's *Tomorrow's Bread* (1938) can't stop sleeping around on his wife, he stays steadfastly loyal to his union. Sometimes mistaken as anti-Semitic propaganda, another batch of novels—Samuel Ornitz's *Haunch, Paunch and Jowl* (1923), Jerome Weidman's *I Can Get It for You Wholesale* (1937), and Budd Schulberg's *What Makes Sammy*

Run? (1941) are the best examples—manifest their sympathy with socialist causes covertly by presenting nightmarish portraits of capitalist exploiters. As one of the characters in Daniel Fuchs's *Summer in Williamsburg* (1934) puts it, "Everybody who makes money hurts people."

By mid-century, Jewish writers began to use their novels to promote a broader range of political and religious values. Irving Shulman's pulpy *The Amboy Dukes* (1947), about vicious Jewish street gangs, aimed to spur educational and real estate policy reform, just as Upton Sinclair's muckraking *The Jungle* (1906), which focuses on non-Jewish Ukranian immigrants to Chicago, had led to the creation of the Food and Drug Administration. Herman Wouk's *Marjorie Morningstar* (1955) can be read as an extended tract against premarital sex, and it would be difficult to read Leon Uris's *Exodus* (1958) as anything but a rallying cry for American Zionism. As young Jewish activists reevaluated the previous generation's commitments in the 1960s, novels about ideology became more ambivalent, as in E. L. Doctorow's *The Book of Daniel* (1971), Irvin Faust's *A Star in the Family* (1975), Joseph Heller's *Good as Gold* (1979), and Philip Roth's *American Pastoral* (1997), which represent American politics as dangerous or absurd. A different reaction to the politics of the 1960s, Mark Helprin's *Refiner's Fire* (1977), meanwhile, provides a revealing glimpse into the formation of the neoconservative imagination, which is certainly one of the crucial developments in American Jewish thought and culture of the late 20th century.

Movements

Other sociological trends from the final third of the 20th century also make strong appearances in these fictions, belying Irving Howe's infamous *kvetch* that once the immigrant experience faded from the memories of American Jews, they would no longer be able to produce a valuable literature. Prominent among the recent concerns has been the expansion of Jewish religious institutions and the increasing institutional domination of Orthodoxy in American Jewish life. Conservative and Reform Judaism pop up occasionally, usually in books with rabbi protagonists, such as Harry Kemelman's *Friday, the Rabbi Slept Late* (1964) and Jonathan Rosen's *Joy Comes in the Morning* (2004), while the new spiritualist movements of the 1970s and afterward have been represented in experimental works such as E. M. Broner's *A Weave of Women* (1978). Beginning with Chaim Potok's novels, meanwhile, and continuing in the work of younger authors including Faye Kellerman, Ehud Havazelet, Pearl Abraham, Nathan Englander, and Tova Mirvis, American ultra-Orthodox and modern Orthodox Jews have been represented with the artistic techniques—realistic, magical, nostalgic, or satirical—that have long been conventional in fiction about secular American Jews. As in earlier contributions such as Isaac Rosenfeld's *Passage from Home* (1946) and Ben Field's *Jacob's Son* (1971), the attitudes of this recent wave of fiction range from longings for a lost pious past to outright rejections of the promises of religion.

The Holocaust and Israel

For at least the past 60 years, meanwhile, the American Jewish community has found itself increasingly enthralled by two other issues, the Holocaust and Israel, and both of these are thoroughly treated in fiction. The persecution and murder of the Jews by the Nazis informs books such as Edward Lewis Wallant's *The Pawnbroker* (1961), Raymond Federman's *Double or Nothing* (1971), Arthur A. Cohen's *In the Days of Simon Stern* (1973), Cynthia Ozick's *The Shawl* (1989), and Jonathan Safran Foer's *Everything Is Illuminated* (2002) as well as hundreds of other novels excluded here because they are set mostly or entirely in Eastern Europe, and including such worthwhile works as André Schwarz-Bart's *The Last of the Just* (1959), and Susan Fromberg Schaeffer's *Anya* (1974)—not to mention memoirs or the tens of thousands of video testimonies.

Fictions about Israel, written by American Jews, have likewise been popular. The Land of Milk and Honey serves as a minor or peripheral setting in many American Jewish novels, and Zionism, as a powerful if not always central belief. In others, such as Leon Uris's blockbuster *Exodus* (1958) or Philip Roth's dizzying *Operation Shylock* (1993), the question of Jewish life in the American Diaspora has been treated as implicitly tied up in the affairs of the State of Israel. These concerns haven't played out just in fiction, but reflect larger trends within American political and social history: many cities in the United States have Holocaust memorials, and the political relationship between the United States and Israel has been a significant investment on the part of American politicians in recent decades.

Eclectic Visions and Revisiting Old Themes

Not all of the books discussed in this guide can be categorized easily: not all are *about* Israel or intermarriage, ideology or immigration—and, in a sense, novels aren't *about* anything at all, except the individual stories they tell and the words they arrange into meaningful patterns. The bizarre Master Yehudi in Paul Auster's *Mr. Vertigo* (1994) fits no model, nor does the lyric mysticism in Paul Goodman's *The Break-Up of Our Camp and Other Stories* (1949) or the historical fantasias of Ben Katchor's *The Jew of New York* (1998). Even piling on further categories to the list of motifs and themes articulated here (perhaps the city, the family, education, food, or art) wouldn't establish a pigeonhole for every one of the remarkably varied fictions discussed. So many of the books—especially the short story collections, which are eclectic by nature—touch on several of these themes, or all of them, within a scant few pages, and then move on to something else. While it is useful to note the consistencies in the field over more than a century, the more noteworthy phenomenon, as far as most readers are concerned, is the zealous drive with which writers have managed, over and over again, to transform the same old experiences into new, unpredictable, and revelatory narratives.

What You Can Expect Here

Immigration and cultural development, politics and religion, Zionism and the Holocaust—you'll encounter them all, repeatedly, in the novels and short stories discussed in this guide book. Each entry that follows introduces you to one of these books and to its author, gives you a sense for what might be worth attention in that particular work of fiction, and—when it's relevant—provides background information on the reception or composition of the book. Every entry includes a "further reading" section to point you onward to other titles by or about the author or to novels that are comparable thematically or stylistically. These entries are organized chronologically, starting in the mid-19th century and ending with novels published in 2007.

That's what you'll find in this guide. The rest of this section of the introduction outlines what's *not* here: the many deserving and worthwhile sorts of books that could not be covered due to concerns of space, coherence, and the author's sanity.

First of all, this guide has had to define "American" as relating to the United States of America, a choice that won't make sense to everyone. (Try telling a Jew from Montreal or Montevideo that he or she doesn't live in America—you might get a funny look.) What this means is that superb works of North American Jewish literature—the novels of Canadians such as Mordecai Richler, Adele Wiseman, A. M. Klein, Aryeh Lev Stollman, and David Bezmozgis as well as Mexicans such as Rosa Nissan—and the extraordinarily robust Latin American literature published in Yiddish, Spanish, and Portuguese, have all been summarily excluded. Readers interested in these fields are encouraged—please!—to seek out resources such as Michael Greenstein's *Contemporary Jewish Writing in Canada* (2004), the Jewish Latin America series published by the University of New Mexico Press, and the online bibliography of Latin American Jewish literature maintained by the UCLA library.

Second, novels with nothing to say about the United States—even if they were written by American Jews—have mostly been left out. No guide could cover every piece of American fiction that happens to have been written by a Jew, so this one focuses on those that relate directly or indirectly to the experiences of Jews in America. A few exceptions have been made for Milton Steinberg's *As a Driven Leaf* (1939) and Howard Fast's *My Glorious Brothers* (1948), both of which take place in Palestine, centuries before the New World was even a twinkle in the European explorers' eyes; for Leon Uris's Zionist epic, *Exodus* (1958), set in Europe and Palestine and never setting foot on American soil; and for Chaim Grade's *Tsemakh Atlas/The Yeshiva* (1967-68), which concerns life in Eastern Europe. These books have been included according to the notion that their composition and reception in the United States reveal essential truths about Jewish experience in this country. Many other novels could have been added following the same logic—retellings of Torah stories such as Anita Diamant's blockbuster *The Red Tent* (1997); historical fictions about Jewish life set in medieval or early modern Europe or during the Holocaust or the Spanish Inquisition; science fiction tales of Jews in space—but these have been left out so as to maintain focus on the representation of American Jewish life. The "further reading" sections for *As a Driven Leaf* and Marge Piercy's *He, She, and It* (1991) point to some bibliographical resources for Jewish historical and science fiction, though.

On the other side of the coin, this guide excludes books that do not mention Jews. It's enchanting to learn that the children's book series *Curious George* was dreamed up by two German-born refugees from Nazi-era Paris who escaped by bicycle and eventually settled in Cambridge, Massachusetts, but it would be a stretch—and a disturbing one, at that—to identify the curious little monkey as somehow Jewish himself, just because of the heritage of his creators. With this principle in mind, this guide has avoided interpreting Jewishness into books where it does not already inhere, or has not been noticed by critics, simply on the basis of an author's Jewish lineage. With the possible exception of two short novels by Nathanael West, *Miss Lonelyhearts* (1933) and *The Day of the Locust* (1939), which mention Jews in passing, and Kafka's *Amerika*, this guide focuses on fictions with something explicit, if often ambivalent, to say about Jewish people. On the basis of this criterion, the guide also happily includes novels by non-Jewish authors, such as Edward King, John Updike, and Gish Jen, that feature American Jews in prominent, rather than marginal, roles. For a survey of the importance of minor Jewish characters in canonical American fiction, see Appendix A.

This guide covers fiction and *only* fiction, which means no poetry, no drama, and no autobiography. The first two genres are easy to distinguish from book-length fiction: rarely do readers confuse a sonnet with a novel. Memoir and autobiography, in contrast, are hard to tell apart from fiction, and for good reason. Even the most scrupulous autobiographer cannot help stretching, or distorting, the truth on occasion—a point made resoundingly in one of the crucial American Jewish autobiographies, Mary Antin's *The Promised Land* (1912). As the literary scholar Werner Sollors has pointed out, Antin remarked, after having been informed that the flowers she remembered from her Russian girlhood as having been dahlias were actually poppies, that it didn't matter: "I have nothing against poppies. It is only that my illusion is more real to me than reality." Few memoirists can claim that they have never chosen a foggy memory over an unrecoverable fact, so all autobiographies, once you scratch the surface, look a little like novels. Several works discussed here could be said to participate in the genre-bending category of "autofiction"—part memoir, part invention, very much a recognition of the challenges inherent in the autobiographical genre—including Chaim Grade's *The Yeshiva*, Leslie Epstein's *San Remo Drive* (2003), and a couple of novels that are formally autofictional in that their main characters share the names of their authors: Philip Roth's *Operation: Shylock* and Jonathan Safran Foer's *Everything Is Illuminated*. Still, whatever might be said of their veracity or lack thereof, works that have conventionally been published and discussed as factual—such as Elie Wiesel's *Night* (1958), Art Spiegelman's *Maus* (1986–91), and John Sanford's five-volume *Scenes from the Life of an American Jew* (1985–91)—have not been covered here.

Hewing to a principle established by JPS in 1888, this guide discusses only those novels and short story collections that are available in English, whether because they were originally published in that language or because they have been translated. Unfortunately, this means that many Yiddish and Hebrew novels about America that have not yet been rendered into English have once again been marginalized. This is a tremendous shame, and it emphasizes a flaw in the way publishers have approached the translation of Jewish literature for American audiences. If we're going to go to the trouble of translating a novel from Hebrew, publishers have seemed to feel, it had better be a quintessential expression of Israeli culture, or if the book is coming from Yiddish, it must evoke the lost world of Eastern Europe for its readers. Such an attitude not only misrepresents literary geography—erroneously relegating Hebrew to the Middle East and Yiddish to Europe—but also cheats readers of splendid novels. Those who can read in Hebrew or Yiddish should consult Appendix B, and those who can't should pester any publishers they happen to meet to pursue more translations into English of American novels in Yiddish and Hebrew.

Unlike most bibliographical resources, each entry in this guide discusses not an author's complete works but a single book. The advantage of this arrangement is that novelists who published only one relevant title can be included here just as easily as authors who returned to American Jewish themes again and again throughout their careers; this allows for broader and more eclectic coverage than most bibliographic guides. On the flip side, less attention is devoted to major authors than they deserve: a fan of Philip Roth might bristle at only four of his books being covered ("How could you leave out *Sabbath's Theater*, *The Human Stain*, or *The Ghostwriter*?"), and similar objections could be made by partisans of Saul Bellow, Cynthia Ozick, and other major authors who get just one mention. However, once you've discovered Roth or Bellow or Ozick, it shouldn't be hard to find more of his or her work—every librarian will be able to show you half a dozen relevant titles—while many other authors, such as Vera Caspary, would be difficult to discover on one's own. One of this book's primary goals is to alert readers to less famous figures—the Jo Sinclairs and Raymond Federmans—whom they might not otherwise encounter. While this guide can't claim to be comprehensive, let alone exhaustive—and while my own biases and predilections are reflected in the selections—I do hope to point an average reader to enough fiction to keep him or her busy for years. If you happen to be a bibliographic junkie or are looking for information about a specific author not covered here, Appendix C provides a list of resources to consult.

11

Finally, books have been excluded if they are simply too hard for an average reader to locate. A decade ago, that condition might have meant that all out-of-print books would be disqualified, but because of the way the Internet has transformed the sale and distribution of used trade books, many out-of-print novels are now just a few mouse clicks away. The only books that have been excluded on the grounds of scarcity, then, are those that are truly rare—like Aben Kandel's *Rabbi Burns* (1931), Konrad Bercovici's *Main Entrance* (1932), Melvin Levy's *The Last Pioneers* (1937), and the multivolume Polonsky family saga that established Charles Angoff as a major voice in American Jewish letters—in the sense that they can be found in few libraries and cannot readily be purchased through online booksellers for the cost of a new hardcover.

Using the international library catalog WorldCat, librarians at your local public library or university can track down nearby copies of just about every book discussed below, and with websites like Bookfinder, ABEBooks, Alibris, and Amazon, you will in most cases be able to purchase a copy of your own, often for less than the cost of a brand-new book, occasionally as little as four dollars, shipping included. Even better, virtually all of the books discussed here that were first published before the year 1923—and are therefore no longer protected by copyright—can be downloaded, for free, from one of the many services that digitizes old books. As of this writing, Nathan Mayer's *Differences* is available only through the Wright American Fiction Project, hosted by Indiana University (http://purl.dlib.indiana.edu/iudl/wright2/wright2-1686), but most of the others can be found on Google Books (http://books.google.com), Microsoft's Live Search (http://books.live.com), and Project Gutenberg (http://gutenberg.org). Many relevant books were also digitized by Harvard University Library's Open Collections project, *Immigration to the United States, 1789–1930;* check the Harvard library catalog, HOLLIS (accessible at http://lib.harvard.edu), for links to the individual titles.

If you're struggling to track down a copy of one of the books mentioned in this guide, or if you feel—as I expect almost every reader will feel—that a particular author or novel has been unfairly neglected, or if you would like to discuss your responses to these novels with other readers of American Jewish fiction, please visit this book's companion website, http://AmericanJewishFiction.com, where you'll be able to do all of these things and contribute to a collaboratively edited bibliography of American Jewish fiction that will become, with your help, a truly exhaustive resource.

. . .

Nu, what exactly is American Jewish fiction, then? Why have the books in this field won so many prizes, sold so many copies, and influenced so many writers in the United States and around the world? Who is American Jewish fiction for, and what does it do?

The best way to answer these questions is simple: Read the books. You'll quickly figure out what American Jewish fiction means to you.

~Titles~

. . . .

1 ~ *Differences*

By Nathan Mayer

BLOCH AND CO., 1867. 462 PAGES.

By the second page of Nathan Mayer's novel *Differences*, the reader has learned that Louis Welland hails from Germany and that he has, therefore, a poetic and slightly foolish temperament. A couple of pages later, the narrator enumerates Welland's physical characteristics, which include "the chest of a Hercules" as well as "that elegance of appearance, which results from perfect symmetry of form"—in other words, he's a looker. Coyly, though, Mayer withholds until page 48 the fact that Welland—respectful, honest, courageous—also happens to be Jewish, and, when he reveals his faith to the Goldmans, a family of his coreligionists in northeastern Tennessee, they respond with "a pause of astonishment," as if to say: *You? Really? You're Jewish?*

Welland soon tumbles into love with Antonia, the Goldmans' beautiful and literary-minded daughter (she's a fan of Goethe and George Sand), but, in the fashion of traditional romances (not to mention contemporary romantic comedies), circumstances conspire to keep the lovers apart. As the tensions of the 1860s mount, local rabble accuse Welland of abolitionism and then chase him out of Tennessee. After his arrival in New York, miscommunications and the jealousy of Antonia's brother Charles convince Antonia that Welland is two-timing her. Soon the Civil War breaks out, and Welland fights on the side of Union, while Antonia, a loyal Southern belle, cheers on the Confederate troops. Thanks to Welland's unflinching gentlemanliness, though, all of the issues are eventually resolved, and the book ends with the coming together not only of the Union and Confederacy but also of Jews and non-Jews. The book's closing lines ("United in love . . . notwithstanding former differences . . . United forever") speak to the hope of healing concord ardently desired not only in postbellum America but also by generation after generation of American Jews.

Mayer's book, a fascinating document of its times, has been called the first American Jewish novel of significant literary interest. In addition to presenting period detail, ranging from kosher recipes to the reading habits of the upper classes in the 1860s to elaborate battle scenes, the novel deliberately refutes the prevalent stereotypes of the 19th century of Jewish men as degenerates, sissies, or cutthroat mercantilists. Such Jews do appear in *Differences:* the unsubtly named Mr. Sellington Sharp, the Goldmans' *shochet* and associate, and later a faithful go-between for Welland and Antonia, is described as having a "hook nose" and "a good deal of cunning and vulgarity"; he also finds firearms terrifying. A young New York associate of Charles Goldman, meanwhile, is so allured by wealth that he refers to his potential dates by the names and products of their father's companies ("Don't you know her? Krakowwitzer & Co, Gents' Clothing and Furnishing Goods"). Welland, in contrast, demonstrates that Jewish masculinity can be everything and more than its non-Jewish counterpart—while the novel, with its approving commentary on intermarriage (as long as the non-Jewish partner converts!) and on the vigorous Jewish participation in the nation's bloodiest and most consequential war, suggests Mayer's hopefulness about the future of Jews in the United States.

Further reading: Very little information on Mayer has survived; even academics haven't devoted much attention to him. He may or may not have modeled the surgeon who makes a cameo in *Differences* on himself. An entry in the *Norton Anthology of Jewish American Literature* offers a few details about Mayer's life, as well as an excerpt from another one of his novels, a historical romance called *The Fatal Secret* (1858). Those interested in the history of the period can consult Bertram W. Korn's *American Jewry and the Civil War* (1951) or the edited letters of a real-life Jewish Civil War colonel published under the title *Your True Marcus* (1985). A much more recent historical novel, Peter Melman's *Landsman* (2007), features the wartime experiences of a Jew from New Orleans, and if you have a high tolerance for sentimentality, also seek out Belva Plain's *Crescent City* (1984).

. . . .

14

2–*As It Was Written: A Jewish Musician's Story*
By Sidney Luska (Henry Harland)

Cassell and Co., 1885. 253 pages.

Sidney Luska didn't exist, but that didn't stop him from becoming the first Jewish novelist to hit it big in America. The apparent author of stories of Jewish life, including *Mrs. Peixada* (1886) and *The Yoke of the Thorah* (1887), Luska was created in the 1880s by Henry Harland, a young non-Jewish writer with large ambitions. The pseudonym was basically a marketing tactic: if he put "a Jewish name on the title page," Harland remarked in a letter to his godfather, "the sale of the book would be vastly increased. I believe lots of Jews would buy it for that reason, if for no other."

The first of Luska's novels, *As It Was Written*, proved this strategy successful; it sold a respectable 50,000 copies even before it was reissued in 1900 (with Harland's name now printed alongside Luska's). The book tells the tragic tale of Ernest Neuman, an uncannily talented violinist, and the woman he loves, Veronika Pathzuol, who is quite the musician herself. That these young Jews should discover each other through music, Luska intimates, is fateful and appropriate, for "music is the art in which the Jews excel." (Note that this was written before the rise to international fame of such violinists as Jascha Heifetz and Mischa Elman.) Some of Luska's characters have even more complimentary things to say about "the ancient and honorable race"; one enlightened philo-Semite gushes to the effect that "the whole future of America depends upon the Jews."

As suggested by the complexity of his authorial identity, though, Harland's/Luska's ideas and plots weren't all quite so sunny; *As It Was Written* describes Veronika's sensational murder, a crime for which her fiancé is arrested and tried. In the typical fashion of the 19th-century potboiler, the plot progresses through mysteries and coincidences, revealed legacies, mesmeric trances, and improbable curses, all spiced with Harland's sometimes loopy attempts to include "authentic" details of Jewish language and rituals. The final implication about the narrator, Ernest, is that while his heritage has given him remarkable gifts, it has also burdened him in ways that are frankly disturbing in what they suggest about Judaism and its legacies. There's no sense reading *As It Was Written* (or any of Luska's novels) for the truth about Jews in late-19th century America, but the book reflects what bohemians and denizens of high culture were thinking about them then. And while the final twist of the plot may prove a little predictable for contemporary audiences, Harland doesn't mince words and manages to provide some fast-paced, creepy thrills.

Further reading: Karl Beckson's *Henry Harland* (1978) is the only biography available of this eccentric author; Luska's novels are discussed in Leslie Fiedler's essay *The Jew in the American Novel* (1959). Jewish musicians occupy central roles in George Du Maurier's smash *Trilby* (1894)—in which the nefarious Jew Svengali mesmerizes an innocent girl into success as a singer—as well as Sholem Aleichem's *Stempenyu* (published in Yiddish in 1888 and first translated into English in 1913).

. . . .

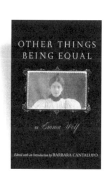

3 – *Other Things Being Equal*
By Emma Wolf

A. C. McClurg, 1892. 275 pages.

The most durable of American Jewish concerns—the temptation of intermarriage to a non-Jew—is also, unsurprisingly, the most ubiquitous of American Jewish literary plots, and not only where the infamous *shikse* (non-Jewish woman) is concerned. With her successful first novel, published when she was just 27, Emma Wolf made what was then, and continues to be today, a radical point, at least from the perspective of traditional Jewish culture. If they come from similar perspectives when it comes to social and economic life and find each other congenial, she suggested, a Jew and a Christian can be as happy together as any couple. As Wolf phrased it, "The humanest love knows no sect."

Unlike many novels that flirt with intercultural romance only to revert to endogamy, Wolf's novel manages to reconcile the fidelity of its protagonist, Ruth Levice, to her family and particularly her father, on the one hand, with her passion for her Unitarian beau, Dr. Herbert Kemp, on the other. Kemp appears on the scene to treat Ruth's mother, who is suffering from hysteria—that most typical women's disease of the late 19th century. Kemp prescribes a rest cure—made famously ominous in Charlotte Perkin Gilman's contemporaneous "The Yellow Wallpaper" (1892)—which boils down to getting Ruth's mother to stop hobnobbing with well-to-do Jews in San Francisco like herself and stay in bed. Admiring his medical prowess, and in thrall to the force of his personality, Ruth accompanies the doctor to the houses of his indigent patients. Eventually, despite a marriage proposal from Ruth's cousin Louis, a recent immigrant from France, Ruth and Kemp fall in love. Her wise old father pronounces that he will not support their marriage but neither will he prevent it; Ruth can't bear to break his heart, though, and she knows that she would if she married Kemp. (Wolf likely based this dilemma on that of her sister Alice, who married a Protestant.) The novel's denouement offers a solution to this impasse, proposing that vigorous Jewish pride and complete intimacy with a non-Jewish partner are not mutually exclusive possibilities.

Enchanting as it relates the salon conversations of upper-middle-class Jews of French origin in the San Francisco of the 1880s—not the typical demographic of fin de siècle American literature—*Other Things Being Equal* received supportive reviews across the country and was reissued half a dozen times. Its set pieces provide a guided tour to the experiences of rich Jews in the final decades of the 19th century: Ruth and Kemp attend a performance of Shakespeare's *The Merchant of Venice* and disagree about how to interpret the character of Shylock; they discuss the supposed Jewish genius in music and theater, and where it might come from; their courtship is subjected to the gossip that inevitably develops in small communities (and which the word *yenta* has evolved to describe). At times sentimental and at others surprisingly honest, Wolf's book deserves a spot among the pioneering works of American Jewish literature.

Further reading: Wolf's other novel on Jewish themes, *Heirs of Yesterday* (1900), also takes up the questions of marriage and ethnic loyalty, but it is considerably harder to find. *Other Things Being Equal* can be downloaded for free online, but the reprint edition (2002), edited by Barbara Cantalupo, is more than worth the price: Cantalupo's introduction includes a remarkable biography of the author (who, crippled by polio, was confined to a wheelchair for much of her life) and covers the reception of Wolf's novels and her epistolary relationship with Israel Zangwill. It also mentions various relevant books worth seeking out, such as Harriet Lane Levy's *920 O'Farrell Street* (1947), which is set among the Jewish community of San Francisco during Wolf's lifetime.

4—*Joseph Zalmonah*

By Edward King

LEE AND SHEPARD, 1893. 365 PAGES.

Like Hollywood or comic books, the union movement in America wasn't an entirely Jewish phenomenon, but Jews played pivotal roles from early on. One typical mover and shaker was Joseph Barondess (1867–1928), an immigrant who organized a cloakmaker's union as a young man and later went on to participate in the founding of both the International Ladies' Garment Workers' Union and the Hebrew Actors' Union, among other accomplishments. The eponymous hero of Edward King's only Jewish, and his last, novel, Joseph Zalmonah, shares much more than a first name with Barondess: King, a non-Jewish newspaperman at the New York *Morning Journal*, based almost every detail of Zalmonah's life and personality on Barondess's.

King did diverge from Barondess's story somewhat in insisting on the absolute purity of Zalmonah's goodness. A charismatic speaker in half a dozen languages, Zalmonah is a hero to every impoverished Jew in New York, completely incorruptible (offered a bribe, he says, "I scorn and spit upon them"), self-sacrificing in his duty to the point of asceticism, and handsome, to boot. Imagine a Jewish Robin Hood, but with less of a sense of humor, and that's a reasonable approximation of Joseph Zalmonah, who comes complete with a Little John–like sidekick, a pushy pushcart vendor named Ben Tzion who isn't above smacking a few sweatshop owners around. Zalmonah's enemies include not only the "sweaters" and industrialists who exploit poor Jews, but also the "party of force"—socialists and anarchists who believe nothing short of a violent uprising will help the poor and that unionism delays the inevitable revolution. In opposing Zalmonah to these two parties, King attempted to show his readers—presumably gentile Americans—that Jews could be something other than frightening communists and greedy capitalists.

King's plot chugs along with more verve than one might expect from a book about trade unionism: a narrow escape from a burning tenement, a mysterious baby, and a visit to a phony "wonder rabbi" amp up suspense, while Joseph fends off the temptations of a gorgeous femme fatale assigned to win him over to the socialists. Minor characters include a proverb-spouting impresario of the Yiddish theater, a "poet of the people" who sparks a riot with a sentimental ballad, and a tragic host of pious laborers fated to suffer in the misery of the sweatshops. King's good intentions and reportorial acumen notwithstanding, he doesn't always nail the details of Jewish life in late-19th-century New York, but his fanciful or sentimentalized versions of Yom Kippur, Purim, Passover, and quotations from the Talmud are themselves fascinating in the perspective they provide on what a smart, sympathetic non-Jew could make of Jewish culture toward the beginning of the massive wave of immigration that would change the country forever.

Further reading: There's not much out there to read about King, and his novel hasn't been a darling of criticism. Arthur Bullard's *Comrade Yetta* (1913) is a similarly idealistic portrait of a leftist, in this case a woman; see also Beatrice Bisno's *Tomorrow's Bread* (1938). Readers curious about Jewish proletarian and left-wing culture in general should consult Irving Howe's cultural histories, such as *World of Our Fathers* (1976). For a more recent scholarly history focused on Yiddish-speaking milieus, see Tony Michels's *A Fire in Their Hearts: Yiddish Socialists in New York* (2005).

. . . .

5 – *Yekl* and *The Imported Bridegroom and Other Stories of the New York Ghetto*
By Abraham Cahan

DOVER PUBLICATIONS, 1970. 240 PAGES.

As editor of the *Forverts*, which he built up into the most widely circulated Yiddish-language periodical of all time, Abraham Cahan introduced his immigrant readers to the wonders of America, from slang to baseball to trade unionism. Before he took that fateful job, though, he had already made a name for himself doing the exact opposite thing: writing stories about Jewish life for non-Jewish readers, in shockingly elegant English (for a man who'd lived in another language into his 20s). Published before the beginning of the 20th century, Cahan's early fictions—the novella *Yekl* (1896) and the collection *The Imported Bridegroom and Other Stories of the New York Ghetto* (1898)—are skillful and sympathetic Jewish counterparts to the local color tales of rural America, which were routine exercises in exoticism in the waning years of the 19th century.

How can we tell that Cahan's stories were for non-Jewish readers? For one thing, he translates Jewish terms, explaining in parentheses that "rabbitzen" means "a rabbi's wife," and, in a footnote, that "mazol-tov" means "good luck" (which it does, literally—though the phrase is more often used to mean "congratulations"). For another, the tales trade on the tragic struggles of the Jewish immigrants in a mode familiar from more recent fictions of this sort. In one story, a law school graduate in Russia, having discovered that "the government was bent upon keeping the Jews out of the forensic profession," packs up his college-educated wife and winds up on the Lower East Side of New York. With no hope of employment in the legal field, he ends up doing piecework in a pearl-button factory, and his sweetly intellectual home life, under the yoke of abject poverty, begins to crumble. A century later, publishers were offering nearly identical stories about Indian and Asian immigrants, trained as cardiologists or physicists back home, forced to drive taxis or serve take-out in the United States.

With that caveat in mind, the stories are gems. *Yekl* concerns a ladies' man who is shocked when his wife from the Old Country, who he has been keeping a secret, appears unbidden in New York. In a twist on the same idea, *The Imported*

Bridegroom deals with a Talmud prodigy sent to America, who finds himself drawn away from traditional learning. Eventually, his prospective father-in-law, who paid a fortune to bring him over and sees where he is headed, declares dejectedly, "A convert Jew is worse than a dead one." Cahan provides vivid details of immigrant life—textured descriptions of the dance halls, boxing matches, weddings, restaurants, and tenement houses of turn-of-the-century Jewish New York. In other words, though these fictions were originally intended to expose uptown WASPs to the harsh conditions and intense emotions of immigrant life, they can now fulfill that same function for readers of any background.

Further reading: Cahan's own Yiddish translation of Yekl as *Yankl der Yankee*, published in the *Arbeter Tsaytung* [Worker's newspaper], has unfortunately never been printed in book form. He wrote an autobiography, translated into English as *The Education of Abraham Cahan* (1969). His writing is sensitively analyzed in Jules Chametzky's *From the Ghetto: The Fiction of Abraham Cahan* (1977), and he receives coverage in all of the major anthologies and critical surveys of American Jewish literature as well as in literary studies of turn-of-the-century America. A selection of letters translated from the advice column Cahan inaugurated can be found in *A Bintel Brief* (1970), and Edward Steiner's *The Mediator* (1908) is another early chronicle of immigration to the United States.

. . . .

6 – *Children of Men*

By Bruno Lessing (Rudolph Edgar Block)

McClure, Phillips, and Co., 1903. 311 pages.

At the beginning of the 20th century, magazines were booming. Monthlies such as *McClure's*, *Munsey's*, and *Cosmopolitan* (long before its 1960s remake) sold for a dime and offered reams of general-interest reporting, cultural features, and fiction in each advertising-packed issue. Historians credit this phenomenon as the first blossoming of a real mass culture in the United States and as a precursor to television, because of the tremendous appeal of these publications to wide audiences. Whether it was with tender tales of romance or muckraking exposés of industry, as long as you were middle class, the monthlies wanted to entertain you and break your heart. And what would be more entertaining and heartbreaking than tales of the impoverished Jews of the sweatshops?

First published in magazines such as *McClure's* and *Cosmopolitan* and later reprinted in newspapers including the *Chicago Tribune* and the *Washington Post*, Bruno Lessing's brief sketches of Jewish life on the Lower East Side present a tiny universe of immigrant striving and unfulfilled desire. Beautiful young girls work themselves to death in sweatshops, and earnest young men attempt to alleviate their suffering, as in "The End of the Task." Recent arrivals find themselves unable to fit in, either because they're still reeling from pogroms in their native lands, like "Queer Scharenstein," or because other immigrants won't tolerate their traditional ways (as in "The Americanisation of Shadrach Cohen," one of the most successful of these stories). As would be expected, several of the tales turn tragically on ill-fated romances between Jewish girls and Christian men. In one of them, "A Daughter of Israel," so torn is Bertha between her desire for her lover and her respect for her father, a rabbi, that she flings herself into a river. In another, mutual knowledge of the Song of Songs helps yet another rabbi's daughter and a Catholic altar boy end up together despite prejudice on both sides.

Many of Lessing's stories are brief sketches without much plot, and all of them are at least a little melodramatic. Like one of his characters, an artist, Lessing seems to have been drawn to Hester Street in a "search for the picturesque"—which was what the turn-of-the-century magazines, more than anything, hoped to sell to their readers. At the same time, although he does not seem to have been Jewish himself, Lessing's attitude to Judaism is unquestionably sympathetic: in "Unconverted," when an idealistic reverend hopes to bring the poor Jews to Christianity, he is shown the error of his ways and disabused of his plans. More generally, the Jewish immigrants in Lessing's fiction are inevitably hardworking, honest, and faithful, despite terrible living conditions. Such a picture is not quite realistic or historically accurate, but it does capture one of the many truths about the early phase of Jewish life in the United States.

Further reading: Little has been written about Lessing, whose real name was Rudolph Edgar Block. His later books, including *With the Best Intention* (1914), are hard to find. According to newspapers, it was while "covering a cloakmakers' strike on the East Side that he became interested in the Jews and their frightful suffering and poverty." He edited comic strips for the Hearst syndicate and later in life, among other things, amassed the world's largest collection of walking sticks. Herman Bernstein's *In the Gates of Israel* (1902) is a comparable but much more difficult to locate collection of short stories that reprinted pieces first published in forgotten venues ranging from *The Menorah* and *Jewish Comment* to *Ainslee's Magazine*.

7 - Q.E.D.
By Gertrude Stein
In *FERNHURST, Q.E.D., AND OTHER EARLY WRITINGS.* LIVERIGHT, 1971. 80 PAGES.

If she's ever neglected as a writer and doyenne of the American expatriates in Paris, Gertrude Stein will always be remembered for her epigrams. She is the person to whom Ernest Hemingway attributed the phrase, "You are all a lost generation," in the epigraph to *The Sun Also Rises* (1926), thus naming one of America's most famous literary cohorts (though apparently the actual coiner was a garage owner in the Paris suburbs). Stein also described Oakland, the town in which she was raised, saying, "There is no there there." This is pure Stein: a deformation of conventional English syntax and rhythm, with a stunning use of repetition, that somehow expresses briefly what it would be difficult to express any better at length. The inventive syntactic and stylistic experiments of American modernism—think Hemingway and John Dos Passos—would be impossible to imagine without Stein's influence.

Composed in 1903 at the beginning of her career, the novella *Q.E.D.* is much less self-consciously experimental, much less linguistically startling, than the work Stein began to publish in 1909. Even as she churned out dozens of impenetrable books, this earlier piece went unpublished during her lifetime: a limited edition was printed in 1950, and the first widely available one in 1971. (Now it is available in various editions of Stein's early writing.) Why the delay? The explanation is that *Q.E.D.* takes up in relatively explicit terms—about as explicit as Stein would ever be, on any subject—the subject of lesbian desire, as well as the relationship of Jews to other Americans. Stein describes each of the novel's three characters as bearing "the stamp of one of the older civilisations": Helen the English, Mabel the Italian. And Adele, the protagonist? Stein only hints that she is Jewish. "I have the failing of my tribe," Adele remarks, referring to her tendency to talk and talk and talk and talk; a page later, annoyed with the other two, she exclaims, "I always did thank God I wasn't born a woman," echoing the *Birkat ha-Shachar* (morning blessing) recited by Orthodox Jews at the start of each day and also signaling the complexities of gender identity at work here.

The plot tracks these three young American women in Europe, Baltimore, and New York, as well as Adele's dawning consciousness of the mutual attraction between herself and Helen. "Why . . . it's like a bit of mathematics," she notes, of her realization of the feelings between them. "Suddenly it does itself and you begin to see" which also explains why the story's title refers to the Latin formula *quod erat demonstrandum*, usually used to announce the solution of a mathematical proof. A triangular situation develops, in which Adele envies Mabel's patronage of Helen ("Oh it's simply prostitution," she whines, as Mabel buys Helen's affection with antique jewelry); but Adele is also confused about what she wants. Though easier to read, in a way, than Stein's incredible "Melanctha," (itself said to be a revised version of *Q.E.D.* set among African Americans rather than lesbians), the early novel is elliptical and peculiar—but what else can we expect at a time when the issues at hand could barely be treated in private conversation, let alone prose?

Further reading: "Melanchta," an excellent introduction to Stein's prose, appears in *Three Lives* (1909). Stein's opus, *The Making of Americans* (1934), went through many versions; an early one, often published alongside *Q.E.D.*, is much clearer than the standard edition about the story's interest in Jewish immigration—and Stein's unpublished notebooks for the project are full of systematic comparisons between Jews and Anglo-Saxons. An astounding document on Stein's approach to Jewish identity was republished in the scholarly journal *PMLA* in 2001: in it, the 22-year-old Stein argues vociferously that even atheist Jews should resist intermarriage. Stein's most famous book is *The Autobiography of Alice B. Toklas* (1933), and she has been the subject of dozens of critical studies, reminiscences, and biographies, though the question of how and whether we can read her as a Jewish writer has only recently been taken up.

. . . .

8 – *Motl, the Cantor's Son*

By Sholem Aleichem (Sholem Rabinovitch)

YIDDISH: HEBREW UNIVERSITY PRESS, 1997. 360 PAGES.
ENGLISH: TRANSLATED BY HILLEL HALKIN, IN *THE LETTERS OF MENACHEM-MENDL AND SHEYNE-SHENDL AND MOTL, THE CANTOR'S SON*. YALE UNIVERSITY PRESS, 2002. 214 PAGES.

Immigration to the United States is often dangerous and painful, and it usually means leaving behind friends, family, and familiar sights. But Sholem Aleichem's Motl, who is featured in a series of short stories first published between 1907 and 1916, has a special talent for looking at the bright side; when his father, a respected cantor, passes away during the holiday of Shavuos, Motl famously exclaims, "*Mir iz gut—ikh bin a yosem!*" (Lucky me—I'm an orphan!).

This is a classic joke, but Motl's elation stems from solid reasoning: having lost his father, he's excused from school and choir practice, and no one dares smack him around anymore, not even his older brother, Elye. Of course, Motl's statement can be interpreted more broadly: Motl's father was a traditionalist, and Motl's destiny is enlightenment and the modern world. After a few disastrous attempts to earn a living in their hometown of Kasrilevke and spurred on by the entrepreneurial Elye and his poetic friend, Pinye—a devotee of "Kahnegi," "Rahknfelleh," and "Vendehbilt," to whom America is "the only country in the world with real freedom and equality"—Motl and his family sets their sights on "Ella's Island." Their trip winds westward through Germany, Austria, Belgium, and England, and eventually they reach New York, where they proceed to mangle the English language with stunning perspicacity. Hillel Halkin's inventive translation offers the English-language reader access, of a sort, to Sholem Aleichem's signature wordplay, rendering the family's endeavors to speak English in phonetic form and modifying puns when necessary: where does the word "foinitsheh" (that is, furniture) come from, Motl wonders—maybe from "fein" (fine) and "tsheh" (chair)? When he's not playing with pronunciation, Sholem Aleichem can't resist literalizing an idiom or two: settled in New York just long enough to feel superior to more recent arrivals, Motl, who aspires to a career as a painter, draws a picture of an immigrant "with a big green horn on his forehead"—in other words, a "grinhawn."

Sadly, Sholem Aleichem died in 1916 while writing the second half of Motl's story, which ends just as the family begins to taste the prosperity made possible in America. A newspaper account claims that 100,000 mourners flooded the streets of New York on the day of the author's funeral. One can't help wondering

22

where the author, whose trips and final relocation to New York inspired this tale, would have taken his characters if he had lived longer; but we're lucky to have even this much of an American odyssey from the writer known as the Yiddish Mark Twain and one of the all-time greats of modern Jewish literature.

Further reading: Thanks to the unstoppable Broadway shmaltz-fest *Fiddler on the Roof* (filmed in 1971), there is no doubt that Sholem Aleichem's most enduring character will be Tevye the dairyman—whose story is also available in an exceptional translation by Hillel Halkin (1987); Menachem-Mendl, meanwhile, whose epistolary tale is available in the same Yale University Press volume as Motl's, is a destined-for-failure entrepreneur, last heard from on his way to try his luck in the United States. Maurice Samuels's *The World of Sholem Aleichem* (1943) is a well-intentioned introduction for English readers of the Yiddish master's oeuvre and background. Also available in English translation, *From the Fair* (1985) is Sholem Aleichem's autobiography in the third person.

. . . .

9 – *The Tether*
By Ezra Brudno

J. B. LIPPINCOTT COMPANY, 1908. 326 PAGES.

In a brilliant essay from 1958, Leslie Fiedler observes that the Jewish American novel "must be a problem novel, and its essential problems must be identity and assimilation"—because the drama of being an American Jew so often centers on the question of how Jewish, and how American, one can or should be. "What is unexpected," Fiedler continues, "is that these problems be posed in terms of sexual symbols. . . . It is in the role of passionate lover that the American-Jewish novelist sees himself . . . and the community with which he seeks to unite himself he sees as the *shikse* [non-Jewish woman]." Half a century before Fiedler made this canny observation, Ezra Brudno published a novel that dramatizes it expertly. Referring to his protagonist, David Sphardi, and his attraction to the daughter of a well-to-do Baptist, Brudno writes, "Instead of a personal matter, his love for Mildred presented itself to him in the form of a general question, a problem to be solved—the problem that had faced his race in all lands and at all times."

Though he was born in Lithuania, David really starts living at the age of 14, in Boston, when a wealthy gentile painter, Miss Helen Truesdale, offers to teach him English if he'll sit for portraits. The son of a peddler, David not only learns to read and write English through Miss Truesdale's influence but discovers a natural affinity to art and poetry. In high school, he doesn't fit in—a class performance of *The Merchant of Venice* (which was one of the most frequently taught plays in American schools at the turn of the century) mortifies him, and as his classmates celebrate Christmas, he can't help feeling that "he was amongst them and yet outside; in their midst and yet separated." He enrolls at Harvard and, after his patroness's nephew invites him to join a selective student club, finds himself being courted by the nouveau riche Jewish dandies, but he has no stronger link to them than to his traditional, superstitious father or to the non-Jews. He muddles through college, writing lyric poetry, and, in the third section of the novel, meets Mildred Dalton while vacationing in the lake country north of Toronto.

The novel dawdles over their courtship, then speeds to conclusion at a frenzied clip: on the way to elope, the couple encounters typical anti-Semitism (they had hoped to honeymoon at a resort hotel that turns out to have a policy of "Hebrews need not apply"), and their relationship fractures under the pressure. David's father, meanwhile, suffers a paralytic stroke upon reading in a Yiddish newspaper that his beloved son has run off with a *shikse*. David, grasping at straws and despairing of options for himself and for the Jews as a people, takes up Zionism; but at the Zionist Congress in Switzerland, he sees only the movement's flaws, and his contribution is a call to "Disband, brothers, disband!" The novel ends with the disturbed ramblings of David's journals and then, to hammer the point home, with his tombstone, which reads: "Strangled By His Tether." David's somewhat melodramatic fate constitutes Brudno's striking comment on the impossibility of reconciling Jewish and American identities. In the century that has followed, others have taken similar as well as drastically different stands on the same basic questions (for example, Woody Allen's 1977 film *Annie Hall* and Philip Roth's 1969 novel *Portnoy's Complaint*), but it is fascinating to discover a precursor to these works in Brudno's readable and charming novel.

Further reading: Brudno, born in 1877, attended Yale and worked as a lawyer in Cleveland. He published a handful of books that are now nearly impossible to find, including *The Fugitive* (1904), set in Russia and America; *The Little Conscript* (1905); *One of Us* (1912); and *The Jugglers* (1920), about legal practice in Cleveland—not to be confused with Michael Blankfort's *The Juggler* (1952), set in Israel. Unfortunately, little has been written about Brudno, even by scholars of American Jewish literature. In contrast to *The Tether*, and like a number of the earliest American Jewish novels, Elias Tobenkin's *Witte Arrives* (1916) portrays a comfortable intermarriage—and the rapprochement between Americans and Jews that it symbolizes—as a definite possibility.

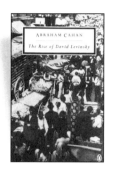

10 – *The Rise of David Levinsky*

By Abraham Cahan

HARPER AND BROTHERS, 1917. 530 PAGES.

Abraham Cahan's epic masterpiece is the American novel of immigration par excellence, as it should be: no one knew the millions of Eastern European Jews who arrived in America between 1881 and 1924 better than Cahan did. As the longtime editor of the *Forverts*, the Yiddish daily newspaper that at its peak claimed more than 200,000 subscribers, Cahan communicated directly with his readers in an advice column (the famed "Bintel Brief") and knew their triumphs and suffering firsthand.

Cahan's writing in English benefited from the support of the turn-of-the-century literary heavyweight William Dean Howells, and *The Rise of David Levinsky* took inspiration from Howells's *The Rise of Silas Lapham* (1885). At the same time as he was being embraced by readers of the nation's most prestigious magazines, though, Cahan was also a fierce socialist and staunch supporter of the working men and women in the trade unions. The novel, which describes the rise of the title character from an orphan in Russia to the owner of a major cloak-making firm in New York, registers these tensions: fabulously wealthy by the book's end—he even learns to savor unkosher delicacies, thanks to a non-Jewish associate—Levinsky never quite finds satisfaction.

Levinsky's aimlessness comes through most powerfully in his romantic relationships. After losing his mother to mob violence in the old country, Levinsky dallies with one woman after another—a divorcee with revolutionary ideas, a prostitute, the wife of one of his best friends, the daughter of a Hebrew poet—but never meets his match. Unlike characters of the same period who solved this problem by marrying out of the fold, Levinsky remains alone and ambivalent about the overall trajectory of his life: "I cannot escape from my old self," he admits. "My past and my present do not comport well." Experiencing the pull of the Old World and the rush of the New, the thrills of capitalism as well as its stings, Levinsky captures much of what it meant to be an American Jew in the first decades of the 20th century.

Further reading: Susan Glenn's *Daughters of the Shtetl* (1991) and Daniel Soyer's *A Coat of Many Colors* (2005) offer historical descriptions of the development of the garment industry, complementing the fictional portrayals in Cahan's novel. See also Meredith Tax's novel *Rivington Street* (1982).

11 – *The Chosen People*

By Sidney Nyburg

J. B. LIPPINCOTT CO., 1917. 343 PAGES

One of the problems with most descriptions of the American Jewish experience is that there is no single experience shared by all Jews in the United States. Even if we allow for a reasonable amount of simplification, the successive waves of immigration and geographical spread of the country led to the formation of various communities, each with its own unique features. A finely detailed and cunningly constructed novel of ideas, Sidney Nyburg's *The Chosen People* is distinguished not only by its unusual setting, Baltimore in 1915, but also by its vigorous description of the social chasm separating the city's German Jews from their Russian-born counterparts.

As the novel opens, German Jews have been in the United States for generations, practice "reformed Judaism," and have achieved extraordinary success as leading manufacturers and surgeons. The Russian Jews have only recently arrived, speak Yiddish, subscribe to traditional Orthodoxy, and labor for mean wages in taxing jobs—often in factories owned by the wealthy Germans, one of whom refers to them as the "scum of Europe." That tensions exist between these groups should not shock anyone, but it does surprise Philip Graetz, an idealistic dreamer fresh out of rabbinical school at the age of 24. Hired as the rabbi of Temple Beth El, "the largest and wealthiest synagogue in Baltimore," Graetz hopes to convince his congregants to apply Jewish ethics to their business dealings. A strike at a clothing factory owned by his synagogue's president provides a test for his principles, but his attempts to broker a compromise show him how little he knows about either of these communities.

Graetz faces another, not unrelated dilemma: should he marry the fabulously wealthy Ruth, who hangs on every word of his florid sermons, or the non-Jewish Ellen, a socialist nurse for whom he feels real desire? In making this decision, and in sorting out the battle between labor and capital, Graetz receives aid from the cynical, atheistic, but not unsympathetic David Gordon, who was himself born in Russia but has become one of the city's most respected lawyers. Given that Nyburg himself was a practicing lawyer, it is perhaps to be expected that Gordon's wisdom and politicking prove more successful than Graetz's idealism, or that the book ends with Gordon shrugging his shoulders at the *mishegoss* of his coreligionists. While Nyburg's plot chugs along effectively enough, many of the characters in the book obviously stand for political philosophies, from Zionism to socialism to unabashed market capitalism, and the fiction's main purpose is to explore these various ideologies as they apply to American Jews before the First World War; along the way, Nyburg offers an effective portrait of well-to-do Jewish life and a welcome reminder of the diversity of American Jews.

Further reading: Nyburg published a handful of other books, none of which deals with Jewish life; and, unfortunately, aside from Stanley Chyet's introduction to a 1985 reprint of the novel, not much has been written about Nyburg at all. Those interested in Jewish Baltimore should seek out the novels of Robert Kotlowitz, including *Somewhere Else* (1972), as well as Barry Levinson's films, such as *Diner* (1983) and *Avalon* (1990).

· ·

12 – *Fanny Herself*
By Edna Ferber

FREDERICK A. STOKES, 1917. 323 PAGES.

Edna Ferber's single novel about American Jews stakes out two contradictory positions about the nature of Jewish tradition and heritage. On the one hand, her plucky heroine, Fanny Brandeis, discovers that it is a serious mistake to deny the responsibilities and gifts conferred by her heritage; on the other, Ferber is broad-minded about how exactly Jews can do honor to their Jewish roots. Fanny, like Sholem Aleichem's Motl, in *Motl, the Cantor's Son*, has "an authentic gift of caricature" and illustration, while her brother is a violin prodigy; less conventionally, the suitor with whom she inevitably ends up, Clarence Heyl, is predisposed through his Jewishness to be a mountaineer and newspaper columnist. In other words, Ferber believes that Jewish "suffering breeds genius," but she is not picky about what types of genius, precisely, it breeds. 27
 Raised in small-town Winnebago, Wisconsin, Fanny learns the ways of commerce from her mother, "an extraordinarily alert woman, mentally and physically, with a shrewd sense of values." The opening section of the novel provides a detailed, if idealized portrait of the life of Jewish shopkeepers in rural America, building upon Ferber's real-life experiences in a town called Appleton. Taking the lessons learned in Brandeis's Bazaar, the family store, with her, Fanny, as a young woman, decamps to Chicago to run the infants' wear department of a massive mail-order operation, which sounds suspiciously like Sears, Roebuck and Co. (which, don't forget, was largely a sales juggernaut because of the leadership of a Jewish executive, Julius Rosenwald). Fanny couldn't be more of a hotshot—she revolutionizes the operation in her first week by suggesting that the stock boys could travel around faster on roller skates—but the millions of orders and dollars rushing in leave her cold. What she was born to do is draw; but it isn't just "a case of being able to draw. It's being able to see life in a peculiar light, and to throw that light so that others get the glow." Eventually, she learns to value this ability from her naturalist friend, Heyl; he also teaches her how to throw a mean uppercut, a skill she puts to use when her infatuated boss tries to put the moves on her.
 Having been trained as a journalist, Ferber writes slick prose, and her book contains an expertly modulated mix of humor, sweetness, and pathos, with topical references to the First World War, a smattering of dialect jokes, and some gentle didacticism about the dignity of Jewish tradition thrown in. It is no

surprise that *Fanny Herself*, like many of Ferber's better-known novels—the Pulitzer Prize–winning *So Big* (1924), *Show Boat* (1926), and *Giant* (1952)—was adapted into a film, in 1921 (titled *No Woman Knows;* it has not survived). Ferber's novel itself refers to movies and comic strips continually, and assertive Fanny resembles a toned-down version of the daring heroines of the movie serials of the mid-1910s such as the *Hazards of Helen* or *The Exploits of Elaine*. With insights into the sales end of the garment industry as well as Jewish involvement in the arts, the book may come off as quaint to some but will undoubtedly charm most contemporary readers.

Further reading: Ferber's first autobiography, *A Peculiar Treasure* (1939), is of particular interest because of its response to the rise of Nazism and fascism, and Ferber's great-niece, Julie Goldsmith Gilbert, also wrote a biography of the author (1978). Fannie Hurst was a similarly prolific writer of slick short stories and novels, most famous for her narrative of African American passing, *Imitation of Life* (1933); her short fiction has been recently republished as *The Stories of Fanny Hurst* (2004), and she discusses her Jewish background in her autobiography, *Anatomy of Me*, published in 1958.

. . . .

13 – *Salome of the Tenements*
By Anzia Yezierska

BONI AND LIVERIGHT, 1923. 184 PAGES.

Yezierska's debut novel, first published in 1923, is ripped from the headlines, so to speak: Sonya, a poor Russian Jewish immigrant, falls for a millionaire philanthropist—just like the real-life sweatshop worker Rose Pastor, who rose to national celebrity in 1905. Despite poverty, Sonya is wild and passionate for beauty, and from the perspective of her paramour, John Manning, she embodies "the intensity of spirit of the oppressed races." The book's title refers to a New Testament character, but Yezierska is concerned less with the original Salomé and more with the turn-of-the-century craze for her, which took the forms of Oscar Wilde's 1893 play of that name and the many risqué Dances of the Seven Veils performed throughout the world.

A story of passion and desire, Yezierska's rags-to-riches narrative unearths the complexities and discomforts of Jewish success in America. For one thing, living the American dream often involves turning your back on your history: as she rises to fame and fortune, Sonya encounters Jacques Hollins, who drapes wealthy New York aristocrats in the finest Paris fashions. Like the contemporary fashion icon Ralph Lauren, whose name was originally Lifshitz, Jacques was once called Jaky and grew up in the same Lower East Side ghetto as Sonya. More centrally, there is trouble in paradise when Sonya and her high-class husband encounter each other's peers: Sonya finds the WASP establishment desiccated and judgmental, while Manning finally betrays a streak of genteel anti-Semitism.

Rendering her characters' speech in Yiddish-inflected dialect, Yezierska's novel raises crucial questions about intermarriage and about charity, which remain unresolved today: Can a Jew and a gentile overcome their differences through shared passion? What's the best way to help the working classes?

Though neglected by readers for decades, Yezierska's work provides a crucial example of the leftist feminist position that was more common than one might expect among immigrants in the early 20th century. When Yezierska writes, "Sonya was like the dynamite bomb and Manning the walls of tradition," she reveals some of her own experiences: she married and divorced, forged a bond with the famed educator John Dewey, and protested exploitation, whether by capitalists or by patriarchal Judaism. Her work found admirers both among the literary elite (she was one of the first Jewish guests at the MacDowell Colony, a prestigious artists' retreat) and in Hollywood, where a number of her works, including *Salome*, were adapted for the screen.

Further reading: Two biographical volumes explore Yezierska's life and her own intense relationship with a non-Jewish beau, respectively—Louise Levitas Henriksen's *Anzia Yezierska: A Writer's Life* (1988) and Mary Dearborn's *Love in the Promised Land: The Story of Anzia Yezierska and John Dewey* (1988)—and the author's own reminiscences can be found in *Red Ribbon on a White Horse* (1950), which takes its title from a famous talmudic statement about poverty.

14 - *Haunch, Paunch and Jowl*
By Samuel Ornitz

BONI AND LIVERIGHT, 1923. 300 PAGES.

One of the literary debates that never seems to get resolved is whether a book that depicts a Jewish character as scheming, criminal, or downright evil is automatically anti-Semitic. We don't hold literature about non-Jews to that same standard, of course; Shakespeare's *Macbeth* tells the tale of a couple of repulsive social climbers, but rarely is it thought of, nowadays at least, as propaganda against the Scots. Ultimately, the meaning of a literary work depends on the circumstances in which it is consumed and how its readers react to it—so, with some clear exceptions, asking whether a particular book is anti-Semitic or not is less practical than asking whether the way the book has been read by certain people is anti-Semitic. Samuel Ornitz's *Haunch, Paunch and Jowl*, a breathless novel of Jewish life written in the 1920s, has often been castigated as a work of unadulterated self-loathing; but, as is often the case, this book is more complex than such a knee-jerk reaction suggests.

The protagonist and narrator of this novel, which is sometimes titled *Allrightniks Row*, is a true immigrant child, born aboard ship between Europe and America; his mother calls him *zigelle*, little goat, because a goat's milk helped him survive the journey. Meyer Hirsch grows up in New York City in the last couple of decades of the 19th century; he is a wiseguy in the making who matures over the course of the novel from gang fights to nightclub debauchery to crooked politics. In formless Yiddish-spiced dialect and stream of consciousness, Hirsch describes his impoverished neighborhood and the bright Jewish boys who rise from it to become doctors and famous songwriters; he recounts the speeches given by the incipient socialists, aesthetes, and sociologists around him, though ultimately he sides with his uncle Philip, a pragmatist who makes his fortune by running a sweatshop even more merciless and exploitative than usual. He tells his nephew, "Meyer, respectableness is a lot of rot," and informs him that his father, Meyer's grandfather, was a horse thief. Living up to this pedigree, Meyer becomes a crooked lawyer and then a crooked judge, playing the system like a pro and embracing blackmail, bribes, and any other dirty tactic he can think of to rise to power and prominence.

Meyer is no paragon, but Ornitz doesn't intend him to be admired. Many characters in the novel live up to a considerably higher moral standard, and if their idealistic aims are frustrated by Meyer and those who play his games, that only suggests the undeniable truism that being honest is more difficult than cheating. Ornitz himself fought against discrimination, fascism, and anti-Semitism throughout his life. In Hollywood as a screenwriter, he was one of the organizers of the Anti-Nazi League; he was later one of the Hollywood Ten who resisted McCarthy's crusade against the movie business. If his first and most successful novel—which was reported to have sold over 100,000 copies and was adapted for the stage by the famed Artef proletarian Yiddish theater—still smacks of the unsavory, perhaps that is due to its attempts to provide sensational thrills to the readers of the Jazz Age. While his is not the most finely turned prose in American Jewish literature, Ornitz crams in a great deal of snappy dialogue and period detail as well as an enduring Yiddish-tinged *joie de vivre*.

Further reading: In addition to many screenplays, Ornitz published two other uneven novels—one satirizing Catholicism and another, *Bride of the Sabbath* (1951), exploring the varieties of Jewish life in America. Most of the writing about Ornitz focuses on his role as one of the Hollywood Ten. Later fictions similarly, and erroneously, dismissed as self-hating anti-Semitic propaganda include Jerome Weidman's *I Can Get It for You Wholesale* (1937), Budd Schulberg's *What Makes Sammy Run?* (1941), and Mordecai Richler's *The Apprenticeship of Duddy Kravitz* (1959); for a truly bitter and possibly even self-hating novel, see Ben Hecht's *A Jew in Love* (1931).

15 – *Bread Givers*

By Anzia Yezierska

DOUBLEDAY, 1925. 297 PAGES.

Yezierska's most frequently read book, *Bread Givers*—unlike *Salome of the Tenements*—renders the story of poor Jewish immigrants in an idiom based on Yiddish. Yezierska wasn't the first to write in the linguistic amalgam that has come to be known as "Yinglish": dialect stories were common in late-19th-century America, and starting in 1914 Harry Hershfield's comic strip character Abie Kabibble spoke Yiddish-inflected English to millions of newspaper readers. But Yezierska achieves remarkable results by eschewing phonetic spellings and relying instead on unusual syntax to evoke the native language of her characters. By way of introduction, the novel's narrator, Sara Smolinsky, remarks, "From always it was heavy on my heart the worries for the house"—which is a near-literal translation of what one might say in Yiddish.

The novel relates the strong-willed narrator's endeavor to escape the indignities of poverty and the tyranny of her father, whose cruelty and small-mindedness, Yezierska suggests, typify unenlightened, patriarchal, Old World Judaism, no matter how pious it pretends to be. As vicious a character as can be found in American Jewish literature, Mr. Smolinsky forces his family to provide for him so that he can study Torah, and he refuses to work even if that means his daughters must live in brutal conditions (by the family's unfortunate standards, the frivolous Masha, Sara's sister, is indulging in extreme luxury when she buys herself a toothbrush and some soap for 30 cents). When he tries to engage in business, he fails miserably, conned by scheming Americans.

Sara, nicknamed "Blood and Iron" for her stubbornness, manages to avoid the awful fates of her sisters and to educate herself. She attends college, wins a speech contest, becomes a public-school teacher, and falls in love with a man who combines the best of Europe and America. Though her father has done nothing to help her, she even nobly takes him into her home when he has no one else to care for him; ultimately, though she believes in education and assimilation, she recognizes that the past cannot be shrugged off. "It wasn't just my father," she realizes finally, "but the generations who made my father whose weight was still upon me." Less florid than *Salome*, *Bread Givers* nonetheless strays into embarrassingly purple passages, but overall it remains a gripping story with many virtuoso flourishes of Yinglish phrasing.

Further reading: Yezierksa's other novels include *Arrogant Beggar* (1927) and *All I Could Never Be* (1932), and her short fiction is collected in *How I Found America* (1991). For other proto-feminist voices, see Mary Antin's famous memoir, *The Promised Land* (1912), and the poetry of Emma Lazarus; Lazarus's compelling life story is told expertly in Esther Schor's biography, *Emma Lazarus* (2006).

16 – *Amerika*

By Franz Kafka

GERMAN: KURT WOLFF VERLAG, 1927. 391 PAGES.
ENGLISH: TRANSLATED BY MICHAEL HOFFMAN. PENGUIN, 1996. 216 PAGES.

Franz Kafka never set foot in America, and, boy, does it show. The first factual error crops up even before the end of the introductory paragraph of his fictional travelogue, as his teenaged hero, Karl Rossman, arrives in New York harbor: "A sudden burst of sunshine seemed to illumine the Statue of Liberty, so that he saw it in a new light," and "the arm with the sword rose up as if newly stretched aloft." Lady Liberty, as we all know, has two hands: one holds a torch, the other a tablet. The image of a pale green sword-wielding Amazon looming over the entrance to the United States captures perfectly the genius of Kafka's art: a neurotic and paranoiac, and easily one of the greatest fiction writers of the 20th century, he manages to reach the truth by dismembering the facts.

Over the course of this fragmentary novel, which Kafka began to write in 1912 and only a small part of which he ever saw published during his life, young Karl, who has been "packed off to America" because he impregnated a servant girl, experiences a rather narrow swath of the American landscape. He is at first welcomed by his uncle, Jacob, who is a wealthy and powerful senator, but soon manages to offend him; setting off on his own, he meets a couple of drifters, an African American and an Irishman, then ditches them for a job as a hotel's elevator boy. He reunites with his multicultural companions in a suburb, where a woman more or less enslaves him. After observing a terrifying political rally, he joins up with the mysterious Nature Theater of Oklahoma, "the biggest theater in the world." The importance of these plot points resides less in their relation to whatever might have happened to a real-life European immigrant in turn-of-the-century America and more in the opportunities they provide for Kafka to spin out his characteristic fantasies and nightmares: endless hallways, Sisyphean labors, grotesque characters, grim jokes. Kafka's America, like ours—and perhaps a little like the travelogues upon which he based his work—is a place of both opportunity and danger, surreal possibility and vague threat.

In what ways is Kafka's *Amerika*—also known as *Der Verschollene* [The man who disappeared]—Jewish? This question, like most regarding Kafka's works, has been fodder for literary critics and scholars for generations, and it resists any single answer. Though the book is in no explicit sense concerned with Jews, writing a tale of American immigration when he did, Kafka must have been pondering the fate of the millions of his coreligionists from Central and Eastern Europe who were pouring into Ellis Island each year. Though his fiction in general never mentions the word "Jew," Kafka's diaries and letters, and many biographies about him, make clear his connections to and disconnections from the Jewish community: he was a fan of Yiddish theater, and among other things he studied a little bit of Hebrew and daydreamed about moving to Palestine.

That his neurotic or paranoiac fictions had a universal appeal does not undermine the extent to which they were the product of a particular Jewish man's experience of alienation. Like Sholem Aleichem's Motl, in *Motl, the Cantor's Son*, Karl is Kafka's vehicle for speculating about the question of whether America would be the solution to the world's, and the Jews', problems. That a world master addressed this issue, in characteristic form, testifies to the increasing centrality of America in the story of the Jews at the start of the 20th century.

Further reading: Kafka's works, most of which were published posthumously—his novels, *The Trial* (1925) and *The Castle* (1926), and shorter fictions like "The Metamorphosis" (1915) and "The Hunger Artist" (1924)—are prominent among the acknowledged classics of modern world literature. His letters and diaries, available in various collected editions, make captivating reading, too. Biographies of this major figure abound, ranging in approach and depth. Philip Roth's story "'I Always Wanted You to Admire My Fasting'; or, Looking at Kafka" (1973) imagines what might have happened if Kafka himself had ended up in the United States, as does one story, "Receding Horizon," in Jonathan Lethem and Carter Scholz's collection of fictional homages to Kafka, *Kafka Americana* (1999).

. . . .

17 – *The Island Within*

By Ludwig Lewisohn

HARPER AND BROTHERS, 1928. 350 PAGES.

One could carp that Ludwig Lewisohn always wrote about his own peculiar situation, even when his ostensible subjects were social movements, ancient eras, or distant lands. Luckily, Lewisohn was a thoroughly intriguing personality and a brilliant thinker, so reading about his personal dilemmas never grows tiresome. He grew up in Berlin and South Carolina, received a master's degree when he was 19, partied with James Joyce in Paris, and was psychoanalyzed by Freud. Through all of it—except for a brief assimilationist phase in his youth, which he soon saw as childish folly—he remained passionate and uncompromising about his identity as a Jew and an American. An extraordinarily prolific career as an author, editor, translator, poet, essayist, and lecturer spanning the first half of the 20th century makes him one of the paramount figures of Jewish literature, and Jewish history, in the United States.

The Island Within (1928) is a sensible place to start exploring Lewisohn's legacy, as it is a wide-ranging grab bag of many of the themes and motifs that would occupy him throughout his career, tied together by Lewisohn's stately prose and perspective. The central narrative concerns Arthur Levy, a native New Yorker and stand-in for the author who grows up in a thoroughly assimilated but still Jewish home only to discover, after his marriage to a Christian minister's daughter, that neglecting his Jewish heritage leads directly to neurosis and anxiety: "It's a kind of an argument, isn't it, against mixed marriages?" his wife asks him at one point, and he replies, "One among many others."

Yet Arthur meets Elizabeth only two thirds of the way through the book; Lewisohn's tale begins much earlier, in the year 1840, with Arthur's pious great-grandfather. Through the generations, Lewisohn tracks the family's drift from Jewish insularity and religious belief to secular culture and society. In addition, Lewisohn starts each of the novel's sections with an essayistic meditation on Jewish and world history ("But we have paid two-and-a-half dollars for a story, not for a treatise!" he imagines his readers reacting to the first of these); and Arthur's decision to join a fact-finding mission on the situation of Jews in Eastern Europe is influenced by an ancient text, belonging to his ancestors, that describes in detail the martyrdom of medieval Jews during the Crusades. In each of these generically diverse texts, which are stitched together into one more or less coherent book, Lewisohn approaches the question of Jewish distinctiveness and survival from a slightly different direction; and at the same time, Arthur's work as a psychologist in New York allows Lewisohn to include Freudian notions about sex and marriage, while he even finds a little space to discuss German culture in America. Though occasionally pedagogical, Lewisohn acknowledges that there are no easy answers—even the difficult ones he comes up with tend to be somewhat vague at best. His status as a foremost representative of intellectual culture in the United States, and an indispensable voice of modern Jewish thought, rests on his unflagging commitment to posing and struggling with the crucial questions.

Further reading: In addition to Lewisohn's autobiographical volumes, *Up Stream* (1922) and *Mid-Channel* (1929), he wrote dozens of books of fiction and criticism, the vast majority of which are sadly out of print but easy enough to find. Ralph Melnick's massive two-volume biography (1998) can tell you everything you'd ever want to know about Lewisohn's work and highly complicated personal life, and then some.

. . . .

18 – *Arnold Levenberg*
By David Pinski

YIDDISH: DOVID PINSKI BIKHER, 1938. 466 PAGES.
ENGLISH: TRANSLATED BY ISAAC GOLDBERG. SIMON AND SCHUSTER, 1928. 401 PAGES.

Plenty of writers in English, Anzia Yezierska and Bernard Malamud among them, have represented Yiddish-language milieus without actually using much Yiddish. The opposite phenomenon—Yiddish fiction primarily about English-speaking Jews—is less common, which makes the playwright David Pinski's debut novel, *Arnold Levenberg*, a rare gem. The book's eponymous protagonist, a wealthy and effete uptown German Jew, doesn't speak Yiddish, and, what's more, he doesn't even *recognize* the language when he hears it at a banquet of leftist intellectuals honoring the Russian revolution.

Drafted in the wake of World War I, in 1919 and 1920—though not published for almost a decade—Pinski's novel takes place before, during, and just after that war, beginning with an appropriately harrowing dream of an annihilated Manhattan in which "all New York was dead; [Arnold] was the only living being." Upon awakening from this vision, Levenberg, a well-connected pacifist and loyalist to Germany, spends most of his time pondering which woman he should wed. His choices range from the sexy, immoral daughter of dissolute adulterers, to a prim and proper heiress, to the socially conscious doctor who introduces Arnold to the culture of impoverished Russian Jews. Partying with these Yiddish-speaking communists, socialists, poets, and Zionists, Levenberg is introduced to yet another love interest, Olga Mankoff, whose dedication to her causes eventually sends her to Palestine. Tracking the developments of Arnold's stalled romantic life, Pinski attends meanwhile to the major political and historical developments of the day: the split interests of German Jews when the United States declares war on Germany, the optimism and faith of leftists in response to the revolution of 1917, the superficial patriotism and jingoism of American interventionists, and, most of all, the malaise and depression brought on in sensitive types, like Arnold, by the wholesale slaughter of innocent young men in the trenches of Europe. The guidance of a Yiddish labor leader and a military posting in Washington, D.C., are not enough to jolt Arnold into action. Eventually, he meets his match in a woman who can't even bear to speak of the war, and though he still hasn't found a purpose for his life, at least he has someone with whom to share his "withdrawal from the world."

Though largely neglected by scholars, *Arnold Levenberg* couldn't be more relevant to contemporary life: any one of Pinski's prescient discussions—of American imperialism, of capitalist-driven military campaigns, and of the obstacles hedonism and apathy pose to genuine political engagement—could have been pulled from last month's magazines. The book's many sidedness can be glimpsed in its variant, punning subtitles: "The Man of Peace" in English, "*Der Tserisener Mentsh*" (The torn man) in Yiddish. Though perhaps not as iconic as Pinski's best plays, this often thoughtful, sometimes sensational novel nonetheless provides an invaluable panorama of New York Jewish life during the first great conflict of the 20th century.

Further reading: A major figure in the world of Yiddish letters, Pinski comes in for treatment in most major studies of Yiddish or Yiddish American writing. Several collections of Pinski's plays, and a book of short stories, *Temptations* (1919), are available through Google Books in Isaac Goldberg's workmanlike English translations. Like his first novel, Pinski's second, a generational saga titled *The Generations of Noah Edon* (1931), appeared in English translation and only later in the original Yiddish. The final two volumes of John Dos Passos's *USA Trilogy* (1930–36) cover a similar time period and, in part, treat the role of a Jewish communist.

19 – *Singermann*

By Myron Brinig

FARRAR AND RINEHART, 1929. 446 PAGES

Myron Brinig's first novel, *Singermann*, can be thought of as a little-known Jewish counterpart to Sherwood Anderson's *Winesburg, Ohio* (1919). Anderson's book earned its secure position in the American canon by informing the literary vanguard of the post–World War I years that the nation's small towns were just as full of unexpressed longings, dark secrets, and flaring passions as the big cities. *Singermann* does the same for American Jewish life, for it takes place not on the teeming Lower East Side or in the well-to-do neighborhoods of suburban Boston or Baltimore, but in a frontier town, Silver Bow, modeled on Brinig's childhood home of Butte, Montana.

As in Anderson's collection of linked short stories, each of *Singermann*'s chapters describes the frustrations and desires of a different conflicted individual; in Brinig's book, though, all of these characters belong to the same titular family. The patriarch, Moses, arrives in the United States from Romania at the relatively advanced age of 30, and through his energy and hard-headedness manages to become one of his small town's most respected merchants. He's a lusty and vital fellow—in the Old Country he was a tavern keeper, and he still loves his homemade wine—and despite a sometimes adversarial relationship with his strong-willed wife, Rebecca, he fathers seven children, six of them boys. In the chapters devoted to them, each of the Singermann kids stirs up drama. The youngest, Michael, is the one most modeled after the author, and the book begins with his *bris* and ends with his departure for college in Chicago; Joseph, the oldest, marries a shrewd Jewish girl with an interest in Christian Science who isolates him from his family; David, a handsome go-getter, falls in love with a prostitute who treats him like dirt; while Rachel, the only daughter, falls for a romantic Russian who, it turns out, has not one, but two previous wives. Perhaps the most interesting chapter focuses on Sol, Harry, and a violent riot by the town's striking miners. Sol, the strongest and most doltish of the Singermanns, decides—like many Jews of the early 20th century—that his destiny will be found in the boxing ring, while Harry, an intelligent and effeminate young man, is receptive to the seductions of a high-school teacher; his dawning consciousness of his homosexuality, described sympathetically if somewhat vaguely, is a remarkable first in American Jewish literature.

Brinig's lyricism occasionally rings false, and his plots border on melodrama, but the book paints a vivid portrait of Jewish life in the American West. Spiced with untranslated Yiddish phrases and details of life in a mining town, *Singermann* is irreplaceable as a reminder that Jews have lived just about everywhere in the United States and compelling as a family saga and social history of Montana.

Further reading: Brinig's debut was successful enough to merit a sequel in 1932, *This Man Is My Brother* (also known as *Sons of Singermann*), and the author published more than a dozen other books, some of which, like *Anthony in the Nude* (1930) and *Footsteps on the Stair* (1950), also feature sympathetic gay characters. Earl Ganz's *The Taos Truth Game* (2007) fictionalizes Brinig's adult life in Taos, New Mexico, based in part on Brinig's unpublished (and reportedly not-so-interesting) memoirs; it might be easier to find Ganz's novel than Brinig's books themselves, which—until they are reprinted—must be sought out at well-stocked libraries. Later Jewish novels that deal with homosexuality include Sanford Friedman's *Totempole* (1965), Gene Horowitz's *Privates* (1986), and David Sadownick's *Sacred Lips of the Bronx* (1994); see also the work of Lev Raphael (including 1990's *Dancing on Tisha B'Av*) and David Leavitt.

. . . .

20 – *Bottom Dogs*
By Edward Dahlberg

PUTNAM, 1929. 269 PAGES.

In selecting the subject matter of his first novel, Edward Dahlberg scraped the very bottom of the economic barrel, long before it was fashionable to do so—before novels of junkies and drifters, lunatics, and street children had become common literary fare. The panoramic view of American low life in orphanages and petty jobs and business scams that came to be called the proletarian novel as well as the modern American road novel (the most famous example of which is Jack Kerouac's *On the Road,* published in 1957) both owe a great deal to the example Dahlberg provided in *Bottom Dogs*. In a supportive introduction for the novel's first publication, D. H. Lawrence hoped that Dahlberg's book was a "ne plus ultra," an unsurpassable peak in the description of hopelessness and destitution, for, he wrote, "the next step is legal insanity." If that's the case, a great swath of American literature in the 1930s and afterward is fit for an asylum.

Dahlberg's autobiographical hero, Lorry Lewis, is raised by his mother, Lizzie, in Kansas City, Missouri. Lizzie—who shares a first name, a job, and many other characteristics with Dahlberg's real-life mother—runs a barbershop near the train station and proceeds to entangle herself with any number of creeps. One of these sketchy characters convinces her to send Lorry off to an orphanage in Cleveland, a terrifying place where corporal punishment, hazing, and spoiled food are the regular amenities. Having survived this hostile environment and even managed to discover the pleasures of literature in the process, Lorry finds he can't stay still or settle down back in Kansas City, or anywhere else. Learning the tricks of "boing" (not a sound effect, but a verb, shortened from "hoboing"), Lorry rides the rails and hitchhikes west to California, where he winds up at a Los Angeles YMCA filled with yet another set of outlandish characters, as loudmouthed and passionate as the orphans he has known. These experiences are related in a quick-moving, flat dialect studded with local expressions, slang terms, and occasional old-fashioned vulgarity—all of which Lawrence referred

37

to as "sheer bottom-dog style, the bottom-dog mind expressing itself direct, almost as if it barked"; later on in a long career, Dahlberg disowned his early work as "dunghill fiction."

Bottom Dogs is essentially autobiographical, with Lorry standing in for the author—but Dahlberg edits his past with a free hand—removing many of the cues that would alert readers to the Jewish elements of his experiences. In real life, the institution Dahlberg grew up in was the Jewish Orphan Asylum of Cleveland. His father was a no-good Jewish barber, and his mother seems to have had a thing for dishonest Jews, as she was later scammed and mistreated by Harry Coen, a supposed baker and entrepreneur, the sort of guy who burns down a stable after heavily insuring his horses. Jewish elements do occasionally appear in the book: one of the drifters at the YMCA, for example, is Hyam Davidd, a British Jew to whom Lorry reaches out. *Bottom Dogs* isn't a book about people connecting, though, but an influential exploration of a loner's disaffection.

Further reading: Dahlberg's long career was marked by prolixity, a turn to a ponderous style, and his insistence on bad-mouthing his contemporaries. His third novel, *Those Who Perish* (1934) deals with the rise of Hitlerism and the passivity of American Jews. Those interested in the conjunction between Dahlberg's life and his first novel can compare the stories in *Bottom Dogs* to Dahlberg's highly praised autobiography, *Because I Was Flesh* (1964), which covers much of the same material, as well as Charles DeFanti's biography of the author, *The Wages of Expectation* (1978).

· ·

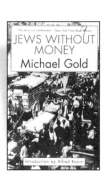

21 – *Jews without Money*

By Michael Gold (Irwin Granich)

LIVERIGHT, 1930. 309 PAGES.

In a preface to his autobiographical novel, *Jews without Money*, published five years after the book's initial release, Mike Gold relates an anecdote about a German radical friend of his who was translating a chapter from Gold's book when she was interrupted by a Nazi. The title amuses the soldier: "How could there be Jews without money, when as every good Nazi knew with Hitler, Jews were all international bankers?" As a staunch communist, the notion of all Jews being capitalists turned Gold's stomach; to him, Jewish bankers—like bankers of any other religion or race—were fascists, pure and simple. But poor Jews in America, exploited in sweatshops and struggling to eke out a meager living, could be exemplary proletarians.

The novel describes the childhood of one such worker, modeled on Gold himself, and given his name (though the author's birth name was actually Irwin Granich). This precocious child grows up on a Lower East Side choked with prostitution and gangsters, on the one hand, and naively religious peasants, on the other. The narrator's father, Herman, is a Romanian immigrant who finds himself screwed out of job after job, first by a corrupt partner, then by lead poisoning and a tumble from scaffolding. He winds up, to his shame, peddling bananas for pennies from a pushcart. Meanwhile, his wife, the narrator's mother, is a paragon of virtue—not only slaving long hours at a restaurant and running a clean home but also reaching out to her neighbors, Jewish and gentile, and fighting for the rights of the poor against landlords and bosses. That every plot development reminds the reader of the tragedies made inevitable by the capitalist system and Tammany Hall should be no surprise; Gold introduces a sweet younger sister for his protagonist, for example, only to have her run over and killed by a delivery truck.

Gold was a communist first, and a writer second. He published just this single novel, compared to the hundreds of essays and polemics against capitalism and corruption he churned out at rapid speed; his most lasting impact on American culture may have been as the editor of *The New Masses*, the premiere communist journal of its day. *Jews without Money* was a major success, though, and was translated into more than a dozen languages, including Chinese, Swedish, and Esperanto. Part of its international appeal was, of course, the call to revolution in its final pages ("O workers' Revolution . . . You are the true Messiah" reads about the same in any language) and its status as one of the first major proletarian novels to be published in America. If only a series of vignettes, Gold's novel is still among the most sympathetic and textured tales of the Lower East Side, and as an expression of communist thought, it reflects a major trend in the politics and ideology of early Jewish life in the United States.

Further reading: Gold's life was fascinating: poverty forced him out of school at 12, but as a young man he briefly attended Harvard; he knew many of the literary eminences of his day and was praised in Sinclair Lewis's Nobel Prize address. Some biographical coverage of Gold can be found in books on left-wing writing in America, such as Daniel Aaron's *Writers on the Left* (1961) and Alan Wald's *Exiles from a Future Time* (2002). His essays are collected in two somewhat hard-to-find volumes, *The Mike Gold Reader* (1954) and *Mike Gold: A Literary Anthology* (1972).

39

. . . .

22 – *By the Waters of Manhattan*
By Charles Reznikoff

CHARLES BONI BOOKS, 1930. 255 PAGES.

Charles Reznikoff's first and most famous novel, *By the Waters of Manhattan*, tells a familiar tale of American Jewish life, starting with Eastern European origins and hardships and immigration, and climaxing with uneasy acculturation to the United States. What distinguishes the book is the oddness and singularity of its narration, which might be less startling to readers who know that Reznikoff is primarily remembered as a poet and as a primary force in the small but influential group dubbed the Objectivists. (Not to be confused with followers of Ayn Rand's philosophy, these Objectivists were influenced by William Carlos Williams and Ezra Pound.)

The first half of the narrative focuses on the Volsky family of Elizavetgrad, Russia, and relates detail after detail of their struggle to earn a living and dodge persecution. They move, change jobs, and farm out their kids to friends and relatives so often that it becomes hard to keep track of them; more than once, the birth of a child flies by in a single sentence. In this way, Reznikoff creates a sense of the inexorable press of time and the necessary intricacy of family dependencies caused by poverty and political instability. Gradually, the narrative focuses on Sarah Yetta, the Volsky's eldest and most willful daughter, who happens to have the same name as Reznikoff's own mother. Smart and hardworking, she is too poor to spend time reading, but she builds up a business with four sewing machines and eight employees. Refusing to be deluded by religious optimism, and yet unwilling to forego tradition entirely, Sarah Yetta sees no future for herself in Russia. In New York, she marries and continues the struggle to put food on the table, and the narrative turns to her cerebral son, named Ezekiel after her father. Living off the labor of his parents and siblings, and having made "the Forty-second Street library his hang-out," this young aesthete decides to open a bookstore in Greenwich Village. Making a moderate success of it, he finds himself attracted to a customer, Jane Dauthendy, whose grandmother was a "Jewess," and proceeds to court her tentatively throughout the remainder of the novel; the book ends without much of a conclusion, as Ezekiel rushes to her house to give her a photograph of himself. More significant than the progress of Ezekiel's business or love life are his lyrical reflections on New York City in the early 20th century; he is a poet in training, modeling himself on his namesake, his grandfather, who "went about the country on business, writing page after page of verse to hide in his baggage—until his widow found the bulky manuscript and burnt it."

Since Reznikoff's career as an artist was frequently stymied by financial and critical obstacles, his interest in the struggles of both of these Ezekiels to bring beauty into the world is understandable: for them and for Reznikoff, the Jewish situation in the Diaspora is one that challenges, if also inspires, literary production. It makes sense, too, that the novel's title alludes to Psalm 137, a timeless statement on the fraught relationship between art and exile; as the psalmist asks, "How can we sing the songs of the Lord while in a foreign land?"

Further reading: In addition to his first novel, Reznikoff published a historical novel, histories, and translations; his complete poems were collected by Black Sparrow Press in two volumes (1976, 1977)—and, later, in a single convenient paperback. His objectivist counterparts included Louis Zukofsky and George Oppen. *Charles Reznikoff: Man and Poet* (1984), edited by Milton Hindus, contains relevant biographical and critical essays.

23 – *Thicker Than Water*

By Vera Caspary

LIVERIGHT, 1932. 426 PAGES.

Willa Cather once remarked that she wanted to write "novels without furniture"—efficient fictions stripped bare of all nonessential social and environmental detail. By contrast, Vera Caspary packs her second novel, *Thicker Than Water*, full of furniture, quite literally: every time one of the novel's linked families redecorates, Caspary invariably tells us whether the new bureau is made of Circassian walnut, golden oak, or bird's-eye maple. And she devotes equal attention to details of decor and wardrobe, limning the brocades and taffetas of women's gowns and the trimming of their hats with flair and precision. Caspary doesn't include these particularities for their own sake, though, nor simply because they illustrate the lifestyles of her entitled Chicago Jews. Rather, Caspary emphasizes furniture because it offers a window onto their desires and envies, their lusts and loyalties. As one character observes, "the shining damask and silver, the thin gold-edged china," are "symbols" of the family's values.

A protracted family saga spanning nearly half a century, the novel centers on Rosalia Piera, a proud Jewess of noble Portuguese descent whose family has already been in the United States for five generations. Because she lives in Chicago, though, and not near the well-established Sephardic community of New York—and because she is neither especially wealthy nor attractive—Rosalia agrees to marry a Jew of more recent German extraction despite her family's feeling that these Germans are nouveau riche and déclassé. As decades pass, the Pieras' early prejudice against Germans seems quaint, as younger members of the clan—the novel follows not just Rosalia but also her brother and cousins, as well as their parents and children—wed Russian "kikes" (as some of the less-tolerant German Jews call them) and, even later, elope with non-Jews, while the phenomenal financial triumphs of the new immigrants erode class distinctions. Caspary meanwhile keeps an eye on the declining fortunes of the family's millinery business and on the differences in Jewish practices from household to household. For this extended family "never-ending birthday and anniversary celebrations," not to mention holidays, provide constant justifications for elaborate celebratory feasts, and tastes range from kosher standbys to fashionable delicacies, from stuffed cabbage to well-chilled Veuve Clicquot and shrimp cocktail.

The grand historical narrative (the Spanish-American War, the invention of the automobile, World War I, Black Tuesday) remains in the background, while Caspary focuses on the effects of world events on her characters' relationships. Something of an early feminist, Caspary catalogs the desires and obstacles facing her female characters with particular sensitivity, and she describes not only their teenage crushes and suffocating marriages but also—if more obliquely—their abortions. The novel can't help indulging in sentimentality from time to time, especially as Rosalia ages and watches over her daughter's and granddaughter's foibles; but Caspary earns her emotional and sensational flourishes with her precise storytelling and portraiture. One of the few novels to tell the story of the Sephardic Jews who were the first to establish themselves in the United States, *Thicker Than Water* will especially please lovers of grand, old-fashioned novels.

Further reading: In her long writing career, Caspary rarely touched on Jewish issues or themes; she is remembered today for mystery novels, such as *Laura* (1942), and award-winning screenplays. *Thicker Than Water* is somewhat autobiographical; Caspary describes her upbringing in a Portuguese Jewish family in Chicago, as well as her wild experiences in the 1920s and her turn to communist affiliation during the Depression, in an autobiography, *The Secret Lives of Grown-Ups* (1979). Emma Lazarus, the poet famous for penning the verses inscribed on the Statue of Liberty, grew up in an aristocratic Sephardic family not unlike the Pieras; for her biography, see *Emma Lazarus in Her World* (1997) or Esther Schor's *Emma Lazarus* (2006).

. . . .

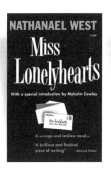 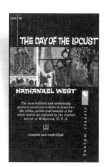

24 – *Miss Lonelyhearts* and *The Day of the Locust*
By Nathanael West

LIVERIGHT, 1933. 213 PAGES.
RANDOM HOUSE, 1939. 238 PAGES.

"**M**en have always fought their misery with dreams. Although dreams were once powerful, they have been made puerile by the movies, radio and newspapers. Among many betrayals, this one is the worst." So muses Miss Lonelyhearts, and the sentiment could stand as the motto for both of these exquisite short novels. More powerfully perhaps than any other artist, Nathanael West argued through his fiction that imagination and fantasy had been commoditized and debased by the mass media (what Theodor Adorno and Max Horkheimer would later call the "culture industry") and that people have consequently been stripped of their sympathies for one another. And just think: West never even saw television. Imagine how he would have felt about *that.*

West's novels manage to be hilariously funny while remaining resolutely grim, in part due to his genius for stark and shocking violence and uncompromising exaggerations. The setup for *Miss Lonelyhearts* sounds like a hoot, but it turns into a nightmare: a young intellectual man takes a job, as a joke, as a newspaper's advice columnist. Soon, though, "the joke begins to escape him"; the letters he receives "are profoundly humble pleas for moral and spiritual advice . . . inarticulate expressions of genuine suffering." He hears from the ill and the abused, and he has no idea what advice to offer. The one answer that works reliably—Jesus—he's not thrilled with, being a nonbeliever himself. *The*

Day of the Locust, meanwhile, takes on the mother of all dream-devouring industries: Hollywood. Tod Hackett, an artist wasting his talents as a scene painter, is the focal consciousness through which the excesses and revulsions of La-La Land are observed. That prostitutes figure into this critique shouldn't surprise anyone, but the raw violence against animals—quails getting their heads snapped off, a cockfight in which two birds tear each other to bloody pieces—ups the ante in terms of disaffection. The disorienting scene in which Tod strolls through a studio lot, passing in a few minutes lifelike sets of deserts and Paris and Greek temples and Napoleon's Waterloo, the trappings of which will end up sooner or later on a garbage heap, is postmodernism *avant la lettre* and a gorgeously self-contained exposition of how 20th-century culture grinds up all that is fine and grand from the past in its inexorable and insatiable jaws.

What does any of this have to do with the Jews? Quite a lot, actually. For one thing, West, the son of immigrants from Russia, was born Nathan Weinstein (he changed his name, legally, at the age of 23); it's up for debate as to how West's Jewishness inflected his literary perspective. For another thing, though, both before and after West's time, Jews have been highly involved in both newspaper advice columns—not just the prominent Ann Landers, Dear Abby, and Dr. Joyce Brothers, but also Abraham Cahan, who penned the famed "Bintel Brief" advice column in the Yiddish *Forward*—and, of course, in the movies (for the story of Jews in early Hollywood, see Neal Gabler's history, *An Empire of Their Own*, published in 1989). In his short career—he died at the age of 37, having produced little enough fiction that it can all fit comfortably in a single volume— West took seriously the ways that the technological and cultural shifts of the 20th century changed the way we think and feel, and though his vision was unremittingly bleak, it has for that precise reason remained distressingly relevant for American Jews and for everyone else who lives in a media-saturated world.

Further reading: Jay Martin's biography, *Nathanael West: The Art of His Life* (1970), unearths the story behind the author's career, while *Critical Essays on Nathanael West* (1994), edited by Ben Siegel, gathers dozens of varied responses to the published works. In several essays, including *Love and Death in the American Novel* (1960), Leslie Fiedler also offers exemplary readings of West's work. The grotesque dark comedy West refined became much more prevalent in the decades following his death; Joseph Heller, Thomas Pynchon, and Flannery O'Connor are three major authors who in different ways owe stylistic debts to West.

on its own; the only reason to group them this way is to make them a great bargain—which they are, at any price—in the hopes of alerting a few more readers to Fuchs's deserving, enduring achievement.

Further reading: After his first trilogy failed to sell, Fuchs stopped writing novels and headed to Hollywood, where screenwriting earned him a living and an Oscar, for *Love Me or Leave Me* (1955), with Doris Day and James Cagney. Fuchs's short stories continued to appear, however, and have been collected in *The Apathetic Bookie Joint* (1979) and *The Golden West* (2005). Though Fuchs hasn't received the attention he deserves, a few scant monographs discuss his work, including Marcelline Krafchick's *World without Heroes* (1988) and Gabriel Miller's *Daniel Fuchs* (1979).

. . . .

27 – *The Education of H*Y*M*A*N K*A*P*L*A*N*
By Leonard Q. Ross (Leo Rosten)

HARCOURT, BRACE AND CO., 1937. 176 PAGES.

Leo Rosten is mostly remembered for *The Joys of Yiddish* (1968), a bestseller offering enlightenment to Jews and gentiles perplexed by the massive amounts of *mameloshen* that get tossed around in American speech. Rosten's career as a humorist was long, though, and three decades before *Joys* he published, under the pseudonym Leonard Q. Ross, *The Education of H*Y*M*A*N K*A*P*L*A*N*, a collection of episodes culled from the pages of the *New Yorker* that could have been subtitled *The Oy-oy-oys of Yiddish Speakers.*

The stories take place at the American Night Preparatory School for Adults, where the genteel Mr. Parkhill attempts to impart American panache ("English—Americanization—Civics—Preparation for Naturalization") to a horde of bumbling immigrants, the most indefatigable of whom is Mr. Hyman Kaplan. In the grand tradition of Jewish dialect humor, which is itself part of a general American literary obsession with regional speech patterns stretching back to the 19th century, Rosten renders Kaplan's language with exuberantly phonetic orthography. Kaplan's favorite American writers, for example, are "Jeck Laundon, Valt Viterman, and the author of 'Hawk L. Barry-Feen,' one Mocktvain." Kaplan has a genius for grammatical errors, a gift for finding ridiculous homonyms, and he approaches English with his own bizarre logic: "to die" is conjugated as "die, dead, funeral." Because Kaplan's mangled speech was designed to entertain fluent English speakers, the puns and jokes still manage to amuse even 70 years after they were first published.

Obviously, Kaplan and most of his classmates—Miss Mitnick, Mrs. Moskowitz, Mr. Bloom—are Yiddish-speaking Jewish immigrants. Yet the author remains coy about their origins: Kaplan remarks that "for som pipple is Chrissmas like for *odder* pipple is Passover," but he never says outright that he is one of those odder pipple. The Poland-born Rosten, writing under his Anglicized pseudonym, aligns himself with the prim Mr. Parkhill, who speaks a high-minded English peppered with Latin and French phrases; and while the satire is light and kindhearted, it is not free of condescension. Nor does Rosten acknowledge the grim side of immigration in the interwar period: since 1924, the numbers of Jews who could come to the United States from Eastern Europe had been severely limited by quotas, and by the mid-1930s, tens of thousands of German-Jewish immigrants were flooding Manhattan each year, fleeing Hitler's Germany—hardly a barrel of laughs. Still, the night school experience has been shared by new Americans from all over the globe throughout the generations, and the book is a sweet portrait of that quintessential and hilarious element of the immigrant experience.

Further reading: Rosten churned out a couple of sequels to this first Hyman Kaplan book, and his *Joys of Yiddish* is a riot (though not a reliable Yiddish lexicon). While no biography of the humorist has yet appeared, *The Many Worlds of L*E*O R*O*S*T*E*N* (1964) offers a partial introduction to the scope of his writings (in addition to his humorous work, he also wrote political novels and screenplays). Fans of Jewish dialect humor should consult the works of Arthur Kober, Milt Gross, and, if they can find it, Harry Hershfield, whose long-running comic strip character Abie Kabibble spouted a wonderful Yinglish and occasionally even wrote theater and film reviews in that argot for the *New York Evening Journal* (despite the fact that he was a fictional character). Myra Kelly's stories set in the public schools of the Lower East Side, such as *Little Citizens* (1904), can also be read as literary antecedents of Hyman Kaplan's adventures.

. . . .

28 – *I Can Get It for You Wholesale*

By Jerome Weidman

SIMON AND SCHUSTER, 1937. 370 PAGES.

Harry Bogen, the hard-boiled antihero of Jerome Weidman's best-selling debut novel, knows that you can't have it both ways: "You couldn't reach for the big dough and listen to your mother's lessons in morals. . . . You took one or the other." Forced to choose, he doesn't hesitate: he joyfully screws over his co-workers, dispatches an innocent partner to jail, and, despite his loving mother's advice, chooses a slick non-Jewish actress over a kind, "Jewish-looking" girl from the Bronx. A little dishonesty? "That's the way things are," he says. "In business you got to be that way." Having started out as a shipping clerk at $15 per week, he waltzes out of his venture into the Seventh Avenue garment industry with a sweet $20,000, a plush apartment, and a flashy car. Not bad for a kid still in his 20s.

Like *Haunch, Paunch and Jowl* (1923), *What Makes Sammy Run?* (1941), *The Apprenticeship of Duddy Kravitz* (1959), and other novels of scheming Jew-boys on the make, Weidman's novel has offended some readers and delighted millions.

Despite a use of frank language shocking for its time—Weidman himself was surprised that his publishers hadn't pruned the "raw elements"—the only censorship mounted against the book has come from its publishers; both Simon and Schuster and Avon, the book's paperback publisher, attempted in varying ways to assuage outraged readers in the Jewish community. Far from an endorsement of Bogen's cutthroat behavior, or from a claim that dishonesty in business is typical of Jews, though, *I Can Get It for You Wholesale* is the author's attack on the moral depravity of the capitalist system, in which jerks like Bogen profit at the expense of the world's ethical *schlemiels*. What makes Weidman's version of this common story stand out is the author's familiarity with the details of the garment trade (he worked his way through college as an accountant in a ladies' wear firm), Bogen's shameless voice, and the exhaustingly snappy dialogue, in which questions are always answered with questions and sarcasm runs high. What, you need an example?

Bogen is vile, even by the cynical standards of our own times. He exploits the labor movement; he hurls hateful epithets at every minority he comes across, including Jews; he patronizes whorehouses, preys on his secretaries, and lies to his mother—for whom, it should be mentioned, he has what seems to be an unnatural passion. Nonetheless, though, the character has enthralled millions of readers and has spurred adaptations of the story into a movie in 1951—which changed the plot almost entirely, transforming Harry Bogen into Harriet Boyd, a gentile fashion model—as well as a more faithful Broadway musical in 1962 that featured the debut of a teenaged Barbara Streisand in a supporting role.

Further reading: In a long career, Weidman published more than two dozen books, including many novels, short story collections, travelogues, essays, and an autobiography, *Praying for Rain* (1987). Harry Bogen's story continued in *What's in It for Me?* (1938). Weidman's *The Enemy Camp* (1958), a look at anti-Semitism, is worth reading, too.

. . . .

29 – *Tomorrow's Bread*

By Beatrice Bisno

JEWISH PUBLICATION SOCIETY OF AMERICA, 1938. 328 PAGES.

Like many American Jews in the first half of the 20th century, Beatrice Bisno grew up in labor movements: her father, Abraham Bisno, was the president of the Chicago Cloakmaker's Union, and for decades she worked as a secretary and right-hand woman to Sidney Hillman, the president of the Amalgamated Clothing Workers of America. What distinguishes her portrait of a charismatic labor leader, *Tomorrow's Bread*, from a large field of ideologically engaged fictions by leftist Jews before and after it, is not its politics but its focus. Bisno, having been immersed in unions throughout her life and taking them almost for granted, does not bother to propagandize for them; instead she exhibits, through her antihero Sam Karenski, the lives people lived in their orbit.

From a tender age, Sam goes his own way. At 14, apprenticed to a tailor in Chattanooga, Tennessee, the business-minded Sam has already drifted from his mother's traditionalism—he can't read Yiddish, and "his morning prayers were the whir of his sewing machine." Though the family relocates to Chicago for its Jewish community—to have "kosher butcher shops," "ortadox *Shuls*," and a "*mikveh*" nearby—Sam continues to be drawn to atheistic, political, and sexual leftism. A fiery speaker, if not an intellectual, Sam soon rises to the presidency of a Chicago union through his support of closed (that is, union-only) shops and his simple but persistent reliance on the socialistic principles of Marxism. His long career has highs—a well-paying position as a government inspector, for example, enforcing workplace regulations he helped draft—and humiliating lows. Through it all, whether he is making a fortune selling real estate to poor African Americans or getting mugged as a subway ticket taker, he remains loyal to union politics.

More complex are Sam's family and romantic relationships. Though he woos and marries a supportive woman, Sam never stops sleeping around—but when his infidelities are discovered, he refuses to divorce her. As he proclaims, "Other women don't interfere with my marriage." Such "personal sex theories" and his poor hygiene don't win Sam anyone's support—even as some of his ideas become more mainstream in the years after World War I. His sons grow up to resent him for the way he has mistreated their mother, while his daughter, a budding writer, may be the novel's most autobiographical figure. Hardly a stylistic masterpiece, this readable novel features some subtle Yinglish syntax and abundant period detail, offering a broad panorama of turn-of-the-century Chicago and its Jews. It also offers a reminder of how much Jewish culture—from unionism to everyday speech—has been assimilated into mainstream Americana: in the late 1930s, the word "*begel*" was still unknown enough that it had to be included in the novel's glossary!

Further reading: Though she remained active in the labor movement for decades afterward, Bisno published only this single book. Little has been written about her life. Fictional treatments of Jewish involvement in the labor movement include Arthur Bullard's *Comrade Yetta* (1913), while a jokey perspective on immigrant Jews in the needle trades can be found in Montague Glass's bestseller, *Potash and Perlmutter* (1910).

30 — *As a Driven Leaf*
By Milton Steinberg

BOBBS-MERRILL, 1939. 480 PAGES.

For the most part, historical novels set somewhere other than America have been excluded from this guide (even if written by an American and relevant to contemporary Jewish life). There is no reason for this exclusion, other than the impossibility of doing justice to the vast number of such books, which retell biblical stories, fictionalize the Spanish Inquisition, and reimagine Eastern Europe. For *As a Driven Leaf* it is worth making an exception, though, because this is an extraordinary novel in so many ways. One of the few novels of literary quality written by a practicing rabbi, it is also unusual for what it accomplishes: an imagined biography of a shady talmudic character, pulled together from narrative scraps strewn throughout the textual tradition.

Steinberg invents a life for Elisha ben Abuyah, also known as Akher ("Other"), and familiar to talmudists as the archetypal apostate. In doing so, he offers a vibrant reconstruction of life under the Romans in Palestine around and after the year 100 C.E., replete with pagans, Christians, and the rock stars of the Rabbinic world, sages like Rabbi Akiba and Rabbi Meir. The young Elisha reads the *Iliad* with a pagan tutor and retains a wandering intellect into his adult years. Though he rises to a position on the Sanhedrin, the great legislative body of the Jews, he witnesses a bad thing happening to a good person, and that is enough to shake his faith to the foundations: "It is all a lie," he proclaims. "There is no reward. There is no Judge. There is no Judgment. For there is no God." It is not exactly the kind of speech we expect from the great rabbis. After being excommunicated, Elisha sets out to find truth on his own—attempting to reconcile heartfelt Jewish belief in a divine creator with the rational principles of Greek logic. Two thousand years later, many Jews are still trying to work out an answer to that same problem.

Steinberg studied at the Jewish Theological Seminary with Mordecai Kaplan, the founder of Reconstructionism, and served as a rabbi in Indiana and later at the Park Avenue Synagogue on the east side of Manhattan. He died when he was only 46 years old and left an impressive shelf of books behind him, including the widely used *Basic Judaism* (1947). He never wrote a second novel—which is too bad, as the Talmud is filled with characters and tales ripe for fictionalization—but his first has been acclaimed for decades; most recently, it earned a spot on the National Yiddish Book Center's list of the 100 best works of modern Jewish literature.

Further reading: Simon Noveck's *Milton Steinberg: Portrait of a Rabbi* (1978) is a useful biography, if you can locate a copy of it. As for historical novels of Jewish interest, even aside from Anita Diamant's colossal bestseller *The Red Tent* (1997), there are hundreds of examples: from Louis Untermeyer's *Moses* (1928) to the Nobel laureate Pearl S. Buck's *Peony* (1948), about the Jews of Kaifeng, China, to

David Liss's *The Coffee Trader* (2003), set in 17th-century Amsterdam. Rosalind Reisner's *Jewish American Literature* (2004) contains a sizable list of such titles.

. . . .

31 – *What Makes Sammy Run?*
By Budd Schulberg

RANDOM HOUSE, 1941. 299 PAGES.

Jews were making movies in Hollywood before Hollywood was Hollywood, so it should come as no surprise that they have also written several of the best novels about the American film industry. Budd Schulberg moved west as a kid after World War I, and as his father became a major player in the movie business, he found himself well-positioned to overhear all the behind-the-scenes gossip. He returned to California after graduation from Dartmouth College, hacked away at screenplays, and after a few years published *What Makes Sammy Run?*, a runaway bestseller that remains both a peek into Hollywood's soul and a durable parable on the perils of American ambition.

In the book, Sammy Glick, a poor Jewish teen in New York City, hustles his way from the bottom of the barrel to the very top, doing anything necessary to get there. Clawing his way out of East Side poverty, he runs errands for a newspaper, then inaugurates a radio column. He teams up with and exploits a shy writer named Julian Blumberg, and, stealing his partner's script, decamps for Hollywood. Soon after arriving, he is already sporting "one of those California tans" and scheming his way up through the ranks of screenwriters; before he is finished, he has become a genuine mogul, having pushed aside an older executive. Every step of the way, his achievements come at someone else's expense—and he shows no remorse for the carnage he leaves in his wake, remarking, "If you haven't learned by this time that it's every man for himself, it's no skin off my ass. It's your funeral." The genial narrator, Al Mannheim, tracks Sammy's progress, bewitched and repulsed by the kid's amoral drive, and wondering if he'll ever know why it is that Sammy was always hustling. Schulberg plots his novel with extraordinary efficiency, and his dialogue is always snappy, as befits his subject.

What Makes Sammy Run? is often dismissed as anti-Semitic and self-hating, perhaps because it first appeared during the Holocaust and because its unforgettable title character long remained the paradigm of scheming, stop-at-nothing youth. Admittedly, Schulberg's portrait of Sammy is far from flattering. Yet as Schulberg himself has pointed out, virtually all of the novel's cast is Jewish, including many likeable characters and most of Sammy's victims; Sammy's Jewishness cannot rationally be used to explain his ethical lapses. The question of how close Sammy comes to being an anti-Semitic stereotype remains worthy of discussion, though, as does the always perplexing problem of how Jewish communities can encourage and take pride in the achievements of Jewish youths without promoting Sammy-like competitiveness.

Further reading: Schulberg's *Moving Pictures: Memories of a Hollywood Prince* (1981) offers the author's real-life experiences, as far as he remembers them. He wrote a number of other novels and nonfiction studies, but his other enduring contribution to American culture was the screenplay for *On the Waterfront* (1954), directed by Elia Kazan and starring Marlon Brando. Other authors who have handled the Jewish experience of Hollywood in various eras include Leslie Epstein, Albert Goldman, and Daniel Fuchs.

. . . .

32 – *Jewish Cowboy* [*Der Yidisher Kauboy*]
By Isaac Raboy

YIDDISH: ICUF, 1942. 311 PAGES.
ENGLISH: TRANSLATED BY NATHANIEL SHAPIRO. TRADITION BOOKS, 1989. 297 PAGES.

From Edward Meeker's turn-of-the-century vaudeville routines to Mel Brooks's *Blazing Saddles* (1974), the notion of a Jewish cowboy has long been a source of hilarity. But to the Yiddish novelist Isaac Raboy, being both a Jew and a ranch hand was no joke: Raboy spent a couple of years laboring on a North Dakota farm, and the autobiographical protagonist of his novel *Der Yidisher Kauboy* does the same, partly in the hopes that "by demonstrating his skills and his willingness to work hard, he would salvage the good name and reputation of the Jewish people."

Jewish Cowboy is not, then, as one might expect, a fish-out-of-water comedy, but rather a sensitive coming-of-age story. Hewing closely to the author's real-life experiences, Raboy's protagonist, Isaac ("Eye," for short), ships out to the North Dakota prairie after graduating from a New Jersey agricultural college. This academic training supplements the intimate knowledge of horses he picked up during his Bessarabian boyhood, and the North Dakotans he meets remind Isaac of Eastern European peasants, so he isn't completely unprepared for the exigencies of farm life. At the same time, much of what the young man knows about the West derives straight from the movies, and his academic training is not respected by the farmers. As one of his professors writes in a recommendation letter, "Isaac knows more about horses than he knows about himself"—or, for that matter, about other people. So while he bonds with the farm's prize stallion, he has more trouble with the exploitative and anti-Semitic ranch owner; the other hired hands; and the only two women in sight, the owner's kindly Chicago-born wife and a young woman who is basically an indentured servant, both of whom fall in love with the young Jew from the East.

The novel's minor plot intrigues—pay disputes, farming accidents, stifled emotional revelations—provide a frame for Raboy to explore his interests in the development of Isaac's poetic sensibility, in the eternal exploitation of the working classes and minorities by the rich, and, most of all, in the nobility of horses and physical labor. After being labeled a "dirty Sheeny," Isaac abandons North Dakota and returns to his family in New York, suggesting how difficult it would have been for a Jew to make a life on the prairie. At the same time, though, Raboy demonstrated how seductive the dream of the frontier was to him and to his readers, milking his stint on the farm for literary inspiration over and over, treating it in his first novel, *Herr Goldenbarg* (1913), and in his memoirs, as well as in *Jewish Cowboy*—which is, for the time being, the only one of his books available in English translation.

Further reading: Raboy was associated with the Yiddish literary cohort *Di Yunge*, and his novels dealt with farm life in Connecticut (1918's *Der Pas fun Yam*) as well as more typical urban and old-country stories. Aside from the standard Yiddish-language sources, biographical material on Raboy can be found in Sol Liptzin's *A History of Yiddish Literature* (1972). Recordings of Meeker's slapstick vaudeville hit "I'm a Yiddish Cowboy" can be found widely online, but both of the silent films titled *The Yiddisher Cowboy*, from 1909 and 1911, have probably been lost to posterity. *The Frisco Kid* (1979) and HBO's series *Deadwood* offer more recent takes on the role of Jews in the Wild West.

· ·

33 – *The Family Carnovsky*
By I. J. Singer

YIDDISH: MATONES, 1943. 518 PAGES.
ENGLISH: TRANSLATED BY JOSEPH SINGER. VANGUARD, 1969. 405 PAGES.

Israel Joshua Singer was born in Poland, but he had already been living in the United States for 10 years, and had been an American citizen for 4, when he first published *Di Mishpokhe Karnovsky* in book form in 1943. So naturally, when his characters, three generations of the Carnovsky family, are forced to flee the persecutions of Hitler's Germany in the novel's third section, Singer brings them to his adopted home, New York City. They're lucky—we know now the horrific fate of those who didn't escape Berlin before the war—but adjusting to the change isn't easy. As Singer writes, "To the family Carnovsky, America was like a new pair of shoes—a pleasure to put on, a pain to wear."

The novel's three books track three generations of Carnovskys, each of which strays farther from the family's roots in Eastern Europe. David, the patriarch, rejects the small-mindedness he sees in his Polish shtetl and moves with his young wife to Berlin, the seat of Enlightenment and culture. His son, Georg, grows out of his youthful aimlessness, and, thanks in part to an attractive female medical student, works his way up to become one of the city's most prominent surgeons. Though highly pursued by Jewish marriage brokers, Georg falls in love with a Christian, Teresa; their son, Jegor, matures in interwar Berlin and assimilates the disgusting racial theories peddled by the Nazis and their flunkies. Singer fleshes out his plot with a supporting cast that includes Solomon Burak, an appealing discount store magnate; Dr. Elsa Landau, a communist firebrand and member of the Reichstag; her father, a vegetarian and philanthropic physician; and Dr. Zerba, a failed mystical poet and pervert who becomes a low-level Nazi spy with a home on Long Island.

Over 110,000 refugees immigrated to America from Germany in the 1930s, and half of them settled on New York's Upper West Side. Singer's novel—incredible for having been written before the end of the war and the revelation of the most awful brutalities—offers a panorama of their experiences, from the prejudices Jews cultivated toward Jews from other lands, to the inconceivable reticence some had about describing the horrors of the homelands they had fled. A document of its time, and a grand family saga, *The Family Carnovsky* is as valuable as it is compelling.

Further reading: Singer's most famous novel, *The Brothers Ashkenazi* (1936), gives similar epic treatment to the city of Lodz, Poland, and is even more powerful. Though he died tragically young from a heart attack in 1944, Singer's oeuvre also includes a number of plays, short story collections, and a memoir, translated as *Of a World That Is No More* (1970). Readers interested in Singer's relationship with his younger and ultimately more famous brother, Isaac Bashevis Singer, will find Clive Sinclair's *The Brothers Singer* (1983) worthwhile (or see Isaac Bashevis Singer's memoirs of childhood), while Anita Norich's *The Homeless Imagination in the Fiction of I. J. Singer* (1991) is the finest scholarly study of the author's life and works.

34 - *Focus*
By Arthur Miller

REYNAL AND HITCHCOCK, 1945. 217 PAGES.

Though best known as a major American playwright—and, secondarily, for having been married to Marilyn Monroe—Arthur Miller wrote a novel that deserves attention in its own right. This searing book, *Focus*, appeared a couple of months after the end of World War II, and it captures the creeping anxieties of the war years, especially as regards the frightening persistence of American anti-Semitism.

Miller's non-Jewish protagonist, Lawrence Newman, prides himself on his ability to spot Jews by their physical appearance; he has long honed this talent in his capacity as a personnel executive who hires employees for "one of the most anti-Semitic corporations in America." As the novel opens, Newman's failing eyesight forces him to wear glasses, and, in an almost magical transformation, this new accessory makes him look Jewish himself; his mother, co-workers, and neighbors all think so. This premise allows Miller to subject Newman to the typical indignities foisted on Jews in the 1940s and earlier: his bosses find an excuse to fire him from his job; other employers tell him they have no openings for him; and, eventually, he is turned away from "restricted" resort hotels that do not care for the business of that "sort of people." Meanwhile, members of a hate group riled up by a vociferously anti-Semitic Boston priest (modeled on the real-life Father Coughlin) harass a Jewish shopkeeper, Finkelstein, on Newman's block. Although Newman is at first ambivalent toward Finkelstein, the two men are drawn together as they are both targeted by the thugs; Newman, persecuted as a Jew, begins to feel Jewish. The character thus embodies the provocative idea, articulated by Jean-Paul Sartre in *Anti-Semite and Jew* (1946), that if Jews didn't exist, anti-Semites would create them.

Evaluated as realism, the novel is not entirely convincing and, in the sense that its premise depends on the notion that Jews can be identified at least some of the time by their physical appearance, it may even be considered offensive by contemporary standards. As a fable of racial hatred, however, it raises many of the crucial questions about personal responsibility, passivity, and resistance that must be dealt with in response to the Holocaust and American reactions to it. Suspenseful and disturbing, the novel reads like a thriller, and though Jews in America are much less vulnerable now than they were half a century ago, Miller's nightmare images serve as valuable reminders of how susceptible we all are to acting on our fears.

Further reading: Miller's plays—including *Death of a Salesman* (1949), *The Crucible* (1953), and *All My Sons* (1952)—are required reading at many high schools. Miller has been subject to perhaps a dozen biographical studies; the author's own impressive autobiography, *Timebends* (1987), is the best place to start. Laura Z. Hobson's *Gentleman's Agreement* (1947), like *Focus*, treats anti-Semitism in the 1940s from the perspective of a non-Jew and was a major bestseller; both books have been adapted into films, and the movie version of Hobson's book is perhaps even better than her novel.

35 – *Passage from Home*
By Isaac Rosenfeld

DIAL PRESS, 1946. 280 PAGES.

The teenage protagonist of Isaac Rosenfeld's *Passage from Home* attempts to do something that conventional wisdom says you just can't do. As a playground saying puts it, you can pick your nose, and you can pick your friends, but you can't pick your family. Bernard Miller, a protagonist as precocious as the author who created him—at 14, he reads Nietzsche, Schopenhauer, and Herbert Spencer—realizes that he is stifled at home. It is not only, or not exactly, that his is a big, typical Jewish family ("a good two dozen of us . . . would sit around the table drinking tea and eating honeycakes and all of us would be talking at once"), but also that he himself is as "sensitive as a burn," particularly to the failings of his father and to everything he owes him: "Everything I did marked me as his son. My whole life was an acknowledgement and a denial."

Bernard finds himself attracted to two outsiders: his aunt Minna, who keeps her distance from the family and has a shelf of jazz records, and a non-Jewish southerner named Willy, who was married to Bernard's cousin before she died. Willy is a no-good charmer who once played semi-pro baseball, has drifted through a couple of dozen countries and can tell a thousand stories, a few of which might even be true; he sings down-home Christian ditties at the family's Passover seder and mentions, off-hand, that he served as a Paris correspondent for a Yiddish newspaper during the war, though he doesn't know Yiddish or French. In this pair of rebels Bernard glimpses the possibility of a more attractive, more fitting family for himself, and he schemes to bring the two together. He succeeds, and ends up leaving home to live with them, only to discover—surprise, surprise—that their lives are neither as substantial nor as viable as models for him as he imagined them to be. Among other things, their house is a pigsty and he ends up sharing a cot with some nasty bedbugs. If there's a transcendent moment that breaks through Bernard's persistent alienation, it is at a *beit midrash* he visits with his grandfather, where he experiences something akin to revelation, or, as he says, "ecstasy." An allegory for the dilemma of American Jews, stuck as they are between a traditional, often parochial home and a sometimes unpleasant, if exciting, wider world, Rosenfeld's only published novel serves as a timeless rendition of the adolescent search for independence. His prose is subtle and, at its finest moments, deeply thoughtful.

Rosenfeld was an outsized personality whose literary career did not live up to what some hoped it would; he has been memorialized warmly by Alfred Kazin, Saul Bellow, and others, and he was the model for Leslie Braverman in Wallace Markfield's *To an Early Grave* (1964). Though some critics prefer his essays to his fiction, *Passage from Home* is hard to equal as a portrait of Jewish life in Chicago and as a psychological study of adolescent angst.

Further reading: Rosenfeld's literary output was small, if influential; aside from the novel, his essays have been collected in *An Age of Enormity* (1962), his stories in *Alpha and Omega* (1966), and a smattering of his work in various genres in *Preserving the Hunger: An Isaac Rosenfeld Reader* (1988). Selections from his journals have been edited and published in literary journals by Mark Schechner, and Steven Zipperstein's critical biography of the author is forthcoming from Yale University Press.

36 – *Wasteland*

By Jo Sinclair (Ruth Seid)

HARPER, 1946. 321 PAGES.

Good therapists are perhaps even harder to find in fiction than they are in life: psychiatrists in novels and movies tend, more often than not, to be comic figures, ridiculous men or women with silly Freudian accents, jargon, and ideas. Jo Sinclair's first novel, *Wasteland*, is an exception to this and many other rules. Sinclair's doctor is subtle and kind; he doesn't press his patient, John Brown, to accept abstract complexes or theories of childhood development. He simply helps him to think critically about the patterns of his relationships, and soon, John—whose real name is Jake Braunowitz—begins to realize why his life is the way it is.

The novel is set during World War II. John/Jake, who is 35 years old, still lives with his parents in a cramped two-bedroom apartment in Cleveland, along with all but one of his adult siblings. Though a successful newspaper photographer, he struggles with tremendous shame and fear, as well as alcoholism. Without quite knowing it, he resents that his parents are poor immigrants, that his older brother is unemployed, that one of his sisters is a sexually active divorcée, and that another sister is a lesbian. And he is terrified to discover that his nephews, children of his eldest sister, have begun to exhibit the self-hatred and antisocial behavior that he sees in himself. The novel consists of Jake's therapy sessions, related through doctor–patient dialogue, third-person passages in which Jake describes his experiences to his therapist, and brief excerpts from the doctor's notes. By the end of the book, the therapy has succeeded: John has accepted his real name, Jake; he has returned to the family's annual Passover seder, which is enormously important to him as a symbol of his identity; and he has even photographed his relatives, using his technical and artistic skills to reflect the dignity and pathos he didn't realize they had. He accepts himself as a Jew and discovers that by doing so he can be a better American.

If a little utopian in its portrait of psychotherapy, the novel is abundant in psychological and sociological details, and it is powerful in its sympathy for people of all backgrounds. This is visible nowhere more than in the book's depiction of Debby, a strong and self-confident lesbian. Debby's biography mirrors that of the author, Ruth Seid: both graduated first in their high school class and worked on WPA projects during the Depression, for example. Seid, presumably hoping to protect her own privacy, published under the pseudonym Jo Sinclair, but as it happened, at least one acquaintance wrote to her, wondering if perhaps Sinclair was just a pen name. Seid received many more astonishing letters from women who identified with Debby and, in some cases, for whom the novel was their first contact with anything resembling gay culture. A technically accomplished and emotionally resonant fiction, *Wasteland* deserves a much more prominent place on the shelf of American Jewish letters than it has as yet received.

Further reading: Sinclair published three more novels, including *The Changelings* (1955), and a memoir, *The Seasons* (1993), as well as numerous short stories and essays. Though relatively little has been written on Sinclair, a splendid essay by Monica Bachmann in the scholarly journal *GLQ* (2000) quotes extensively from the mail Seid received from the readers of *Wasteland*. Other American Jewish writers who have examined the lesbian experience include the poet and essayist Adrienne Rich and Judith Katz, whose novel *Running Fiercely towards a High Thin Sound* (1992) is worth seeking out.

. . . .

37 – East River
By Sholem Asch

YIDDISH: A. LAUB, 1946. 514 PAGES.
ENGLISH: TRANSLATED BY A. H. GROSS. PUTNAM, 1946. 444 PAGES.

Dozens of American Jewish novels handle the issue of intermarriage, and among the most thoughtful of these is Sholem Asch's *East River*. Set in the diverse, impoverished neighborhood of 48th Street and the East River in Manhattan, during the years before World War I, Asch's novel points up one of the inevitable and wrenching consequences of peaceful coexistence between Jews and Christians.

The plot centers on a devout Irish Catholic girl's involvement with the Jewish Davidowsky family. Pious Moshe Wolf Davidowsky operates a grocery, but he can't cover his bills because he extends credit to all of the neighbors—even those, like Mary McCarthy's father ("the block's official anti-Semite"), who are irresponsible drunks. Grateful for the shopkeeper's charity, Mary is attracted first to the grocer's eldest son, Nathan, a paraplegic and intellectual, and then to Nathan's younger brother, Irving, a budding tycoon of the garment industry.

Struggling to rise from poverty together, Mary and Irving inevitably fall in love, though unlike many of their fictional predecessors, they are not at all naive: they realize from the start how difficult life will be for them, and neither is willing to sacrifice either religion or family ties for the sake of their marriage. Asch is often remembered now only for his audacious—some would say perverse—Yiddish-language trilogy dealing with the life of Christ, but in *East River*, his evident fascination with Christianity allows him to humanize Mary impressively. Her faith is treated with respect both by her husband, who does not insist she abandon the church for him, and by the author, who represents it as the equivalent of pious Moshe Wolf's Jewish Orthodoxy in its sincerity and seriousness.

Like any good epic, *East River* makes room for a wide-ranging cast and a series of captivating discourses on social phenomena, including the connection between dance crazes and women's rights, the church's defense of child labor, and the ideologies—from communism and anarchism to Spinozist philosophy and capitalism—that enlivened American Jewish life in the first decades of the

20th century. Asch harrowingly narrates the infamous Triangle shirtwaist factory fire, in which over 100 young sweatshop workers died in 1911, and he is equally notable as a master in rendering the everyday details of Jewish life.

Further reading: Many of Asch's books, like *East River*, were translated into English soon after (or even before) their publication in Yiddish. His best-selling novels may be *The Nazarene* (1939), *The Apostle* (1943), and *Mary* (1949). Those interested in the descriptions of the garment industry found in *East River* will also want to look at his short novel *Uncle Moses* (1920). Ben Siegel's *The Controversial Sholem Asch* (1976) remains one of the only full-length biographical publications on the author, but recently renewed interest in his work (a conference at Yale in 2000 resulted in a collection of essays, *Sholem Asch Reconsidered* [2004], that includes an exhaustive and masterful analysis of *East River* by Dan Miron) suggests that more sources may be forthcoming soon.

· ·

38 – *The Amboy Dukes*
By Irving Shulman

DOUBLEDAY, 1947. 273 PAGES.

*T*he *Amboy Dukes* comes as a sensational shock: was there really a time, not so many years ago, when Jewish teenagers lurked on the streets of Brooklyn, armed with knives, brass knuckles, and homemade pistols, terrorizing each other and the law-abiding citizens around them? Picture *Boyz 'n the Hood*, except everyone's named Goldfarb, Bronstein, or Sachs, and they're still young enough to fit into their bar mitzvah suits.

It sounds ridiculous, and Irving Shulman undoubtedly exaggerates a little, but the world of *The Amboy Dukes* isn't total fantasy. During World War II, as parents worked overtime and older boys fought overseas, 16-year-olds could swagger through their tough neighborhoods and, in some cases, land themselves in serious trouble. Frank Goldfarb, the protagonist of Shulman's novel, isn't the most violent or unbalanced member of his gang, the titular Dukes: he isn't the one who suggests that the boys steal back the money they've paid to a prostitute who has serviced each of them in turn, and he isn't the one who stabs an innocent Puerto Rican on a whim. He contents himself with smoking "reefers" and making time with the neighborhood's loose girls, one of whom is only 12 years old. Thanks to his buddies, though, Frank has soon graduated from such petty crimes to being accessory to a capital offense, and despite his desire to be a supportive brother to his lonely sister, Alice, and a couple brief flirtations with reform in the form of basketball at the local JCC, his fate looms, sordid and grim.

Though hardly subtle, Shulman's prose is taut and propulsive, and he has a remarkable eye for details of dress, architecture, and other cultural artifacts. The novel's immediate aim was sociological; Shulman insists that problems in the schools, in labor conditions, and in the real estate market exacerbate the natural

59

wayward tendencies of youth. Though he is more famous for writing the screenplay for *Rebel without a Cause* (1955), the impact of *The Amboy Dukes*, Shulman's first novel, was hardly insignificant: it sold more than 4 million copies in paperback. Strangely, though, the paperback copies aren't quite the same book; every last trace of Jewishness—copious Yiddishisms, all of the Jewish names, references to kosher meat and Passover—was excised from them, and from the film adaptation of the novel, titled *City across the River* (1949). This transformation was noted by Henry Popkin in an article in *Commentary* in 1952; Popkin wondered why these edits were deemed necessary, as Shulman's book "says no more than that the Jews, like other groups in America, have the problem of juvenile delinquency." What Popkin may not have realized is that within a few decades, after demographics and stereotypes had shifted, Shulman's association of Jewish teens with gang activity would come to seem utterly unbelievable.

Further reading: Shulman wrote two sequels, *Cry Tough* (1949) and *The Big Brokers* (1951), and other novels including *Children of the Dark* (1955), the basis for *Rebel without a Cause*. Those interested in a scholarly history of the neighborhood in which the novel is set can consult Wendell Pritchett's *Brownsville, Brooklyn* (2003). Mathieu Kassovitz's *Hate* (1995), originally titled *La Haine* in French, is an outstanding film centered on a thuggish Jewish teen in the gritty ghettos near Paris.

39 – *My Glorious Brothers*
By Howard Fast

LITTLE, BROWN, 1948. 280 PAGES.

Lighting candles to commemorate Hanukkah is one of the most widely practiced Jewish traditions in America these days: a whopping 72 percent of respondents to the most recent National Jewish Population Survey said they did so. Reading the Book of Maccabees is much less common, especially since it isn't even included in the Torah (only Catholic and Eastern Orthodox churches consider it one of their scriptures). When Jews tell their kids about Judah Maccabee, they tend to sugarcoat the tale: as with so many of the stories in ancient texts, this one is a whole lot bloodier, and more complicated, than the cheery modern festival we've developed to commemorate it. Admirably, Howard Fast doesn't pull any punches in his prize-winning retelling of the Maccabee story, *My Glorious Brothers*, a narrative of armed resistance that remains relevant today.

The basic plotline is familiar: around the year 167 B.C.E., while many of their less faithful coreligionists in Palestine embrace Greek culture, the sons of Mattathias of Modin lead an armed revolt against their colonialist foes. Fast's Jews set the standard for morality and courage: unlike the Greeks, they treat their slaves with respect and free them after only seven years; they value literacy and education; they fight reluctantly, only because their principles demand it, and never for money or fame. At the time a card-carrying communist and throughout his life a champion of underdogs and the oppressed, Fast dedicated his book to "all men, Jew and Gentile" and saw in the Maccabean story "the first modern struggle for freedom, and . . . a pattern for many movements that followed." At the same time, the history paralleled contemporary developments. Fast's Greeks close Jewish schools and legislate an end to the dietary laws, and they want Jews not only assimilated but "wiped from the face of the earth forever"—which, in the 1940s, must have resonated with Hitler's Nuremberg laws and program of extermination. When Fast wrote that "Jews all over the world . . . lifted their heads when they heard the rumor that Judea might be free again," he must have considered how the establishment of Israel, just a few months before his book was published, had a similar effect. The parallels turn stranger and much more disquieting in the 21st century, when Middle Eastern guerrilla fighters continue to use the tactics and even the rhetoric supposedly pioneered by Fast's Jewish freedom fighters—they "trap and countertrap," hide out in caves, regard themselves as martyrs—in order to demoralize the more powerful armies against whom they fight, but in defense of very different religious and political positions.

Fast tells a rousing tale of adventure—at times the novel reads like the script for a video game with its displays of weaponry and its ever-more-threatening enemies to be slaughtered, including some who maraud on elephants—but he is also sensitive to the moral issues. While most of the book is narrated by Judas Maccabeus's brother Simon, one chapter appears in the form of a report by a Roman legate on the status and nature of the Jews, which shows how the principles the Maccabees hold dear look reprehensible from a different perspective. There is no doubt, though, that Fast sympathizes with his band of courageous Jews, as he did with everyone who fought in the "ancient and unfinished struggle for human freedom and dignity."

Further reading: Fast may be the American Jewish writer whose works have been read by the most people, in the most countries around the world: according to one surprising but not implausible estimate, his work has been translated into 82 languages! Most famous perhaps for *Spartacus* (1951), which was adapted into a film by Stanley Kubrick (1960), Fast churned out dozens of novels under his own name and pseudonyms too, only a small portion of which addressed Jewish themes or characters. He was blacklisted and jailed before denouncing communism in *The Naked God* (1957). A pamphlet that he wrote— "Never Forget: The Story of the Warsaw Ghetto" (1946)—was one of the first literary treatments in English of the Holocaust, and it has been made available online. Fast's *Being Red* (1990) tells the story of his own eventful life.

40 – *The Naked and the Dead*

By Norman Mailer

RINEHART AND CO., 1948. 721 PAGES.

While the vast majority of novels written about Jews and World War II focus, sensibly enough, on the European front, the early bestsellers about the war are a reminder that for many Americans, the Pacific theater of operations was of primary interest, and Hitler remained an afterthought. Such hits include James Michener's collection *Tales of the South Pacific* (1947), which was the basis of the well-known musical *South Pacific*, and James Jones's *From Here to Eternity* (1951) as well as *The Naked and the Dead*, which the wunderkind Norman Mailer published to wide acclaim at the age of 25.

An enormous, ambitious novel, *The Naked and the Dead* centers on the invasion of a fictional Pacific island, Anopopei, and on one unit's trek, at the behest of its maniacal sergeant, up the slopes of the forbidding Mt. Anaka. Mailer, who himself served in the Philippines during the war, infuses this tale with gritty detail; rain, dirt, and sweat abound. The men speak a rough soldier's slang, peppered with the word "fug" (which Mailer's uncle, Charles Rembar, an attorney and a literary agent, suggested he use in order to placate potential censors). To enrich his portrait of this small group of men, Mailer inserts "Time Machine" chapters that return to their hometowns and upbringings, reflecting the diversity of American society that came together as a result of the war effort. Mailer's soldiers hail from Texas, Oklahoma, Massachusetts, New York; they are of Polish, Mexican, Irish, and—like Mailer—Jewish descent.

Throughout his career Mailer would maintain only a tenuous relationship with his Jewish identity (in 1968's *The Armies of the Night*, the author remarks that there is only one of his many personas that he finds "absolutely insupportable— the nice Jewish boy from Brooklyn"). Nonetheless, and though they are hardly flattering portraits, two Jews figure prominently in Mailer's fictional World War II platoon. Roth, "a small man with an oddly hunched back," is prone to "the kind of anxiety and panic a child has" and struggles to keep up. Goldstein, though somewhat more sympathetic and capable and acutely aware of Jewish suffering in Europe—of "all the ghettoes, all the soul cripplings, all the massacres and pogroms, the gas chambers, the lime kilns"—is hardly the ideal soldier, either. Other Jews pop up occasionally, and Goldstein's grandfather's mantra, "Israel is the heart of all nations," echoes throughout the book, all of which suggests Mailer's awareness of the impact Jewish participation in World War II would have on American Jews. Though a bleak and merciless piece of fiction—reading it at times feels like hiking alongside the soldiers to an unreachable destination—Mailer's astonishing debut offers a crucial perspective on the war that is too often left out of American Jewish history.

Further reading: There is no challenge in finding biographical material on Mailer (a challenge, actually, would be to find later work by the author that is not overwhelmed by the autobiographical impulse). His *Advertisements for Myself* (1959) is a weirdly irresistible volume of the author's self-consideration, and at least a few of the dozens of critical studies and unauthorized biographies should be available at any library. Irwin Shaw's *The Young Lions* (1948) and Mark Harris's *Something about a Soldier* (1957) also take on the Jewish presence in the army, and Deborah Dash Moore's *G.I. Jews* (2005) is a historian's lively nonfiction recovery of the experiences of a few of the 500,000 Jews who served in the U.S. armed forces in World War II.

· ·

41 – *The Break-Up of Our Camp and Other Stories*
By Paul Goodman

NEW DIRECTIONS, 1949. 160 PAGES.

Paul Goodman is usually remembered as a philosopher embraced by the radical student movements of the 1960s. With *Growing Up Absurd* (1960) and other works of cultural criticism, with his participation in rallies protesting the Vietnam War, and with his revolutionary and occasionally disquieting sexual perspectives (Norman Mailer called him a "sexologue—that is, an ideologue about sex"), Goodman provided intellectual and psychological inspiration for much of what was done on college campuses during the tumultuous 1960s. He had always been a writer, though, or, as he referred to himself, a "man of letters," and the early stories brought together in *The Break-Up of Our Camp* are reminders of the extent to which Jewish experience underwrote his philosophy.

The book's title novella is a series of linked tales told in the voice of one narrator, Matt, and all revolving around "Camp Katonah, a summer camp for Jewish boys," in the woods of Vermont. Yiddish songs abound, but the camp is by no means secular; the kids say *Birkat ha-Mazon* after meals and pray on Friday nights, and the counselors form a minyan so that two of them, brothers, can say *Kaddish* for their dead mother. A few events transpire—a Quebecois canoeist appears on the waterfront one day; the owner, having run the camp into bankruptcy, takes off; Matt, left without any money for a train ticket home to New York, hitchhikes—but Goodman's stories, detailed as they are, serve as dreamlike, mysterious vehicles for his philosophical and poetic explorations rather than realistic evocations of people's lives; the titular story cycle ends with a parable-like reaction to the destructions of World War II in which Matt, the French Canadian canoeist, a Polish survivor, and others join together to construct "a synagogue dedicated to Grief for [the Jews'] own recent disasters and the disasters of all peoples." Hints of eroticism and messianic lyricism flash throughout the rest of the stories, which deal ostensibly with bus trips, a synagogue auction, gamblers, and handball players. In a powerful coda to one story from 1947, which echoes Kadya Molodofsky's Yiddish poem of the same era, "*El Khanun*" (God of mercy) (1945), Goodman offers up "Hints on Planning a Universe," presumably to God—his first piece of advice being, "*Don't* have any 'chosen people.' The fancied advantages of such an arrangement are far less than the complications that arise."

The abstract quality of Goodman's stories may put off some readers, and that's no accident; Goodman felt it wasn't the avant-garde author's job to make things easy for his audience, and he complained that the writers of his generation lacked "daring and absolute aspiration" and were too resistant to "experimentation." What is startling about these lyrical, philosophical fictions is the extent to which Goodman's experience and taste drew him back to Hebrew prayers, which he reproduces in transliteration, and to the everyday details of New York Jewish life.

Further reading: Goodman's oeuvre is broad and varied; in addition to his poetry and short stories (both available in collected editions), he wrote novels, the most well known of which is *The Empire City* (1959); sociology; and even a work on urban planning. He was also a founder of the Gestalt Therapy movement; on his involvement, see Taylor Stoehr's *Here Now Next* (1994). Jewish summer camps have inspired many writers: Philip Roth's first prize-winning story, "The Contest for Aaron Gold" (1955), takes place in one, as does Robert Klane's riotous and hard-to-find *The Horse Is Dead* (1968), and so do several of the essays and short fictions gathered in Eric Simonoff's anthology of 2005, *Sleepaway: Writers on Summer Camp* (including one written by me). Michael Seide also published short stories about American Jews during the 1940s—less bizarre and remarkable than Goodman's—and these were collected in *The Common Thread* (1944).

· ·

42 – *A Stone for Danny Fisher*
By Harold Robbins

KNOPF, 1952. 403 PAGES.

The rise of the mass-market paperback in the middle of the 20th century opened up a new audience of American book buyers: millions of readers without much concern for the finer points of literary style, but with enough spare change to shell out for a potboiler at the newsstand or grocery store, provided it was violent, sexy, or sentimental enough. The masters of this field, from Mickey Spillane and Earl Stanley Gardner to John Grisham, have sold thrillers and detective stories by the millions. Harold Robbins played this game and played it well: though he was no darling of the critics, his publicists claim (straining credibility as much as his fictions do) that the number of his books in print worldwide, in all languages, totals nearly a billion copies.

Robbins's third novel, *A Stone for Danny Fisher*, appeared as a hardcover from a highly respectable publisher, Knopf, and book reviewers appraised it seriously—but it was in cheap paperback editions that it sold a couple of million copies. The book, narrated from the grave by the title character, sketches the sordid life and death of a poor Jewish kid in New York. From neighborhood anti-Semitism ("Why did you kill Christ?") to amateur boxing, from hitting on girls at the soda fountain to tangling with organized crime, Danny's experiences encompass every conceivable cliché of the urban Jewish coming-of-age story. Robbins stuffs in plenty of plot, too: Danny is disowned for marrying a *luksh* ("noodle": that is, Italian) girl; he suffers the indignities of welfare; he throws a boxing match, escapes to Coney Island, and innovates in the field of snack food distribution. The narrative zooms by in a stripped-down prose style notable for its emphatic use of long-forgotten slang and pauses now and again to indulge an unbelievably banal sentimentality. Sex is introduced in clumsy soft-core seduction scenes, particularly in the first hundred pages or so; in the early 1950s, Erica Jong recalled, this "was as close as we got to literary sex education." If the paragraphs, dialogue, and structure often show signs of authorial and editorial sloppiness, you can almost hear Danny himself shrugging it all off: Hey, what else didja expect from a four-bit paperback?

Though Robbins scatters Yinglish throughout the book, the Jewish trappings remain steadfastly superficial. (It isn't clear to what degree Robbins, who was raised as Francis Kane in a Catholic orphanage, then adopted by a Jewish family who named him Harold Rubin, had any deeper connections to Jewish culture.) As an encyclopedia of narrative clichés and as repository of cultural attitudes, Robbins's novel can still be useful: this was the picture of Jewish life millions of blue collar Americans were exposed to in the 1950s, for better or worse. Soon after it appeared, Meyer Levin compared Robbins's book, along with Harry Grey's mob story, *The Hoods* (1952)—adapted into the quintessential Jewish gangster movie, *Once Upon a Time in America* (1984)—to Nazi propaganda and argued that such novels confirm "a sinister image of the typical Jew for the mass-reader." It is a matter of personal taste whether readers agree with Levin and find *A Stone for Danny Fisher* offensive or whether they side with the millions of fans for whom it is a guilty pleasure.

Further reading: Like his mass-market peers, Robbins demonstrated a superhuman ability to churn out books; in addition to two dozen published in his lifetime, he continued, thanks to ghostwriters, to publish a new one each year even after his death in 1997. The bestseller of them all is *The Carpetbaggers* (1961), based on the life of Howard Hughes. *A Stone for Danny Fisher* was, oddly enough, adapted into *King Creole* (1958), a film starring Elvis Presley about an aspiring musician in New Orleans. Andrew Wilson's biography (2007) provides a fittingly slick and glossy introduction to Robbins's sordid life.

65

43 – *The Adventures of Augie March*
By Saul Bellow

VIKING, 1953. 607 PAGES.

In 1948, Saul Bellow found himself in Paris and deeply depressed; after World War II, what thinking person wouldn't be? A Guggenheim grant paid for his trip based on the strength of his first couple of novels, but while there he had a revelation about that early work: "The restraint of the first two books had driven me mad," he recalled half a century later. "I hadn't become a writer to tread the straight and narrow." And with that, off he went: "I am an American, Chicago born—Chicago, that somber city—and go at things as I have taught myself, free-style, and will make the record in my own way." So begins *The Adventures of Augie March*, with Bellow's personal Declaration of Independence: independence from literary tradition, from propriety, from tidy prose.

A capacious world of its own, the novel tracks the title character, a young Jewish American man for whom nothing is off-limits, in his picaresque exploits. Born into a struggling, colorful family in the slums of Chicago, he tries his hand at a number of jobs, some legal and some less so. He earns the affections of a wealthy girl, but she dumps him when she hears that he has assisted another woman in getting an abortion—not wanting to hear the truth, that he was helping out only a friend. To this disappointment and the troubles brought on by the Great Depression, Augie responds by taking off for foreign parts: in Mexico, he and a lover train an eagle to catch snakes, and if that doesn't sound odd enough, he ends up, after a boat he is on is torpedoed, stranded somewhere in the Atlantic in a life raft with a megalomaniac. Linking together all of these vagarious events, and many more, is the novel's inimitable, gorgeous prose, wild and allusive and yet precise, with a lavishness of diction and sentence structure rarely equaled, if often imitated.

Augie's Jewishness informs his adventures—he drops Yiddishisms often and refers to Jewish culture unselfconsciously—but does not limit their scope. The question of what exactly Judaism means to Augie is worth considering; but there is no doubt about what Augie meant for American Jews. The book signaled the emergence of Jewish American writers as a force to be reckoned with when it won the National Book Award of 1954. And, as the Nobel committee noted in 1976 when it awarded Bellow the world's most prestigious prize for literature, it was *Augie* that began the phase of the great author's career that included his most significant works. So long and dazzling that it can, at times, grow tiresome, *Augie* is worth working for: a masterpiece of brilliant verbal acrobatics that elevates the street-smart, rootless Jew into the paradigm of the modern American.

Further reading: Reading through all of Bellow's novels and stories isn't a bad way to spend one's time. James Atlas's long biography (2000) is thorough and compelling, and the large pile of critical studies, appreciations, and biographical sketches of Bellow and his oeuvre has continued to grow in the wake of the author's death in 2005.

44 – *Blessed Is the Land*

By Louis Zara

CROWN, 1954. 394 PAGES.

Long before the first American Jewish writer—more than a century, in fact, before anyone had ever dreamed of a United States of America—the first Jews set foot on the island known today as Manhattan. Not much is known about the party of 23 Jews who arrived from Recife, Brazil, but enough details survived to furnish Louis Zara, a historical novelist and publishing executive, with the beginnings of a swashbuckling tale of pioneering adventure. Zara's chronicle features Ashur Levy, a historical personality verifiable in New Amsterdam's legal records, whose unknown interior life and personal history Zara imagines with admirable gusto.

Zara's Levy is something of a writer himself, if only in his own journal, which makes up most of the novel. The tale begins with the Jews' departure from Brazil, follows them through persecution by seafaring Spaniards, and continues on to their not-so-triumphant arrival in New Amsterdam, where the director, Peter Stuyvesant, barely tolerates their existence. It's impressive that Levy finds time to write anything at all, actually, what with his stints as a soldier, fur trader, tavern owner, lawyer, and cattle farmer. Though a "man of action" rather than a scholar, Levy is no blockhead; he speaks Dutch, German, Portuguese, French, Castilian, Yiddish, Ladino, and eventually English, too. Following the wisdom of the community elder ("Let old men go to old worlds and young men to new!"), Levy embraces the undiscovered continent, while Dutch officials, fearing that the Jews will "multiply, and overrun Manhattan," slap fines on the new arrivals whenever possible. Living what some would consider a prototypical American Jewish tension, Levy claims he would love to establish a dedicated Jewish colony so that his people could finally live in peace, but, in the meantime, he amasses a significant fortune and earns the regard of his non-Jewish neighbors.

Zara published his historical novel in honor of the tercentenary of the Jews' arrival, and not long after the Nazi Holocaust had decimated the Jews of Europe as European colonization had decimated aboriginal Americans a few centuries before. It is not surprising, then, that Zara's Jewish characters reach out to the natives, and vice versa: Levy adopts the son of his back-country guide and raises him more or less as a Jew, while one of his countrymen, a messianic kabbalist, relocates to a tribal village and marries a squaw. Along with a Swedish Marrano and a Jewish child raised as a Christian, these ethnically and culturally hybrid characters suggest that, at least in Zara's view, being Jewish in America is always a complicated enterprise. Hardly a literary masterpiece, Zara's well-researched, charming, and accessible novel nonetheless offers its readers a rousing, atmospheric tour through an obscure but crucial moment of history, the beginnings of Jewish life in the United States.

Further reading: Zara, whose last name was Rosenfeld (though you wouldn't know it from his *New York Times* obituary), began his literary career with *Blessed*

Is the Man (1935), a novel of Jewish immigration that made the Chicago bestseller lists for months. In a lengthy career, he published many historical novels—many set in early America, some featuring famous figures—and worked as a publishing executive. For those interested in the beginnings of American Jewry and its literature, the scholar Michael Kramer has argued that we should acknowledge as the first American Jewish writer one Judah Monis (1683–1764), who taught Hebrew at Harvard and published *A Grammar of the Hebrew Tongue* (1735) after converting to Christianity.

· ·

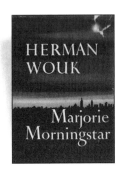

45 – *Marjorie Morningstar*

By Herman Wouk

DOUBLEDAY, 1955. 472 PAGES.

A long and detailed novel of American life, Herman Wouk's best-selling *Marjorie Morningstar* can be summed up in three words: Mother knows best. Or, more precisely, everybody knows best. Wouk's young protagonist, Marjorie Morgenstern, receives sage advice from her parents, her friends, and, in several cases, people she has barely met. They tell her that her

infatuation with this boy or that man will pass; that she is fooling herself with her dreams of becoming an actress (with Morningstar as her stage name); that what she really wants and needs, as much as she denies it, is a comfortable suburban life with separate meat and dairy dishes. What is amazing is that all of these concerned parties turn out to be right, time and again. Marjorie's fate is not to spend her life gallivanting around Paris with the bohemian set, but washing her husband's clothes. From Wouk's perspective, anything else would be impossible fantasy for a sweet, well-raised Jewish girl like her. Recently, he told an interviewer, "I've read an occasional objection to the end as 'disastrous, wrong, too sad, too religious,' and what you will. It's just the truth."

The bulk of the novel takes place in the 1930s and follows Marjorie from the age of 17 to her marriage in her mid-20s; a short final chapter leaps forward 15 years to let us know how it all works out. Beautiful, charming, and well-provided for by her father, a feather importer, Marjorie is the object of adoration of at least half a dozen young men, and the sense is that another several hundred nice Jewish boys, Columbia students and young dentists, would give their right arms for a night alone with her. The romance that takes up most of Marjorie's time is with a dashing ne'er-do-well named Noel Airman (né Saul Ehrmann), played by Gene Kelly in the movie version of 1958. Though the brilliant son of a distinguished judge, Airman lives up to his name, which is a literal translation of the Yiddish *luftmensch*—he dabbles in this and that, occasionally scoring a hit with one of the pop songs he writes, but finding it impossible to settle down to steady work even as he enters his 30s. Marjorie's other suitors include a doctor, a talented radio gag writer one year her junior, and, late in the game, a cynical former Freudian who spends the pre–World War II years smuggling desperate Jews out of Germany. But it is Noel who achieves the unthinkable—persuading Marjorie to give up her virginity out of wedlock; not coincidentally, the momentous event takes place just a few hours after she finally transgresses against her kosher upbringing and eats pork. To Wouk and his characters, Marjorie's fall from virginity is a terrible, if not fatal, "deformity"; after the man she marries finds out about it, "she never again saw on his face . . . pure happiness." In other words, Marjorie's neurotic and bossy mother was right all along.

A romantic panorama of the interwar years with stops in Jewish summer resorts, the theater business, and Paris, Wouk's conservative novel is skillfully, if straightforwardly, wrought, and makes for pleasant reading (though it traffics less in narrative tension, and more in cliché, than Myron Kaufmann's comparable *Remember Me to God*). New generations of female readers continue to identify with Marjorie, and presumably there are many who appreciate and identify with the *heymish* destiny Wouk assigns her.

Further reading: Having won a Pulitzer Prize for *The Caine Mutiny* (1951) and having enjoyed massive sales through a long relationship with the Book-of-the-Month Club, Wouk has had an extraordinary career as a producer of bestsellers; his latest novel, *A Hole in Texas* (2004), appeared when he was a sprightly 89. A religious man and committed Zionist, Wouk explores his commitment to Judaism in *This Is My God* (1959). Though not quite an autobiography, Wouk's novel of 1985, *Inside/Outside*, concerns a character similar, in some regards, to the author; for critical and biographical treatment of Wouk, see volumes by Arnold Beichman (1984) and Laurence Mazzeno (1994).

· ·

46 – *Compulsion*
By Meyer Levin

SIMON AND SCHUSTER, 1956. 480 PAGES.

There's no dearth of murder in American literature; Theodore Dreiser's *American Tragedy* (1925) and Richard Wright's *Native Son* (1940) follow a simple pattern, recounting at great length a vicious crime, the police's efforts to catch the criminal, and finally the trial, culminating with an impassioned oration by a defense attorney that condemns our corrupt society for fostering disobedience and then putting the guilty to death. (It is a model that one imagines having been around forever; in the 1990s it was put to emphatic and seemingly endless use on television in *Law & Order* and its various spinoffs.) Meyer Levin's *Compulsion* is an outstanding example of the genre—a major bestseller, adapted into drama and film, and in many ways more accomplished than either of the books named earlier, though it has received less attention from literary scholars.

Like Dreiser's murder epic, Levin's is based on a real-life sensation, that of Leopold and Loeb, which was called the "Crime of the Century." Levin's version changes the names—his murderers are called Steiner and Straus—but hews faithfully to the particulars of the original case. The pair were prodigies, child geniuses raised in the wealthiest of Jewish families in Chicago; they graduated college while still in their teens, and, for reasons that baffled their families and the world, picked a young boy at random to murder. Levin explores the motivations and the methods of the crime, delving deep into his characters' psychologies: the homosexual relation between the boys, their coddled upbringings, Straus's obsession with detective fiction, and Steiner's with Nietzschean philosophy, all get examined in turn. Levin's brilliant structural gimmick is a narrator, Sid Silver, who is both a classmate of the criminal duo and a cub reporter and, therefore, has access to all of the details of their sordid story and even identifies with them, a little—he, too, graduates college while still in his teens. More fascinating still, this character is based on Levin himself, who covered the Leopold and Loeb case as a cub reporter for the *Chicago Daily News* and did also graduate from the University of Chicago when he was 19.

In addition to its attention to the trial (with an extended closing argument by a character based on the famed lawyer Clarence Darrow), Levin's novel suggests here and there the ramifications of the case's Jewish aspects. For one thing, it was an embarrassing scandal that shocked Jews everywhere; as Levin has the narrator's father say, "It's lucky it was a Jewish boy they picked"—for if it had been a non-Jew, it would have been even more likely to stir up anti-Semitic reaction. Another angle Levin weaves in is the disquieting historical detail that the Nietzschean ideology embraced by the killers—the notion that superior beings, like themselves, are excerpted from conventional moral codes—would underlie, on some level, the Nazi slaughter of Jews that would begin a decade later. A vigorous fictional re-creation of a crime that was already three decades old by the time the book appeared, the novel attempts to capture the spirit of the 1920s (and it should be noted that Levin reproduces the attitudes of characters for whom homosexuality is itself a disease and perversion; it is not clear how much the author, in the 1950s, was able to separate himself from that lamentable position). Written in a taut, reportorial style, and sometimes reading like a court transcript, the novel is not without its flaws, but it remains one of the most successfully executed crime-and-punishment novels in American literature, and it is a window onto one of the most chilling crimes ever committed by Jews.

Further reading: Hal Higdon's *The Crime of the Century* (1975) and Simon Baatz's *For the Thrill of It* (2008) are histories of the actual case, and Leopold, who was paroled after decades in prison, wrote an autobiography while still in jail, *Life Plus 99 Years* (1958). As for Levin, he was prolific, if not always successful; *The Old Bunch* (1937) is a panoramic novel of Jewish Chicago, and *Yehuda* (1931) is notable as one of the first American novels about kibbutz life in what was then still called Palestine. Levin's late career was colored by his advocacy of and conflicted involvement with the publication and adaptation of Anne Frank's diary in America; in addition to Levin's version of the events in *The Obsession* (1973), two histories of this controversy have been published: Lawrence Graver's *An Obsession with Anne Frank* (1995) and Ralph Melnick's *The Stolen Legacy of Anne Frank* (1997). A previous autobiographical volume, *In Search* (1951), covers Levin's earlier years.

47 – *Remember Me to God*

By Myron S. Kaufman

LIPPINCOTT, 1957. 640 PAGES.

A dedicated reader of American Jewish literature, no matter how enthusiastic, will inevitably feel, at one point or another, that he or she would rather browse the tax code than read yet another book about intermarriage. Perhaps that explains why Myron S. Kaufmann's outstanding novel, *Remember Me to God*, is so rarely mentioned anymore; it is, after all, a book concerned with the question of whether Richard Amsterdam, a Harvard student, will marry a Christian girl. With that said, it is tragic that Kaufmann's novel is not more widely read. As is the case with many authors, for Kaufmann intermarriage is a justification for exploring the feelings, frustrations, and philosophies of American Jews about their Jewishness. He takes this as his starting point and produces a fiction of extraordinary insight and emotional depth.

Richard's love interest is Wimsy Talbot, a doltish blue-blooded Radcliffe student. Richard's desire for her grows out of his enchantment with and envy of the wealthy, pedigreed Protestant community of Boston, who are known to Richard's suburban Boston family as Yankees. Egged on by the sly and genteel anti-Semitism that dominates the most prestigious Harvard institutions (he gains acceptance to the Lampoon and the Hasty Pudding Club), as well as his own boyish insecurities, Richard imagines not only that he needs Wimsy but also that he should convert to Christianity. His parents, as one might expect, throw a fit. The prominence accorded to Richard's dilemmas should not obscure the book's careful attention to his sister, Dorothy, a high school misfit—too smart and not confident enough to be popular—as well as his father, Adam, the son of immigrants, orphaned as a child, who has risen from an abattoir to become a judge, even though he still harbors doubts about his own intelligence. While many of the book's long speeches, rendered in the distinct voices of various characters, center on questions of Jewish distinctiveness and survival, the novel ultimately is a family story, in which the intricate psychologies of each member reflect their complicated relationships to the rest.

Kaufmann's massive novel has much to recommend it. A finely detailed portrait of Harvard during World War II, the book is deeply empathetic to its characters and is, furthermore, an unappreciated masterpiece of literary realism. Kaufmann's prose is simple, unassuming, but astonishingly precise; he learned from Hemingway how to write sentences and paragraphs in which everyday words resound with meaning. Kaufmann never tells his reader how to feel about the action he describes—and the book does not offer any didactic solutions to the question of intermarriage—but he orchestrates his scenes so thoughtfully as to make each a powerful window into the minds of his characters. Given its technical accomplishment and intellectual ambitions, it is no surprise that *Remember Me to God* spent more than 30 weeks on the *New York Times* bestseller list; what is shocking, and unfortunate, is that so few people know of it today.

Further reading: Kaufmann's second novel, *Thy Daughter's Nakedness*, appeared in 1968 and his third, *The Love of Elspeth Baker*, not until 1982; all three books take place in Boston and deal intensely and at length with Jewish issues. Though *Remember Me to God* is occasionally mentioned in bibliographies and was praised in Norman Mailer's *Advertisements for Myself* (1959), nothing significant has been written on Kaufmann aside from newspaper reviews of his novels. As of 2008, Kaufmann, who is well into his 80s, is still serving as a *gabbai* for daily services at an Orthodox synagogue in Sharon, Massachusetts. The protagonists of Jack Ludwig's *Confusions* (1963) and James Atlas's *The Great Pretender* (1986) pass through Harvard a decade or two after Richard Amsterdam.

. . . .

48 – *The Assistant*
By Bernard Malamud

Farrar, Straus and Cudahy, 1957. 246 pages.

Though it isn't much to see—there's no headstone, just a nondescript grassy stretch—Bernard Malamud's grave, in Mount Auburn Cemetery, explains quite a bit about his writing and particularly his most famous novel, *The Assistant*. The cemetery, a few miles up the road from Harvard University in Watertown, Massachusetts, serves as the final home of several prominent 19th-century American poets and artists, including Oliver Wendell Holmes, James Russell Lowell, and Winslow Homer as well as the Christian Science pioneer Mary Baker Eddy. What on earth is a master of Yinglish syntax, and a patron of struggling immigrant Jews, doing in this grim bastion of Christian high culture?

One answer is that for Malamud, being Jewish was a way of being connected to everybody else, and especially to Christians—"I try to see the Jew as universal man," he said—so why not get buried alongside Christians? Moreover, in Malamud's view, Jews are Jews because they suffer. Helen, for example, the female lead of *The Assistant*, "felt loyal to the Jews, more for what they had gone through than what she knew of their history of theology." Her father, a shopkeeper named Morris Bober, puts the point even more clearly, having been asked by his Italian assistant, Frank Alpine, why Jews seem to suffer so much: "They suffer because they are Jews. . . . I think if a Jew don't suffer for the Law, he will suffer for nothing." As many critics have pointed out about Malamud's work, this isn't a vision of Judaism—in which asceticism and self-abnegation have rarely been privileged as values—but of Christianity, which makes a primary virtue of Christ's martyrdom and of "turning the other cheek." The novel's plot concerns Frank's slow and tumultuous integration into the Bober home: he robs the store; feeling guilty, he signs on as Morris's assistant; he falls in love with

Helen; he's kicked out for borrowing from the till; and, eventually, hoping to win Helen over, he converts. But again, as Ruth Wisse has noted, "The Judaism to which Alpine converts is really a purer ethical form of his own Catholicism." Many Jews may bristle at the idea of Jewishness as a universal human religion, open to all those who suffer or need, but some—the Kabbalah Center, for example—have shown that this view continues to be marketable today, and others have found good reason to agree with the notion, expressed by Malamud in a rabbi's eulogy for Morris, that "there are many ways to be a Jew."

A meticulous work of fiction, *The Assistant* isn't just a conversion tract. Malamud writes beautifully, painstakingly, of his characters' struggles with their desires and unfulfilled dreams. Frank shimmies up an airshaft to watch Helen undressing in the bathroom, and watching her, he feels "a throb of pain at her nakedness, an overwhelming desire to love her, at the same time an awareness of loss, of never having had what he had wanted most." Such precise observations recur throughout the novel. No wonder it won the National Jewish Book Award and earned Malamud an enduring place alongside Roth and Bellow in the pantheon of the great American Jewish writers.

Further reading: A favorite text of literary critics all over the world, *The Assistant* has been the subject of dozens of interpretations and scholarly articles. It is worthwhile to think about the ways that Malamud's other crucial novels treat the issue of suffering—as in *The Fixer* (1966)—or the mirror experiences of Jews and other minorities, as is his concern, vis-à-vis African Americans, in *The Tenants* (1971). Jewish suffering is figured as Christlike in a vast number of literary works, such as Elie Wiesel's *Night* (1958), as well as in paintings by Marc Chagall, such as *Yellow Crucifixion* (1938).

· ·

49 – *Shadows on the Hudson*

By Isaac Bashevis Singer

English: Translated by Joseph Sherman. Farrar, Straus, and Giroux, 1998. 548 pages.

Isaac Bashevis Singer will likely be remembered primarily for his nostalgic, magical, demon-filled tales of Eastern European shtetls and for his memoirs of his boyhood in Warsaw, but the Nobel Prize–winning author also devoted significant energy to narratives of Jewish life in America. The first major novel that he set entirely in the United States, *Shadows on the Hudson*, originally appeared as a twice-weekly serial in the *Forverts* between January 1957 and January 1958. A massive novel of ideas and adultery with an ensemble cast, in the style of 19th-century realism (think Balzac, Tolstoy, and so forth), the book was not translated until after Singer died, meaning that unlike most of the English versions of his work, it was not edited by the author in the process of translation.

The novel takes place in the waning years of the 1940s, as refugees from Hitler's decimated Europe scramble to reconstruct their lives in their adopted home. Characteristically, Singer's protagonist is a man with a complicated romantic life: Hertz Dovid Grein—a former Talmud prodigy, teacher, and Wall Street broker—already has one wife and two children, not to mention a mistress, when he begins an affair with Anna, a former student of his, who also happens to be married. The couple runs off to Florida and then shacks up in New York, as Grein attempts fruitlessly to alleviate his crushing boredom and aimlessness. Their scandalous courtship animates the novel and serves as the point of intersection for a host of fascinating personalities, many of whom spend their time desperately casting around for something to believe in or hope for after the desolation of the Holocaust: for Anna's father, Boris Makaver, it is piety and traditionalism; for his former study partner, Dr. Margolin, it is science and assimilation; for others, it is spiritualism or Freudianism or hedonism or communism.

None of these turns out to be sustainable as an ideology for Singer's characters, though, and most of them find their world, filled with cheap paperbacks, movies, and television, to be repulsive; in Grein's phrase, "The world is an underworld." In late sections of the novel, the spotlight is stolen by Anna's ex-husband, the vulgar comedian Yasha Kotik. Grein himself, and Boris Makaver, find some solace in their respective returns to prayer and religious ritual, but the outlook for them and for the Jews in general is bleak at the end of the book. And why not? Singer had every reason to be pessimistic, as he had watched the vibrant world of his childhood incinerated and destroyed. Reading his explorations of the American aftermath isn't exactly a barrel of laughs, but *Shadows on the Hudson* provides a dark, stirring Yiddish counterpart to English-language stories of Jewish wartime and postwar prosperity and suburbanization.

Further reading: Like *Shadows*, Singer's *Enemies, a Love Story* (1966, 1972) takes place in New York, and the plot is quite similar—its refugee protagonist, Herman Broder, ends up with three wives, none of whom makes him happy. Yasha Kotik even makes a delightful cameo, in both the novel and in its admirable film version (1989). Singer's other novels set in the United States are *Meshugah* (1981–83, 1994) and *The Penitent* (1973, 1983). See the entry on Singer's *Collected Stories* (title 121) for biographical and critical sources.

. . . .

50 – *Exodus*

By Leon Uris

DOUBLEDAY, 1958. 626 PAGES.

Consider Leon Uris's *Exodus* an American writer's present for the State of Israel on its 10th birthday. Published a little more than a decade after the country's founding, it is perhaps the most passionate (and probably the longest) love letter to Zionism ever written in English. Uris's descriptions of the land say it all: "The flowers never stopped blooming . . . and the air was forever filled with their scent." Built by volunteers with morally refined and biblically ratified dreams, Uris's Israel is an ethical utopia where tireless boys and girls, throwing off the yoke of millennia of exile, persecution, and Diaspora, dedicate their lives to the creation of a homeland for themselves and their children.

There is much truth and beauty to this story, though things are not quite so simple as Uris's claim that "the events in *Exodus* are a matter of history and public record." He did base the novel on a phenomenal amount of reading, travel, and interviews, and he does capture many indisputable details about the rise of the Zionist state. Inevitably, though, in fictionalizing and stylizing this history into the personal experiences of a handful of individuals—Ari Ben Canaan, a heroic and unflappable native-born Israeli, and his circle of family and comrades—Uris distorts facts here and there. More distressingly, given today's situation, the novel hovers between toleration and celebration of "terrorists" (who in this case happen to be Jewish) and certainly sheds no tears over the Palestinian Arabs driven from their villages in the War of Independence. Whether Uris's take on Middle East history will read as schmaltzy and over the top or as pernicious propaganda will depend on where a reader stands politically.

What no one is likely to disagree about is Uris's prose, which at its infrequent best is taut and simple and at its worst is riddled with grammatical errors and the flattest of clichés. Uris's characters are deliberate stereotypes, representing in broad strokes the sorts of people involved in the creation of the state: hard-nosed female sabras like Ari's sister Jordana; unsympathetic gentiles overwhelmed by the charm and persistence of the Israelis, like Ari's American love interest, Kitty Freemont; and tortured, misanthropic survivors of the Warsaw ghetto, like Dov Landau, who through the training and camaraderie of the Israeli army becomes "warm and filled with humor." This is the same literary tactic used by John Dos Passos and Norman Mailer, but with less skill. In fact, it is hard to imagine how any of Uris's characters could come alive for a reader, but somehow they have: the book has sold many millions of copies and has been adapted into a Hollywood movie starring Paul Newman as well as—believe it or not—a short-lived Broadway musical. Reading *Exodus* can be a chore, but it is worthwhile for those interested in American Jewish culture, not only because references to American Zionism pop up incessantly in the book but also because, for better or worse, this novel was the means through which millions of American Jews learned about Israel.

Further reading: Uris wrote several other bestsellers on Jewish themes, including *Mila 18* (1960), which expands upon *Exodus*'s flashback to the siege of the Warsaw Ghetto. Many American Jewish writers, from Meyer Levin to Melvin Jules Bukiet, have written engagingly about Israeli history and culture; fans of Uris's military emphasis may especially enjoy Avner Mandelman's tales of Mossad agents, *Talking to the Enemy* (2006). Of course, several excellent fictions on this subject by Israelis have been translated into English: Amos Oz's memoir, *A Tale of Love and Darkness* (2004), is one worthwhile recent contribution, while Benny Morris's *1948* (2008) is a historian's recent attempt to offer a balanced account of the events around the founding of Israel.

51 – *Goodbye, Columbus and Five Stories*
By Philip Roth

HOUGHTON MIFFLIN, 1959. 320 PAGES.

Philip Roth pulls no punches. Think of him as the lifelong, official "Dennis the Menace" of the American Jewish community, only with a sparkling wit and flawless prose instead of a slingshot. Roth's debut collection peers behind the scenes of rampant Jewish success in the years following World War II, devoting equal time to what is desirable and what is repulsive about suburban life. The result is an always fresh, hilarious, and surprisingly poignant set of stories that launched their young author—he was 26 at the time—to national prominence when he was awarded the National Book Award in 1960.

In the title novella, Roth dissects the summer romance of Neil Klugman, a middle-class 20-something whiling away his days behind the desk of the Newark Public Library, and Brenda Patimkin, the doted-upon daughter of a plumbing magnate. Their relationship is a train wreck in slow motion, and if the issues of desire and longing across class lines are not clear enough in the main plotline, Neil's summer sojourn in the well-to-do environs of Short Hills is paralleled by a young African American boy's passionate but ill-fated relationship with a book of Gauguin's Tahiti paintings. Some readers have objected to Brenda—who is ridiculed for the number of cashmere sweaters she owns and for getting her nose "fixed"—as a vicious caricature of what came to be called the Jewish American Princess, and some consider her the inception of a misogynistic streak running throughout Roth's career. At the same time, in the novella itself Brenda is much less vapid and frigid than the version of her that appears in the well-known movie released in 1969, starring Richard Benjamin and Ali MacGraw; Neil is intimidated not only by the size of her father's fortune but also by her wit and intelligence.

The book's other stories are too good to miss. "The Conversion of the Jews" is perhaps the best piece of writing ever produced about the American *heder*, children's after-school lessons in Judaism that are one of the persisting institutions of Jewish life. "Defender of the Faith," meanwhile, is a meticulously crafted, wrenching tale of what the Rabbinic tradition calls *sinat khinam*—the baseless hatred Jews bear one another in their hearts—set in a U.S. army training camp in the final months of World War II. All of these fictions demonstrate Roth's unparalleled ear for dialogue and his tenderness for the people he mocks, and, besides being both touching and hilariously funny, they set forth the themes that have continued to occupy Roth throughout his career: desire, mortality, and the place of Jews in postwar America.

Further reading: Generations of writers have tried to do for their suburban environments what Roth did so masterfully for Newark—recently, for example, David Bezmozgis's *Natasha and Other Stories* (2004) in Toronto, and Daniel Stolar's *The Middle of the Night* (2003) in St. Louis. Maxine Rodburg's *The Law of Return*

(1999) offers an alternative take on Newark's Jews. Roth's own oeuvre returns to New Jersey again and again (see, particularly, *American Pastoral*). Many scholarly books about Roth and his fiction can be found in any library, and an authorized biography is currently in the works; in the meantime, for more on the author's tortured relationship with himself, see his semi-autobiography, *The Facts* (1988).

. . . .

52 – *The Pawnbroker*
By Edward Lewis Wallant

HARCOURT BRACE JOVANOVICH, 1961. 279 PAGES.

For most of us, remembering the Holocaust takes effort; we listen to the stories, watch the films, read the histories, and tell ourselves to "never forget." The people who have come to be called "survivors" in contrast, didn't get to choose whether to remember or not—as much as they might have liked to leave brutal memories behind in Europe, they couldn't. Sol Nazerman, the protagonist of Edward Lewis Wallant's *The Pawnbroker*, is one such sufferer.

Nazerman runs a pawnshop in Harlem, buying and selling back the personal goods of poor African Americans and Latinos as well as one pathetic, failed Jewish poet. It is a colorful, small-time business, and it doesn't matter whether the pawnbroker turns a profit or not: the operation is only a front for a gangster, Murillio, who pays Nazerman a comfortable salary for his services. With this money, Nazerman supports his sister's family in Mount Vernon, though their middle-class aspirations repulse him. Well-meaning people reach out to Nazerman—a social worker, a young assistant, a customer with intellectual leanings—but all he wants is to be left alone. His dreams are haunted by visions of what he experienced in the camps, gruesome and dehumanizing tortures that are recounted in harrowing italicized passages. (The dramatizations of these scenes on the screen, in Sidney Lumet's admirable film version of 1964, are famous for being the first time the extermination camps were depicted in a Hollywood movie.)

Remarkable for its vivid attempts to dramatize the aftereffects of the Holocaust on its victims as well as the wider world, *The Pawnbroker* is likewise valuable as an exploration of the fraught relationships between Jews and other American minority groups. That this readable novel, which was nominated for the National Book Award, manages to be quite funny, as well as ethically and symbolically weighty, makes it all the more tragic that its talented author died, at the age of 36, the year after it was published.

Further reading: Wallant published two books while he was alive, and two further books were published posthumously: *The Tenants of Moonbloom* (1963) and *The Children at the Gate* (1964). His debut, *The Human Season* (1960), won what was then called the Daroff Memorial Fiction Award, which has since been renamed the Edward Lewis Wallant Award; it remains a respected prize for Jewish fiction. *The Pawnbroker* anticipated an enormous wave of American Jewish novels and films about Holocaust survivors that continues to this day. The only published book-length consideration of Wallant's life and works is David Galloway's *Edward Lewis Wallant* (1979).

. . . .

53 – *Tell Me a Riddle*
By Tillie Olsen

LIPPINCOTT, 1961. 116 PAGES.

Reading is a luxury. A luxury of immense value, yes—and one that some of us feel to be necessary to get through the day—but nonetheless there are times when carving out a free hour from our other responsibilities to enjoy a book is impossible. One of Tillie Olsen's characters remembers herself as a "young wife, who in the deep night hours while she nursed the current baby, and perhaps held another in her lap, would try to stay awake for the only time there was to read"—only to be interrupted, inevitably, by her husband, coming in late from a meeting and demanding her attention. If reading is difficult in such situations, just imagine how impossible writing would be.

That is, more or less, the story of Olsen's life. A gifted writer from a young age, she published stories and essays and then began work on a novel in the early 1930s, but soon she found herself busy with motherhood, and with communist and pro-union causes for which she was twice jailed. She didn't publish her first book, *Tell Me a Riddle*, a collection of short stories, until she was 49, and it is mostly upon this slim volume that her reputation rests; as Margaret Atwood remarked in a review, "Few writers have gained such wide respect on such a small body of published work."

The stories themselves, which should not be overshadowed by Olsen's biography, focus with remarkable sympathy on a group of troubled souls. Emily, the 19-year-old daughter described by her mother in "I Stand Here Ironing" has never fit in, being "thin and dark and foreign-looking"; she is, unfortunately, "a child of her age, of depression, of war, of fear." In "O Yes," the shock of an African American church service on a young Jewish girl becomes a symbol for the sad and seemingly inevitable fade-out of her friendship with her African American neighbor when they reach junior high, where they are subject to social "sorting" into "different places, different crowds." The title story, a novella about the last years in the life of a spirited but bitter grandmother, won the O. Henry Award for the best story of 1961; a moving and spirited portrait of life from the perspective of old age, it is told—like the other pieces—in brief snippets of dialogue, flashbacks, remembered conversations, and held grudges. With their children grown, the woman and her husband bicker about innumerable inconsequential things and about whether they should move to a retirement community; soon she is diagnosed with cancer. She gets annoyed when her daughter asks her to light Friday night candles, and, at the hospital, when a rabbi comes to her bedside; "Superstition!" she complains, rejecting a "religion that stifled and said: in Paradise, woman, you will be the footstool of your husband." Her ideology, rooted in European socialism—she was exiled to Siberia in her youth—is "to smash all ghettos that divide us," yet, chatting unhappily with successful old friends, she feels shame over her children's intermarriages. A beautifully realized set of character studies, *Tell Me a Riddle* is a heart-rending classic.

Further reading: *Silences* (1978) is Olsen's nonfiction volume exploring the reasons people—especially women and the poor—aren't able to write; she also published *Yonnondio* (1974), the unfinished novel she had begun drafting decades earlier. A couple of critical volumes on Olsen's work appeared in the 1990s, including one edited by Joanne S. Frye (1995).

· ·

54 – *Stern*
By Bruce Jay Friedman

SIMON AND SCHUSTER, 1962. 191 PAGES.

Moving to the suburbs: in the 1950s, everybody was doing it, and for the bulk of American Jews who had grown accustomed to city life, this meant a whole slew of new challenges. Stern, the protagonist of Bruce Jay Friedman's first darkly comic novel, confronts just about all of them. A lousy negotiator, he winds up in a house with a caterpillar problem, an hour-and-a-half commute, and awful neighbors. Not long after he arrives with his wife and child, one of the locals, with a house a mile down the road, calls Stern's son a kike and shoves his wife, getting a good look at her private parts in the process. It is just Stern's luck that she isn't wearing any underpants. All this, just because Stern aspires to be a normal suburban American: "We're homeowners," he longs to proclaim. "See how much fun we always have and how we fit in."

Stern epitomizes the schlemiel as modern hero (to borrow the title of Ruth Wisse's landmark study of modern Jewish fiction). He is 34, with a job writing product labels, a penchant for wishful thinking, and little self-esteem. His father is a small-time failure in the shoulder pad industry, and his mother is a relentless, indiscriminate flirt who thinks no one on earth has suffered as much as she. (For more of Friedman's take on the Jewish mother, see his second novel, *A Mother's Kisses* [1964].) Though he received a lackluster Jewish education—his Hebrew-school teacher "concentrated on the technique of wearing yarmulkes and hit kids with books to keep order"—and can "read Hebrew at a mile-a-minute clip" without understanding any of the words, Stern, away at college in Oregon, expresses his Jewishness through self-mocking jokes. He nicknames one of his buddies "Little Gee-yoo," and is called, in turn, "Nose." Eventually, thanks to the neighborhood's menacing "kike man," as Stern calls him, Stern develops a nasty ulcer; for treatment, he spends five weeks in a rest home. There he befriends a group of sickly outcasts and manages to feel better about himself by winning a baseball game and sleeping with a literary Puerto Rican girl. His return to society culminates with the "mildest nervous breakdown in town" and then an entirely ambivalent, if violent, encounter with the "kike man."

Friedman's plot matters less than his mordant humor and his sharp ear for speech; his characters mutter inanities and tell unfunny jokes and do disturbing off-color things as if their only purpose in life were to mortify Stern, and the reader. Stern himself causes some of the trouble, too; like many a confused if well-intentioned liberal, he seems unable to keep his foot out of his mouth whenever an African American is around (a shtick revisited on Larry David's brilliant TV show, *Curb Your Enthusiasm*). It is difficult to tell whether Stern's problems result primarily from his maladjustment to the suburbs, from genuine anti-Semitism, or from his personal *mishegoss*, but the book's satire ultimately attacks, in a broader sense, the clichés of life back in the early 1960s, too many of which survive to this day.

Further reading: Friedman has published continuously throughout the decades to the tune of a couple of dozen of books and plays. Elaine May adapted a short story by Friedman into a movie, *The Heartbreak Kid* (1972), with a script by Neil Simon. *The Lonely Guy's Book of Life* (1978) and *The Slightly Older Guy* (1995) are Friedman's humorous nonfictional takes on the male experience in America, and, if you can find a copy of it, an anthology he edited, *Black Humor* (1965), contains morbidly funny work by Joseph Heller, Thomas Pynchon, John Barth, Vladimir Nabokov, and others. Max Schulz's short and already outdated monograph (1974) is the only book-length study of Friedman's writing so far. Friedman's son Drew is an accomplished graphic artist, whose books include *Old Jewish Comedians* (2006) and *More Old Jewish Comedians* (2008).

. . . .

55 – *Herzog*
By Saul Bellow

VIKING, 1964. 341 PAGES.

In literature, nothing succeeds like failure—what could be more boring than a novel in which everything goes exactly as planned?—and it would be hard to find a more perfect literary failure than Saul Bellow's Moses E. Herzog. Herzog's scholarly work has dead-ended, his marriage has imploded, and on his day out with his daughter he ends up in a police station. More important than his impotence as a practical man, though, Herzog is a failure in theory: well-versed in the intellectual traditions of Europe, he can't find a philosophy that continues to apply, or at least not one that makes any sense. "Go through the comprehensible," he observes, "and you conclude that only the incomprehensible gives any light." The character, whose name derives from James Joyce's *Ulysses*, rages against the inanity and commercialism of modern life, but manages to fail even as a crank: at bottom he remains a believer, even if he can't say exactly what he believes.

Herzog's most endearing habit is to compose letters in his head to whomever he's thinking about. He'll never send these letters, we can be sure, especially when they are addressed to the dead. He writes to his mother, his psychiatrist, his two ex-wives, his new lover, and the former friend who cuckolded him, Valentine Gersbach; he directs missives to academics, to clergymen, to Nietzsche, and to God: "How my mind has struggled to make coherent sense," he tells the Lord. "I have not been too good at it." Like much of Bellow's work, the novel is cerebral, but never dry—Herzog's intellectual battles don't preclude physical ones; at one point, for example, he picks up his father's old antique pistol, with two bullets in it, one each for Herzog's most recent ex-wife and for Gersbach.

Herzog displays Bellow at a high point in his career, and also (whether coincidentally or not) at a moment when his interests in the trappings of Jewish culture were particularly pointed. Descended from a great line of failures—his father manages to fail first as an onion importer, then as a farmer, baker, dry-goods businessman, jobber, sack manufacturer, junk dealer, marriage broker, and bootlegger—Herzog can trace his disaffection back to a pious grandfather, who in 1918 hid out from the Bolsheviks in the Winter Palace in St. Petersburg, and in the process "lost his precious books." His distance from an organic Jewish culture is one of Herzog's main problems; coming from a "genteel" "Yiddish background"—Bellow himself was noted for speaking a lovely Yiddish—he can't stand the way a guy like Gersbach mangles *mameloshen*. A rambling and hilarious novel, *Herzog* remains an unequaled dissection of the confusions and frustrations bound to assail a thinking person, especially if he or she is Jewish.

Further reading: No one quite combines intellectual vigor and range with vulgarity and the vernacular as Bellow could, but many try to capture the experiences of Herzog-like intellectuals nonetheless. Brian Morton, for example, writes excellent novels about the Jewish New York literati, such as *Breakable You* (2006) and *Starting Out in the Morning* (1998), which has been adapted into a well-received film (2007), while Tess Slesinger's *The Unpossessed* (1934) and Lionel Trilling's *The Middle of the Journey* (1947) dramatize the intellectual engagements of earlier generations of cultural critics.

81

. . . .

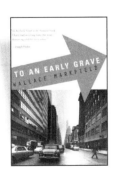

56 – *To an Early Grave*

By Wallace Markfield

SIMON AND SCHUSTER, 1964. 255 PAGES.

In the years after World War II, New York City was the place to be if you happened to be Jewish, middle-aged, and brilliant. A group of brainy, hyper-literate critics who fit that description—including Philip Rahv, Irving Howe, and Alfred Kazin—have come to be known as the New York Intellectuals, and many of their essays and books are insightful and provocative enough that they continue to inspire budding cultural critics in America and abroad. They have also been the subject of a number of novelistic treatments, the funniest of which is Wallace Markfield's first novel, *To an Early Grave.*

The title is literal: four intellectuals pile into a car in Greenwich Village and head to Queens for the funeral of Leslie Braverman, who has died tragically at 40. They remember Braverman as a vigorous, larger-than-life *schmuck*, a miraculously talented writer and raconteur who is not above selling pornographic stories in a pinch (including "a beauty . . . about a Tibetan monk"). The mourner with whom the narrative spends the most time is Morroe Rieff, a fund-raiser and speechwriter for Jewish causes who has moved uptown and feels distanced from the Village scene; he sees himself judged as "something dull and flat and ordinary, an outsider, a *nachshlepper*, a bourgeois, one who held a job and carried a briefcase and set too much store by appearances"—and no one can ever remember his wife's name. The others include a writer for a Yiddish daily; a pretentious New Critic of wide erudition; and a neurotic who makes the nearly fatal mistake of owning a car in Manhattan.

For those familiar with the New York Intellectuals and their writing, the fact that Braverman is modeled on Isaac Rosenfeld enriches the experience of watching these men bumble their way to the funeral home and cemetery; but even if you don't recognize any of the specific individuals caricatured here, the types they represent won't be unfamiliar. Sidney Lumet's movie version, *Bye-Bye Braverman* (1968), deserves a look, too, but Markfield's stew of pop culture, Yiddish, and high culture is a priceless original.

Further reading: The list of available sources on the real-life New York Intellectuals keeps growing; Alexander Bloom's *Prodigal Sons: The New York Intellectuals and Their World* (1986) is not a bad place to start. Mary McCarthy's short novel *The Oasis* (1949) takes on some of the same characters as they form a utopian commune, in a much less cartoony style. As for Markfield, he published four more books, most of which are now sadly out of print—you can track down a copy of *Teitelbaum's Window* (1970) easily enough, though—as well as dozens of essays and stories in journals and magazines.

· ·

57 – *Friday, the Rabbi Slept Late*
By Harry Kemelman

CROWN, 1964. 160 PAGES.

A girl turns up, murdered, in the parking lot of a synagogue in the New England hamlet of Barnard's Crossing. In another place and time—say, Shiraz, Iran, in 1910; Kiev in 1911; or Atlanta in 1913—this would be the setup for a charge of ritual murder and maybe a pogrom. In Harry Kemelman's debut mystery, *Friday, the Rabbi Slept Late*, which won an Edgar Award, it is the occasion for an unusual whodunit in which Jewish brilliance saves the day. "I know very little about these things," Kemelman's hero, Rabbi David Small, admits to the police, "but as a Talmudist," he continues, "I am not entirely without legal training." In fact, Rabbi Small, fresh out of seminary, turns out to be no mean sleuth, and it is a matter of time before he has discovered the unfortunate girl's murderer, surprising not only his congregation and the police chief but also the reader.

The first Jewish hero of a detective novel to achieve wide recognition, Rabbi Small stars in a series of books that offer up the typical enticements of the mystery formula: suspense, clever plotting, surprising solutions, and easy reading. Kemelman also includes two less typical elements: a sociological and historical analysis of Conservative Judaism in a suburb modeled on East Bedford, Massachusetts, as well as a handful of lectures on comparative religion in contemporary America. When he isn't chatting with the police chief, Lanigan, or ferreting out clues, Rabbi Small spends his time educating the locals, Jewish and gentile alike, about Judaism, expounding on the essence of the rabbinical profession, or the relevance of the Talmud to everything from business disputes to criminal detection. Meanwhile, the synagogue's board deals with fund-raising as well as social and administrative issues.

The puzzles in Kemelman's novels remain more or less puzzling, and as time goes on the books become increasingly valuable as repositories of detail about the postwar period. (Among the surprising circumstances crucial to the plot of *Friday, the Rabbi Slept Late* is the fact that no one in Barnard's Crossing would think to lock his or her car door when leaving it in a parking lot.) Kemelman attempts to unseat some of the stereotypes about rabbis and Jews in general— "You Jews are skeptical, critical, and logical," the rabbi is told, and he replies, "I always thought we were supposed to be highly emotional"—but in producing a formulaic series, he nonetheless substantiates a different set of received ideas, and his characterizations tend somewhat to caricature. But that is the nature of the genre, and what is most important about Kemelman's books is how deeply Jewish they can be without diverging from the conventions of the whodunit.

Further reading: The Rabbi Small series has a book for every day of the week and then some. The initial title was adapted for television as *Lanigan's Rabbi* (1977). The most eccentric of the Rabbi Small books is *Conversations with Rabbi Small* (1981), which dispenses with a mystery plot, if not the fictional frame, in order to give the hero direct opportunity to explain what it means to be Jewish. Before inaugurating the Rabbi Small series, Kemelman had published stories starring Nicky Welt, a non-Jewish English professor-cum-detective, which were collected as *The Nine Mile Walk* (1967). For other detective or mysteries novels with Jewish themes and characters, consult the entry in this book on Faye Kellerman's *The Ritual Bath* (1986) or take a look at Laurence Roth's academic study of the genre, *Inspecting Jews* (2004).

58 – *Criers and Kibitzers, Kibitzers and Criers*

By Stanley Elkin

RANDOM HOUSE, 1966. 285 PAGES.

According to some observers, laughing and whining are the two things Jews do best; whether or not that is true, it has doubtlessly been a goal for many Jewish writers to produce stories that are at once sad and also hilariously funny. The title of Stanley Elkin's first collection of short fiction, *Criers and Kibitzers, Kibitzers and Criers*, derives from a character's assessment of the Jewish shopkeepers who share a table at a local delicatessen: some complain, some joke—they are "the two kinds of people like two different sexes that had sought each other out." Elkin's stories likewise dwell on death and suffering, but they manage to do so with comic flair and more than a little absurdity.

The title story concerns a Malamudian grocery store owner, Greenspahn, whose beloved son has passed away at the unfortunate age of 23, and who consequently can no longer abide the petty indignities of his life—like Mrs. Frimkin, an old customer who smears egg yolk on herself so that she can demand a 50 percent discount on a dozen. Similarly morbid, "Among the Witnesses" takes place at a faltering Jewish summer resort that has been shocked by the accidental drowning of a little girl. In "I Look Out for Ed Wolfe"—which, like "Criers and Kibitzers," has appeared in many anthologies—a Jewish orphan, having been fired for being too aggressive as a debt collector, sells off his possessions and wanders around, at a loose end. But summaries don't do justice to the tales in this collection—plot is not Elkin's strong suit; he is better known, and loved, for inventing characters with the gift of gab who follow their instincts wherever they may lead. One, a trumpet player named Bertie, the hero of "The Guest," manages to conduct extensive conversations all by himself. He has been graciously allowed to crash at the St. Louis home of a vacationing friend, and he proceeds to scratch the hardwood floors, drink all the liquor, and enjoy a little mescaline trip, chattering away all the while. Elkin's other characters are equally loquacious; Morty Perlmutter, for example, is a world-weary anthropologist familiar with aboriginal tribes from every corner of the earth who has never found the time to visit New York City, and he gallivants around Manhattan seeking the wisdom of homeless people and subway riders.

The Jewishness of these stories is atmospheric, tonal, a matter of Elkin's syntax and sense of the ridiculous sublime; some are at most allegorically Jewish, like "On a Field, Rampant," about a young man convinced he is heir to the throne of a European nation, though he is not sure exactly which one. Favorites of writers from Cynthia Ozick to the experimentalist Robert Coover, Elkin's stories begin in the familiar precincts of mid-century Jewish fiction, but then spin out in directions exuberant and unpredictable.

Further reading: Though all worth reading, only a few of Elkin's novels have any explicit Jewish content; *A Bad Man* (1967) and *The Rabbi of Lud* (1987) are among those that do. Peter J. Bailey's *Reading Stanley Elkin* (1985) is one of several reasonable introductions to the author's oeuvre, and some of Elkin's sparkling essays—he was a Ph.D. and lifelong professor of English in St. Louis— can be found in *Pieces of Soap* (1992).

· ·

59 – *The Last Jew in America*
By Leslie Fiedler

STEIN AND DAY, 1966. 191 PAGES.

It is a strange pleasure to read the imaginative literature written by an author best known as a critic; the question is always whether the critic's insights into the genre can inform but not overwhelm his fiction—and the answer, almost universally, is no. This is certainly the case of Leslie Fiedler, the author of spectacular works of criticism such as *Love and Death in the American Novel* (1960). In *Waiting for the End* (1964) and the remarkable essay "The Jew in the American Novel" (1959), Fiedler proved himself to be among the ablest interpreters of American Jewish writing, and it is only sporting to admit that these analyses reach insights far more valuable than those found in Fiedler's attempts to write stories and novels. Having said that, even the loopiest of Fiedler's fictions are worth a read for their intelligence, satire, and curmudgeonly humor.

Arguably Fiedler's most successful story, "The Last Jew in America" appeared in a volume in 1966 alongside two similarly titled tales, "The Last WASP in the World" and "The First Spade in the West." Together, the three fictions flesh out life in the improbably named Lewis and Clark City, "a square town, in the very middle of a square state . . . tucked away between Montana and Idaho." Though this description seems to indicate Wyoming, the city itself, distinguished by its university, sounds more like Missoula, Montana, which happens to be the place where Fiedler lived and taught, at Montana State University, from 1941 to 1964. The title story treats the town's Jewish population, mostly composed of "so-called Jews from the faculty" flown in from the Northeast to teach the "sons of ranchers and miners and real estate salesman and used car dealers" who make up the student body. In the story, Jacob Moscowitz tries to round up a minyan on Yom Kippur; following him as he approaches the few Jewish small-business owners, Fiedler explores the variety and tenuousness of Jewish identification in this small western town, inserting details of pop culture and intellectual life wherever he can. He touches on old debates (*Forverts* vs. *Freiheit*, Stalinists vs. Trotskyites), offers his own contemporary rewrite of the *Kol Nidrei* prayer, and demonstrates how even atheistic Jews can strive for fellowship in exile. The second story transports a gentile son of Lewis and Clark City, a prize-winning poet named Vincent Hazelbaker, to a Jewish wedding in New Jersey, reversing the situation: all of his literary associates, love interests, and psychiatrists are Jewish, so Vin stumbles around feeling like an endangered species. So does Ned York, the

85

African American bar owner at the center of the third story. All three fictions treat the experience of being an outsider—a position that inspired Fiedler's fascination and sympathy throughout his life, no matter how persistently people admired and accepted him.

Like his characters, Fiedler showed remarkable facility for outraging people, not only with his polemics but also with personal insults and bad behavior; and even his fiction can be offensive (Fiedler's prominent use of the word "spade," for one example, though perhaps less offensive at the time of publication, is unfortunate). But, like the man, the stories demand to be taken as they are: brash, funny, occasionally brilliant.

Further reading: Fiedler's fictional output was limited to a handful of novels and collections; *Nude Croquet* (1969) contains short stories from a 20-year period and offers a sense for Fiedler's varying tactics and interests as a writer of fiction. *Fiedler on the Roof* (1991) contains the critic's iconoclastic essays on Jewish culture. Mark Royden Winchell's *Too Good to Be True* (2002) offers a critical account of Fiedler's life and works. For an even shtickier take on Yom Kippur than in Fiedler's title story, see Allen Hoffman's novella *Kagan's Superfecta* (1981), and for fiction published by another American Jew better known as a critic, see the collection of Lionel Trilling's stories, *Of This Time, of That Place and Other Stories* (1979).

60 – *Green: A Novella and Eight Stories*
By Norma Rosen

HARCOURT, BRACE, AND WORLD, 1967. 246 PAGES.

Literature is full of gently confused women; Jane Austen's heroines wouldn't be so charming if they weren't so frequently befuddled. Norma Rosen's first collection of stories, *Green*, explores the confusions of Jewish women in the very confusing 1960s, as family dynamics, class concerns, and interethnic relations were all changing. Rosen's title refers not to a person's name, or to the color, but to the adjective meaning "unripe, immature . . . not fully developed"—that is, the same word that produces, paired with "horn," the traditional term for Jewish immigrant naïveté in America. (One of Rosen's protagonists, the daughter of overprotective parents, whines to her mother that though born in the United States, they don't act American; they're "still greenhorns.")

Muriel Ruznack, the 33-year-old protagonist of the title novella, knows she is still green. Her husband, Herb, is tolerant and thoughtful, but she is judgmental, even catty. She loathes her widowed sister's new rich husband and house in the suburbs, and she is fearful that Herb, an undiscovered painter who teaches high school classes to get by, will sell out for a job in advertising. Hoping to bolster her inclinations, she approaches the rabbi in a suburban Reform temple: "Wouldn't it be better sometimes to choose poverty? Hasn't the Talmud foreseen anything like that?" But the rabbi points out that not all wealth is oppressive and not all penury admirable. Many of Rosen's characters find their expectations confounded in just this way and struggle to adjust to the demands of the situation, as in "Apples," where a young husband doesn't know quite how to ask his widowed father to move in with him and his wife. The collection's later stories deal with the interracial dynamics typical of New York's Upper West Side, in terms of the relationships between Jewish mothers and Jamaican baby nurses, in three of the book's most effective tales, and, in the one that concludes the collection, between well-off Jews and poor Puerto Ricans (this was before the gentrification of the neighborhood that pushed most of the low-income families northward). Such stories tend toward sentimentality, but Rosen fends off the typical platitudes about class relations, and her characters, like us, rarely figure out solutions to their dilemmas.

Rosen's ear for language and light prose style amuse throughout the collection (she transforms "dybbuk" into a verb and calls Muriel, "like everyone else, a virtuoso of flawed accomplishments") and couch the seriousness of her concerns in a pleasing form. Many of the strongest stories seem decidedly autobiographical (and a couple of details have been confirmed as such in Rosen's essays, like one story's European husband, more knowledgeable about Judaism than his wife, or the Jamaican nurse who, before Passover, asks her Jewish employers, "What must I say to you?"). Even if the stories provide glimpses into Rosen's personal life—having been raised in a mostly nonobservant family, she began to discover in the 1960s and 1970s the attractions of Jewish faith and community—their primary attraction is the sympathy with which they treat their characters' foibles.

Further reading: Rosen's first novel, *Joy to Levine!* (1962), was rather light and charming like the stories; her second and third, *Touching Evil* (1969) and *At the Center* (1982), deal with weightier issues, such as the resonance of the Holocaust in American life. She has also published a collection of essays, including memoirs and critical pieces, called *Accidents of Influence* (1992), a Passover haggadah (1980), a nonfiction account of Anzia Yezierska's relationship with John Dewey (1989), and a midrashic account of the women in the Torah (1996). Her son is the novelist and editor Jonathan Rosen.

. . . .

61 – *Tsemakh Atlas/The Yeshiva*
By Chaim Grade

Yiddish: Nationaln Arbeter-Farband, 1967–68. Two volumes.
English: Translated by Curt Leviant: Bobbs-Merrill. 1976–77. Two volumes.

Like most Yiddish writers who have lived in America, Chaim Grade was born and raised in Eastern Europe, and specifically in Vilna (now called Vilnius, Lithuania), the sparkling center of Yiddish culture during the interwar period.

Having made a name for himself as a promising poet in the 1930s, and having survived the Holocaust in the Soviet Union, Grade immigrated to the United States in 1948, but—unlike his predecessors, such as the Singer brothers, Sholem Asch, even Sholem Aleichem—Grade never wrote more than a couple of brief poems about his new homeland. "I don't write about America," he told an interviewer in 1980. "I don't feel I understand the psychology of Americans, even the Orthodox here." Such a statement, more than 30 years after his arrival, suggests the enormity of Grade's alienation and loss.

Still, by the time the first volume of his massive autobiographical novel of interwar Poland, *Tsemakh Atlas*, appeared in Yiddish in 1967, thanks to a Los Angeles publisher, Grade had already been in America for nearly two decades. The author's note to the second Yiddish volume reveals his reliance on Americans for support both emotional and financial, as he thanks friends in Grand Rapids and Cleveland (as well as Windsor and Johannesburg). Though the novel portrays the famed yeshivas of Lithuania and their brilliant, tormented students and faculty, one can't help but suspect that Grade's sojourn in the United States inflected his memory at least a little. Americans appear here and there in the book, subtitled (and titled in English) *The Yeshiva*: one woman in Vilna, nicknamed "the American" because she lives off the money sent by her older sister in the United States, has an unstoppable desire for "sweets and expensive fruits," while a vacationing delegation of actual American students have "money but not a crumb of decorum" and speak "with chewing gum in their mouths." Might these jabs at dissolute or disrespectful Americans have been inspired partly by Grade's years as a Yiddish writer in an unsympathetically English-speaking country and Jewish community?

The central conflicts of the book resonated with their immediate, American, context, too. The title character is a charismatic and handsome adherent of Musar, the fiercely ethical and somewhat ascetic branch of anti-Hasidic Judaism according to which a pious Jew must deny all of his desires. Tsemakh has one major problem, though: he is not sure he believes in God. Grade's autobiographical avatar, meanwhile, the teenaged Chaikl Vilner, struggles to reconcile his faith and his loyalty to his saintly teacher with his overpowering sexual lust. Such conflicts—between ethics and faith, tradition and sexual expression—were raging in the 1960s in the Unites States. One long episode in Grade's novel involves the censorship of pornographic and heretical books, and only a year before it was published, the U.S. Supreme Court had ruled it unconstitutional to censor erotic literature. The parallels needn't be overemphasized. Grade's novel is first and foremost a detailed, psychologically and philosophically fertile exploration of the conflicts simmering within the world of the traditional European Jewish scholarly elite before its destruction; a complex self-portrait; and a loving tribute to a major scholar and Jewish leader, the Hazon Ish, who was Grade's teacher before he moved to Palestine and Grade, having rejected religious tradition, decamped to America. On the basis of this masterful novel and a broad oeuvre, many Yiddish scholars felt strongly that Isaac Bashevis Singer's Nobel Prize in literature—almost certainly the last one that will ever be awarded to a Yiddish writer—should have gone to Grade.

Further reading: Grade's most widely available work in English is the oft-anthologized short story/essay, "My Quarrel with Hersh Rasseyner," which was also adapted into a film, *The Quarrel* (1991). A handful of Grade's books have been translated into English, including *The Well* (1967), *The Abandoned Wife* (1974), *Rabbis and Wives* (1987), and *The Sacred and the Profane* (1997). In addition to the autobiographical material available in *The Yeshiva*, those interested in Grade's personal life should seek out *My Mother's Sabbath Days* (1986), a memoir that appeared in Yiddish in 1955. Like Grade, several other Yiddish writers lived in America but wrote mostly nostalgic, or bitter, fictions about the lands of their birth, such as Joseph Opatoshu—see his *In Polish Woods*, published in Yiddish in 1921 and in English translation in 1938. Curt Leviant, whose English translation presented Grade's masterpiece to a new audience, is a noteworthy novelist himself; his books include *The Yemenite Girl* (1973) and *Diary of an Adulterous Woman* (2001).

. . . .

62 – *Waiting for the News*
By Leo Litwak

DOUBLEDAY, 1969. 312 PAGES.

Detroit's Jews have experienced a few highs and a lot of lows: while the city was the home of one of baseball's Jewish greats, Hank Greenberg, and now boasts a sizable, prosperous Jewish population, the region has also been distinguished as a center of race riots, Jewish organized crime, and influential anti-Semitism from Henry Ford's *Dearborn Independent* to Father Coughlin's radio broadcasts. One grisly local tragedy occurred on a Saturday morning in 1966, when a young graduate of the University of Michigan stepped up to the *bimah* of a new suburban synagogue, berated the members of the congregation for their spiritual emptiness, and then shot the rabbi and himself. Perhaps, then, it is only fair to forgive Leo Litwak if his novel of Jewish life in Detroit in the late 1930s and early 1940s is a tiny bit grim.

The book's central personality, Jake Gottlieb, is a larger-than-life labor leader who rebelled against his pious family in Russia, survived Siberian exile, fought in World War I, and now aims his relentlessness at unionizing the Motor City's laundry truck drivers. The novel, narrated by Jake's teenage son Vic, details a successful, if brutal, strike, through which the union earns recognition from the industry. Barely tolerated by his boss or by the violent-tempered "Jewish toughs" at the local dairy restaurant, Jake doesn't know the meaning of the word "compromise," and he isn't afraid of taking a beating. He shuns violence, though, and grieves deeply when some of his lieutenants employ undue force. Jake unerringly honors his pledges, too, and he expects Vic and his elder son Ernie to fulfill their promise to avenge him if he meets an untimely fate. The anxiety Vic and Ernie experience—regarding not only the potential violence that will be done to their father but also Hitler's contemporaneous military victories in Europe—affects them in different ways. Vic remains fiercely loyal, while Ernie falls in with an aspiring hoodlum, shoplifts, and visits a prostitute across the Canadian border, in Windsor. As the title suggests, though, both boys spend most of their time waiting: for news of their father's death, for Hitler's latest atrocity, for an opportunity to live up to Jake's impossibly high standards.

The effete Marxists, Orthodox astronomers, corrupt politicians, and thugs they encounter don't offer Vic and Ernie much in the way of models for a life as honest as Jake's but less fraught with danger and violence. Since some of this material seems based on historical detail, perhaps it is no wonder that Litwak himself left Detroit for San Francisco. Highly praised by Irving Howe, and the recipient of several Jewish book awards, *Waiting for the News* captures the gritty tension that results from attempting to live honestly in a rough city.

Further reading: Litwak's other books are *To the Hanging Garden* (1964), also set in Detroit; *College Days in Earthquake Country* (1971), a nonfiction account of student and faculty protests at San Francisco State University, where Litwak taught for decades; *The Medic* (2001), a fictionalized version of Litwak's experiences in World War II; and *Nobody's Baby* (2005), a collection of short stories, including the top O. Henry Prize winner of 1990. Litwak's father, Isaac, was, like Jake Gottlieb, a labor leader in the Detroit laundry industry, and he has been mentioned in connection with one of Jimmy Hoffa's scandals in the late 1950s; Isaac Litwak's career receives some attention in Steve Babson's history, *Working Detroit* (1986). Another captivating novel about union organization, in which a Jewish leader features prominently, is Chester Himes's *Lonely Crusade* (1947). Those interested in Jewish Detroit should also seek out Elliot Feldman's dark comedy *Sitting Shiva* (2002), and Sidney Bolkosky's history, *Harmony and Dissonance* (1991).

· ·

63 - *Portnoy's Complaint*

By Philip Roth

RANDOM HOUSE, 1969. 274 PAGES.

*P*ortnoy's Complaint is the most notorious, talked-about novel in the American Jewish tradition; it also happens to be one of the finest. Though Roth has spent more energy developing the character of Nathan Zuckerman, and in recent years has written exceptional novels starring none other than Philip Roth, it seems clear that 100 or 200 years from now, the author will be remembered as the creator of Alexander Portnoy—sex-crazed, often impotent, obsessed with the slings and arrows of his Jewish family.

Portnoy tells the story of his life in a hilarious rant, wheeling through the events of his childhood and adult life with a stand-up comic's sense for incident and a postmodernist's eye for subtle underlying patterns. Having barely survived his early years with a stereotypical Jewish mother—straight out of Dan Greenburg's nonfiction bestseller, *How to Be a Jewish Mother* (1964)—and a perpetually constipated father, the young Portnoy soon discovers his first love, masturbation, which he practices with a ferocious intensity rarely matched by anyone, except perhaps just about every teenage boy on the planet. "My wang was all I really had that I could call my own," he explains. His second object of fascination, *shikses* (that is, non-Jewish girls), carries him well into his 20s. He applies a nickname to each of his non-Jewish girlfriends: there's the Pumpkin, the Pilgrim, and finally the Monkey, who matches his nymphomanic lusts but can't spell (she leaves a note for the maid asking her to "polish the flor by bathrum *pleze* & don't furget the insies of windose"). By the end of the novel, Portnoy has landed in post-1967 Israel, where he finds himself as out of place and neurotic as ever. The book then shudders to a stop with an unforgettable "PUNCH LINE," spoken by Portnoy's Freudian analyst: "Now vee may perhaps to begin. Yes?"

Sensibly enough, many readers have found the attitude toward women in *Portnoy's Complaint* repulsive; a smaller number have also objected to the book as an unsavory portrait of the modern American Jew. At the same time, many serious readers—both male and female—have found it not only a riotously comic emblem of late 1960s culture, but also a lasting work of art with something important to say about American Jewish life. One could argue that all the sex in the novel is highly traditional, though expressed in an X-rated vocabulary that became available only in the mid-1960s, thanks to a series of anti-censorship court decisions. Critics like Leslie Fiedler have suggested that telling stories about who sleeps with whom and who marries whom has been one of the major ways Jewish writing has approached questions of Jewish nationhood, identity, and continuity, starting as far back as the Torah itself. In this light, Portnoy's lusts and impotence can be read as Roth's explorations of a potential diasporic Jewish identity in the face of Israeli machismo and the temptations of assimilation. That is one reading, at least—the wonder of this novel is that you can read it and reread it, and each time you'll laugh out loud again and emerge with a different response to its brilliant provocations.

Further reading: Roth's novel was adapted into an unremarkable film in 1972. A controversial blockbuster like *Portnoy* was bound also to inspire imitations and ripostes, which include Gail Parent's *Sheila Levine Is Dead and Living in New York* (1972) and Barbara Bartlett's *The Shiksa* (1982). The novel figures prominently in the historian David Biale's wide-ranging cultural history, *Eros and the Jews* (1992).

64 – *Are You There, God? It's Me, Margaret*

By Judy Blume

BRADBURY PRESS, 1970. 149 PAGES.

At first glance, there seems to be no link between the two primary themes of Judy Blume's classic novel for young adults, *Are You There, God? It's Me, Margaret*: after all, what does having your first menstrual period have to do with picking a religion? Margaret Ann Simon, the book's protagonist, hopes to do both before the end of sixth grade, and when she runs into trouble on both fronts, she worries she is not normal.

Hardly a cosmopolitan herself—though a habitué of Lincoln Center's concerts, she has never sat on a plane—Margaret is nonetheless tapped into the currents of her time, an era during which American Jews entrenched themselves in the suburbs, led the sexual revolution, and confronted a host of changes within traditional Jewish communities, including growth in the rate of intermarriage.

Whether she realizes it or not, Margaret is touched by each of these developments. Her family has just moved from the Upper West Side of Manhattan to suburban Farbrook, New Jersey. Margaret's dad grew up Jewish, her mom Christian—though both profess no religion now—and her doting Jewish grandmother always wants to know whether Margaret has any boyfriends, and whether or not they're of the tribe. More dramatically, Margaret's experience of puberty is marked by new possibilities of sexual frankness: not quite 12, she has seen more than her share of *Playboy* centerfolds, and her sixth grade class is subjected to an awful sex ed film, *What Every Girl Should Know*. None of this teaches her much, and her new gang of suburban friends only adds to the muddle. As a result, Margaret—like J. D. Salinger's Holden Caulfield and even Huck Finn himself—projects a charming blend of world-weariness and wide-eyed innocence as she struggles to figure out who she is. Although she has been informed that she is not religious, she regularly confides in something she calls God—not grasping the irony as she begs, "I'm the only one without a religion. Why can't you help me?" In other words, Margaret's a preteen version of Bellow's Herzog, a believer despite herself.

She has also been a remarkable prizewinner: in 2005, for example, *Time* magazine called *Margaret* one of the 100 best novels published worldwide in English since 1923. Blume, who unlike her character grew up with two Jewish parents, is said to have sold more than 75 million copies of her books, and she has won a dizzying array of awards, capped perhaps by a special National Book Award for lifetime achievement in 2004.

Further reading: Blume has spun out a library full of beloved treasures for young adults, like *Blubber* (1974) and *Superfudge* (1980), as well as a few novels for more mature readers. Some biographies of the author, aimed at young readers, have been published, and the author maintains a website at http://www.judyblume.com/; for brief comments on how religion informed her writing of *Margaret*, see *The Half-Jewish Book* (2000), pages 31–33. There are of course hundreds of other worthwhile books of Jewish interest for teens and younger children—Sadie Rose Weilerstein's K'ton Ton books are also classics—even if there are few that are, like *Are You There God?*, remarkable enough to recommend to adults. Several bibliographies of Jewish children's books can be found easily online, though, and the Sydney Taylor Award annually recognizes distinguished works in this field. Other novels that feature the children of intermarriage include Samuel Yellen's *The Wedding Band* (1962) and Anne Bernays's *Growing Up Rich* (1975).

· ·

65 – *Bech, a Book*
By John Updike
KNOPF, 1970. 206 PAGES.

By the late 1960s, Jewish writers so dominated the field of American literature that non-Jews began to get jealous. In 1968 a Protestant novelist, Edward Hoagland, published a piece in *Commentary* called "On Not Being a Jew," which explicated the disadvantage that his non-Jewish heritage had conferred in the literary marketplace. Just one month earlier, and much more aggressively, Truman Capote had carped about the "Jewish literary mafia" in a *Playboy* interview. John Updike, who could with only a little facetiousness be called the most well regarded non-Jewish writer of his generation, perceived the same situation as Hoagland and Capote, but his response exhibited much more charm and wit. If you can't beat 'em, Updike suggested, why not join 'em?

The result was a durable alter ego for Updike, specifically a curmudgeonly American Jewish writer named Henry Bech who began to star in short stories in the *New Yorker* in the mid-1960s and has persisted for decades. Bech's first set of comic adventures in the world of letters draws upon Updike's own: Bech serves as a cultural ambassador on visits beyond the Iron Curtain to the Soviet Union, Romania, and Bulgaria, as Updike did. He lectures at a women's college in Virginia, smokes pot for the first time, deigns to be interviewed in London, and is inducted into an organization resembling the American Academy of Arts and Letters (which Updike joined in 1964, the same year as Bernard Malamud). Through it all, Bech remains resolutely ambivalent; a devotee of high culture, unsure what to think about his own literary work, and running around in literary circles rather than writing a new novel, Bech never misses the opportunity for a snappy rejoinder ("Your drinking is famous," he is told; "Like Hitler's vegetarianism," he fires back). He simplifies his correspondence by having rubber stamps manufactured with which to rebuff his admirers ("IT'S YOUR PH.D. THESIS; PLEASE WRITE IT YOURSELF"). And Updike caps all this fun off with a delightful Bech bibliography, a finely wrought parody including citations for all of Bech's uncollected essays and stories in various magazines of the 1950s (*Commentary*, the *Saturday Evening Post*) as well as the articles supposedly written about him by critics such as Alfred Kazin, Norman Podhoretz, and Leslie Fiedler.

Cynthia Ozick, as strident as ever, complained that Bech was even more ignorant than typical "indifferent disaffected de-Judaized Jewish novelists" and characterized Updike's sprinkling of Yiddish and Jewish nostalgia throughout the text as the superficial work of "the Appropriate Reference Machine." The point of the Bech stories, though, is not an exploration of the depths of Jewishness but the comedy, and pathos, of the experience of being a writer in the United States: in a playful self-interview ostensibly conducted by Bech in 1971, Updike commented that in *Bech, a Book* he wanted to write "about a writer, who was a Jew with the same inevitability that a fictional rug-salesman would be an Armenian." In other words, Updike was simply tipping his hat to the massive achievements of Jews in American fiction, and it is not like doing so took him away from his closer-to-home excavations of suburban and small-town American life (one of his finest novels, *Rabbit Redux*, appeared just a year after the first Bech collection). Bech may be only as Jewish as a non-Jew's imagination could make him, but he is still very sympathetic—and a sign of his times.

Further reading: *The Complete Henry Bech* (2001) collects the first batch of stories along with those published as *Bech Is Back* (1982) and *Bech at Bay* (1998), plus one bonus story. Updike's novels include the tetralogy of Rabbit Angstrom books, published under one cover in 1995 and 2003, as well as 1968's *Couples*. Updike has been the subject of much criticism, and, amazingly prolific as he is, has published hundreds of essays and reviews as well as a memoir, *Self-Consciousness* (1989). Joyce Carol Oates—a non–Jewish American writer who is about as prolific as Updike—has also written about Jews, for instance in *The Tattooed Girl* (2003). For a mirror image of the non-Jew writing as a Jew, see, among others, Saul Bellow's *Henderson the Rain King* (1959).

. . . .

66 – *The Book of Daniel*

By E. L. Doctorow

RANDOM HOUSE, 1971. 303 PAGES.

It has been reported that E. L. Doctorow tells his students, when it comes to writing historical fiction, "Do the least amount of research you can get away with, and no less." At its best, the historical novel provides more insight than history and more pleasure than a novel; hewing close to the facts but disregarding them regularly for the sake of aesthetic and narrative pleasure, such fiction offers us not only a sense of what happened but also an argument for what it might mean to us. A publishing insider and gifted critic, Doctorow brings a powerful self-consciousness about historical fiction to his own masterful efforts in the genre, including *The Book of Daniel*, *Ragtime* (1975), and *Billy Bathgate* (1989).

The Book of Daniel, Doctorow's third novel, centers on the son of a Jewish couple who were convicted of treason and electrocuted by the U.S. government during the anti-communist witch hunts of the 1950s. They're not Julius and Ethel Rosenberg—in Doctorow's novel, they're called Rochelle and Paul Isaacson, and they have a son and a daughter rather than the two boys the real Rosenbergs had—but they're close. The novel relates the story of their arrest, trial, and execution through the eyes of their son, who is understandably disturbed by the world he has grown up in—it isn't easy being a surviving member of "a notorious family." When he is not out sneering at the counterculture, Daniel spends his time at Columbia University's Butler Library, procrastinating from his dissertation by reading up on the history of the capital punishments, such as knouting and burning at the stake, that preceded death by electrocution. In a fragmented and self-consciously postmodern narrative, Doctorow weaves in remarkable set pieces: a chilling scene from Paul Robeson's concert in Peekskill, New York; a parody of a "Bintel Brief" letter to the Yiddish *Forward*; invocations of the psychedelic prophecies of the biblical book from which the novel takes its title; and learned mock-academic discourses on Disneyland, the history of communism, and a dozen other subjects.

Beneath the raging surface of such virtuosity lies Doctorow's concern for his characters and their suffering as well as his broad interest in what happened to left-wing politics in the United States after World War II. The novel ends with Daniel leaving Butler Library to join the Columbia University student protests of 1968. Though grim in its outlook and subject, the novel engages with politics and eschews hopelessness: it shows the power of fiction to reconstruct, manipulate, and subvert history in the hopes of understanding it.

Further reading: Letters written by the real Ethel and Julius in jail can be found in an edition edited by their son, Michael Meeropol (1994); David Evanier's *Red Love* (1991) also fictionalizes the Rosenbergs. Sidney Lumet adapted Doctorow's novel into film as *Daniel* (1983). Many of Doctorow's novels deal with Jewish subjects; the two others mentioned earlier and *World's Fair* (1985), are among the most interesting. A handful of academic studies have analyzed Doctorow's works and career, including those by Paul Levine (1985) and John Parks (1991), though a complete accounting will have to wait, as Doctorow continues to publish novels at a regular pace. Another outstanding literary treatment of Ethel Rosenberg is Tony Kushner's play, *Angels in America*, which was made into an excellent film by HBO (2003).

67 – *Double or Nothing: A Real Fictitious Discourse*

By Raymond Federman

SWALLOW PRESS, 1971. 202 PAGES.

How can we tell the stories of the Holocaust? This question lies behind the brilliant, inventive writing of Raymond Federman. When he was a teenager, living in Paris, Federman's family was deported to Auschwitz, where they were murdered. He survived because his mother stuffed him, her favorite, into a closet—he crawled out a day later and found his way to a farm in the south of France where he could live out the war. An uncle brought him to America, and he attended school, eventually becoming a professor of French literature and an early supporter of Samuel Beckett.

In his debut novel, Federman's project is not to tell this story but to avoid telling it. Instead of relying on the conventions of autobiography, he erects a clever fictional structure that allows him to concentrate on how such a story might be told, rather than on the tale itself. The novel is peopled by three primary characters: the first, "a rather stubborn and determined middle-aged man," records the activities of the second, "a somewhat paranoiac fellow . . . who had decided to lock himself in a room . . . for a year . . . to write the story" of a third, "the hero"—whose name is often given as Boris, but sometimes as Jacques or Dominique—and whose experiences resemble those of Federman himself. Much of the book consists of the rambling plans of the second man, who has only about $1,200 with which to support himself for his year of writing. Locked in isolation, he hopes to survive on noodles and canned tomato sauce, having carried in with himself toilet paper, coffee, soap, and everything else he will need; his calculations of exactly how many boxes of noodles and rolls of toilet paper he should purchase take up dozens of pages. With the Holocaust hovering so clearly in the background, the symbolic resonance of this character's hypothetical confinement and his computation of the bare necessities of survival hardly need to be emphasized.

Federman's unconventional approach to plot is mirrored by his unique typography: a virtuoso with a typewriter, he lays out each of his pages like a work of visual art, with sentences that trail, twirl, and loop down the page; run backward and upside down; or appear in untranslated French. This book needs to be seen to be believed. Though these tactics might seem sterile postmodernist gimmicks in the hands of a writer with a flimsier subject, *Double or Nothing* is remarkable for its comedy, for its pathos, and for the degree to which its playful format engages, rather than alienates, the reader.

Further reading: Like Federman, many writers use postmodernist tactics to tell and not tell stories of the Holocaust, including Jonathan Safran Foer, Walter Abish, Georges Perec, and the Israeli David Grossman, whose *See Under: Love* (1989) is the masterpiece of the genre. Federman is nothing if not prolific; in addition to books of scholarly criticism, he has also published many novels, including *Take It or Leave It* (1976) and *The Two-Fold Vibration* (1982); though he is in his 80s, he maintains an entertaining blog every bit as irreverent and unusual as his fiction. Ronald Sukenick's *Mosaic Man* (1999) is a more recent attempt to bring together the techniques of postmodernism with the American Jewish experience.

· ·

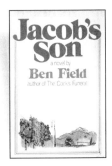

68 – *Jacob's Son*
By Ben Field
CROWN, 1971. 345 PAGES.

In the 1930s, a young Jew in Brooklyn—or anyplace else in America—could choose any number of ideologies. He could join up with communists, perhaps travel to Spain to fight Franco in the Abraham Lincoln Brigade; he could affiliate with the Zionists, yearning to make aliyah to that other Promised Land; he could invest shrewdly, work hard, and build up a fortune in a trade like real estate; he could chase girls. The adolescent hero of Ben Field's final novel, Michael Berkowitz, could follow any of these paths—his friends and companions do—but his interests lie elsewhere. He wants to be a farmer in the United States.

By all accounts a remarkable young man, Michael is not an easy character to like. His father, a devotee of the great Hebrew poet, Chaim Nachman Bialik, passed away during Michael's teens. Any number of men would be happy to fill the empty paternal role, from Freund the proletarian; to Dr. Campbell, a professor of classics; to Dr. Bendel, the principal of the Hebrew school where first Michael's father, and then Michael himself, teach. Michael rejects each of these men in turn, only after winning their admiration. He is so smart that he is offered a job teaching college classes while still an undergraduate and so dedicated that he can build, from scratch, a successful house-painting business. But he acts cold and harsh with his sweet-tempered and sociable mother and even harsher, if that is possible, with himself. He feels he has to reject all sexual temptations, and—like the students of Musar found in Chaim Grade's novels—he sees mostly the self-interest, pettiness, and hollowness in the pronouncements and politicking around him. The one man he does look up to is Reuben, an old suitor of his mother's, a lusty vegetarian follower of Tolstoy, and a full-time farmer. Under Reuben's tutelage and on his land, Michael studies veterinary science and finds his calling as a farmhand.

Published not long before his death, and intended as the first volume in a trilogy that never appeared, Field's novel offers a lusciously textured tour of American Jewish life—and an unusual one, in that it strays well beyond the urban experience. Field's prose is riddled with Yiddish, Hebrew, and manifold cultural references, and it offers everything from the lyrics to the folk song "Oifn

Pripetchik" to bilingual puns, like one on "nahr" (which means "young man" in Hebrew, but "fool" in Yiddish). This thick layer of references and the large cast of characters often necessitate the reader's patience. Fair warning: that patience will not be repaid by Michael's development into a likeable hero—he remains stubborn and idiosyncratic to the book's final pages—but this mostly forgotten novel is well worth the effort it requires, thanks to its depth, robustness, and warmth.

Further reading: Field, who was born as Moe Bragin, published his first book in the 1930s; his little-known and hard-to-find novels include *The Cock's Funeral* (1937) and *The Outside Leaf* (1943). Very little has been written about Field, aside from occasional glimpses in the literary scholarship of Alan Wald.

. . . .

69 – *The Pagan Rabbi and Other Stories*
By Cynthia Ozick

KNOPF, 1971. 270 PAGES.

Cynthia Ozick's first collection of stories, *The Pagan Rabbi and Other Stories*, exemplifies her ability to articulate and explore juicy paradoxes in the fields of art and religion. For example, Ozick views fiction in its essence as contradicting Jewish tradition—because, of course, all art is a form of idolatry. But writing fiction is still her bread and butter. This contradiction hovers over Ozick's story "The Pagan Rabbi," which features Isaac Kornfeld, a Torah scholar and *talmid hakham* who reads Byron, Tennyson, and Keats, and then falls in love with a dryad (that is, wood nymph), a spirit out of pagan folklore. Since in Ozick's view literature and paganism are more or less identical, loyalists of fiction like her, who want to remain Jewish, need some help resolving the contradiction, perhaps along the lines of Kornfeld's argument that "Holy life subsists even in the stone. . . . Hence in God's fecundating Creation there is no possibility of Idolatry." Not that Kornfeld's ideas lead him anywhere pleasant: he ends up hanging himself from a tree.

That fiction contradicts Jewish tradition is not only philosophy for Ozick, either; her novella *Envy; or, Yiddish in America* (reprinted as the second piece in the collection) managed to scandalize the real-life Yiddish *literarishe velt* upon its first appearance in *Commentary*, in 1969. A tale of two Yiddishists—one, Ostrover, a short story writer who is famous around the world because his work is translated into English; the other, Edelstein, an obscure and bitter poet known only to readers of small literary journals in *mameloshen*—*Envy* is a portrait in miniature, with deliberate and gleeful distortions, of the possibilities of Yiddish in postwar America. The satire did not go unnoticed. Sadly, the extraordinary Yiddish poet, novelist, and critic Jacob Glatstein went to his grave in 1971 assuming that Edelstein was a cruel version of himself, just as Ostrover was obviously modeled on Isaac Bashevis Singer. This wasn't the case, Ozick later told an interviewer; "I did not know," she said, "when I wrote that story—just think of my ignorance!—that there had been a great fight between Glatstein and Singer," just like the one in her story. In her defense, Ozick has translated Yiddish poetry by H. Leivick, Abraham Sutzkever, and Glatstein himself, in the hopes of helping these writers reach English-language readers, and *Envy* can be read, as Ozick has said, as "an elegy, a lamentation, a celebration" of Yiddish in the United States.

Though *The Pagan Rabbi and Other Stories* is worth owning for the sake of *Envy* alone, the book also contains "Virility"—a beguiling tale of an immigrant poet, Elia Gatoff, who changes his name to Edmund Gate and owes his fame to an unlikely source of material—and several short weird narratives ("The Butterfly and the Traffic Light" and "The Dock Witch," for example) that beggar summary. The play of Ozick's language and the range of her intellect consistently delight, and if she occasionally strays too far in the direction of the highfalutin or the obscure, she does so for the best reasons, because she aspires to create fiction that enlarges our sense of what art and Jewishness can mean.

Further reading: The biographical essay by Susanne Klingenstein that appears in *Daughters of Valor* (1997) provides fascinating facts about Ozick's life and its relation to her work. A spate of academic studies of Ozick's oeuvre appeared in the 1990s, written by scholars such as Elaine Kauvar (1993), Sarah Blacher Cohen (1994), and Victor Strandberg (1994); a collection of essays edited by Harold Bloom (1986) may be the most useful point of entry into the secondary literature about Ozick's early work.

99

. . . .

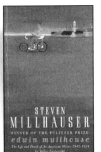

70 – *Edwin Mullhouse: The Life and Death of an American Writer, 1943–1954, by Jeffrey Cartwright*
By Steven Millhauser

KNOPF, 1972. 305 PAGES.

Steven Millhauser's brilliant self-reflexive fictions contain riddles, mysteries, and sly allusions to the interplay between literature and life. Within these labyrinthine, prize-winning works, Jewishness too is buried—so effectively buried that critics have tended to miss it. When a film version of Millhauser's story "Eisenheim the Illusionist" appeared with almost all traces of Jewishness extirpated—it is called *The Illusionist* (2006) and stars Edward Norton, who has elsewhere played the prototypical gentile—a few journalists noticed. None made the connection, though, between this disappearing act and Millhauser's first novel, the tour de force *Edwin Mullhouse*.

Millhauser's book—the winner in 1975 of the Prix Médicis étranger, a French award for the best foreign novel in translation—takes the form of a biography of the great American writer, Edwin Mullhouse, who happens to die on his 11th birthday after having produced a single literary masterpiece called *Cartoons*. Edwin's biographer is his neighbor, Jeffrey Cartwright, older than him by six months, with a "truly inspired memory" that allows him to recall and describe absolutely everything about Edwin's life, starting with his arrival home from the hospital. At great length and in a high style that parodies old-fashioned literary biographies (Boswell's life of Samuel Johnson, for example), Cartwright draws portraits for the reader of Edwin's sister and parents; his hobbies and obsessions with comic books, toys, and animation; his friendships, prepubescent love affairs, and adventures in the school playground. Cartwright's proclivities turn his study of Edwin into a powerful meditation on the relationship between writer and critic, life and art, childhood and what the book calls "the obscenity of maturity."

One thing Jeffrey doesn't seem aware of, though, is Edwin's ethnicity: Edwin's mother calls her son "bubbele" and "kvetch," while his grandfathers hail from Germany and Russia, the latter having "escaped to America from the Czar." The closest Jeffrey comes to spelling this out, though, is when he repeats some playground gossip that "Edwin said he was a Jew" and relates that Mrs. Mullhouse possesses "the pride of her race in its firstborn sons," not to mention a copy of *The Settlement Cookbook* (1903). This is the 1950s in Connecticut, though—when Edwin is ill, Mrs. Mullhouse fears he will be mistaken for a "refugee," which is what Holocaust survivors were called in those years. Dr. Mullhouse, the paterfamilias, seems intent on erasing his Jewishness through an embrace of Anglo American high culture; the only time he touches on his Jewish roots, in fact, is when he is parodying ethnic speech patterns self-consciously or making a pun, in the forest, about "pine Cohens." Of course, the similarities between the names Mullhouse and Millhauser aren't accidental, and Millhauser's father, Milton, was like Edwin's dad a literature professor at a small Connecticut college who wrote an essay in 1959 explaining the benefits of learning Latin for his teenage son (apparently Hebrew and Yiddish were not on the agenda). To what degree is Dr. Mullhouse a version of Dr. Millhauser, and Edwin a version of Steven? This is exactly what Millhauser's novel wants us to do: pursue, and tangle ourselves up in, the troublesome questions inevitably raised when we try to pin down literary Jewishness or perform other sorts of biographical readings. It is a brilliant gambit, and the novel finally suggests the envy of a non-Jewish critic for the imaginative capacities and doting parents of his friend, whom he deliberately labels an American writer, and not an American Jewish one.

Further reading: Millhauser's *Martin Dressler: The Tale of an American Dreamer* (1996), which won the Pulitzer Prize, features a turn-of-the-century entrepreneur who builds an empire of grand hotels—he is not Jewish, but he certainly could have been. For an apposite case study in biography, subtly elided Jewishness, and literary culture, see Leon Edel's monumental five-volume biography of Henry James.

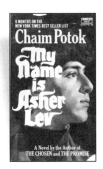

71 – *My Name Is Asher Lev*

By Chaim Potok

KNOPF, 1972. 350 PAGES.

Though less of a blockbuster than his famous debut, *The Chosen* (1967), Chaim Potok's third novel made the bestseller lists for a solid six months and was the first fiction situated so resolutely in the world of Hasidism to make such a splash in the United States. While *The Chosen* dramatizes the schism between modern Orthodoxy and Hasidism in the relationship between two boys, Asher Lev's childhood takes place deep within the folds of Ladover Hasidism; Lev's father is one of the Ladover rebbe's right-hand men, and he grows up in Brooklyn, almost literally in the shadow of the movement's headquarters.

Asher Lev's problem is his gift: he has an uncanny ability to draw. Not yet a bar mitzvah, with no training or instruction, he produces his first oil painting and remarks, "It was as if I had been painting in oils all my life." According to Asher's father, though, "painting is for goyim," and the fact that great artists depict suffering Christs and nude women is further proof that they come from the *sitra achra*, the Other Side, the secular world that some Hasidic Jewish communities shun. Asher's father's rejection of art is more personal than religious, for he himself is a speaker of many languages, a reader of the *New York Times*, and a holder of a graduate degree from New York University; he has been trained, at the behest of the rebbe, so that he can negotiate with governments for the release of Ladover Jews from the Soviet Union, and he is later dispatched to found Ladover yeshivahs throughout Western Europe. (What with its Crown Heights headquarters, international reach, and budding presence on college campuses, Potok's fictional Ladover sect is clearly modeled on the well-known and still thriving Chabad-Lubavitch movement.) The rebbe himself, more sensitive to Asher's needs than the boy's father, recognizes the seriousness of his vocation and arranges for the budding genius to study with a famous, secular Jewish artist who "transformed forever the nature of sculpting as Picasso had transformed forever the nature of painting."

Asher's father turns out to be right: a much-feted young painter is bound to stray beyond the boundaries of *tznius*, or religious modesty. At Asher's breakthrough gallery shows, he exhibits canvases that scandalize the Ladover community. For most artists—and American Jewish writers, too—the answer would be to reject the religious community and seek out temptations in the wider world, but Asher remains *frum*, never shearing his sidelocks or throwing away his yarmulke. If he strays into shmaltz (that is, sentimentality), at least Potok's is an informed and intensely Jewish sentimentality, one with much to recommend it. A moody evocation of the Cold War years in a cloistered American Jewish community, the novel explores the age-old conflict of the artist against tradition—a theme understandably close to the heart of Potok, an ordained Conservative rabbi and one of the most beloved American Jewish writers of all time.

101

Further reading: In 1990, Potok continued the story of the Hasidic painter in *The Gift of Asher Lev*; Potok's *The Chosen* and its sequel, *The Promise* (1969), are some of the most widely read and taught American Jewish novels. Various profiles and obituaries of Potok—who died in 2002—can be found online, and Daniel Walden has edited a collection of conversations with the author (2001). For those interested in the lives of Jewish visual artists, Benjamin Harshav's monumental *Marc Chagall and His Times* (2003) offers comprehensive coverage of the most prominent Jewish painter of the 20th century, and many biographies and critical studies are available on other figures, including Pissaro, Soutine, and Modigliani.

. . . .

72 – *In the Days of Simon Stern*

By Arthur A. Cohen

RANDOM HOUSE, 1973. 464 PAGES.

A back-cover blurb on the original edition of Arthur A. Cohen's best-known novel remarks that "*In the Days of Simon Stern* is very probably a masterpiece." This odd statement—couldn't the publisher find someone to praise the book who was *certain* it was a masterpiece?—reveals quite a bit about this extraordinarily challenging novel. To make a definitive statement about its brilliance, one would need to parse every one of the book's many theologically intricate parables, fables, allegories, and stories-within-stories, and that is more than any single reader could accomplish. Suffice to say that *Simon Stern* is an overwhelming book, and that philosophically minded readers will find it an astounding labyrinth within which to roam.

Though Cohen's approach is solidly within the tradition of the novel of ideas, he does not neglect the basic trappings of plot and character. At the center of the book is one Simon Stern, a New York native born to immigrant parents in 1899, who is also, incidentally, the Messiah. Having amassed an enormous fortune through real estate dealings as a young man, and having caused the death of his parents through his neglect of some faulty wiring, Simon responds to the Holocaust in a peculiar way: he buys up a block and builds an enormous, secret fortress in lower Manhattan, and then he heads to Europe to gather a group of survivors to live there with him. One of them, blind Nathan of Gaza, is the first prisoner liberated at Buchenwald; he becomes Simon's personal scribe (every Messiah needs one, no?) and the narrator of the novel. The book's plot, such as it is, goes on to describe the intrigues among the residents of Simon's survivor haven, including a menacing and mysterious half-Jew, Janos Baltar, and Simon's second-in-command, Dr. Fischer Klay.

But plot isn't the point, really. "My training was in philosophy and theology," Cohen once remarked, "and my passion remains philosophy and theology.

People, unfortunately, don't read philosophy and theology, certainly not Jewish theology"—which is why the author turned to a popular form, the novel, into which he could insert whatever he wanted. He injects, none too subtly, dozens of internal narratives, including epistolary exchanges, private investigator's reports, dreams, a set of meditations written in the personae of Montaigne, Spinoza, and Bar Kokhba, as well as a long independent narrative, "The Legend of the Last Jew on Earth." (Cohen is not the only one compelled by the notion of a "Last Jew": David Pinski, Leslie Fiedler, Yoram Kaniuk, and Noah Gordon all have works with similar titles.) Whether presented in the form of Simon's harangues or Nathan's digressions, Cohen's meditations can be obscure and confusing, but also brilliant—and occasionally even funny. In all, his is an extraordinarily informed and thoughtful perspective on the pressing questions of Jewish existence.

Further reading: The best place to start exploring Cohen's oeuvre is *An Arthur A. Cohen Reader* (1998), which has bits of his fiction—he published five books of fiction aside from *Simon Stern*, one posthumously—and nonfiction. It is largely for the latter, which includes works like *The Natural and the Supernatural Jew* (1963) and *The Myth of the Judeo-Christian Tradition* (1970), that he will be remembered (though he was also influential in his career as a publisher). Those interested in the cropping up of messianism throughout Jewish history should consult Harris Lenowitz's scholarly *Jewish Messiahs* (1998); those more inclined to literature will enjoy Isaac Bashevis Singer's *Satan in Goray* (1935) or Cynthia Ozick's *The Messiah of Stockholm* (1987). Cohen's somewhat grotesque treatment of the Holocaust resembles, to some degree, the approach taken in André Schwarz-Bart's *The Last of the Just* (1959).

103

. . . .

73 – *Fear of Flying*
By Erica Jong

HOLT, RINEHART, AND WINSTON, 1973. 311 PAGES.

In the 1960s, thanks to a series of court battles—often tried by Jewish lawyers—it became possible for reputable U.S. publishers to sell, without expurgation or bowdlerization, "dirty" books such as D. H. Lawrence's *Lady Chatterley's Lover*, Henry Miller's *Tropic of Cancer*, and a moldy old pornographic romp by the name of *Fanny Hill*. A few years later, Philip Roth showed that dirty words and sexual frankness could be put to use in fiction both uproariously funny and, in its own way, deeply serious. A talented 20-something poet and literary scholar named Erica Jong saw all of this going on, and said, in effect, why are the boys having all the fun? In 1973, she published *Fear of Flying*, an exuberant novel dripping with sex and satire that has gone on to sell over 12 million copies in—believe it or not—27 languages.

Jong's highly autobiographical protagonist and narrator, Isadora White Stollerman Wing, grows up in a well-off but loopy New York Jewish family. As the novel begins, she is accompanying her second husband, a Chinese-American psychotherapist named Bennett Wing, to an international psychiatry conference in Vienna—the city, Isadora points out, that Freud fled in 1938. Apropos of this trip, and in good therapeutic fashion, Isadora spins out tales of her troubled childhood and early adulthood, her years in Heidelberg and in graduate school at Columbia, and all the woes of being a woman in a patriarchal world ("Growing up female in America. What a liability!"). She soon finds the ironically named Adrian Goodlove, who, though often impotent, manages to tempt her away from her sullen and taciturn husband. As she guiltily pursues adultery and zips around Europe with Adrian, seeking the enlightenment of self-indulgence, she recounts the traumas of her life to date, including a disastrous first marriage to a brilliant young psychopath, a bizarre visit to her sister in Beirut in the mid-1960s, and all the therapy it took before she amassed enough confidence to submit her poetry to magazines. Through it all, Isadora's Jewishness pops up often, whether she is riffing on Freud and his followers, the peccadilloes of bourgeois New Yorkers, or her acrimonious relationship with Germany.

What makes this novel irresistible is the bright humor and erudition with which Jong lampoons everything in sight, as well as the unbridled diction she employs to explore female sexuality and desire. Though her unabashed dirty words are the same ones that began to appear in sex-pulp paperbacks in the 1960s and 1970s, Jong's aim is not simple titillation—for one thing, the men in her novel are as often flaccid as not. For another, there is an uncanny realism, even pragmatism, to Jong's descriptions of sex and relationships. In general, though the details are larger than life, the book reads more or less like a thinly veiled personal history, exaggerated just enough to be funnier than truth; as Isadora remarks, for herself and her creator, "Nothing quite has reality for me till I write it all down—revising and embellishing as I go." More than one generation of women have found in Jong a guide to self-discovery, and though the novel is an artifact of its era, it still conveys the freshness and verve that first made it a hit.

Further reading: Though she also writes memoirs, such as *Fear of Fifty* (1994), Jong writes fiction so transparently autobiographical that perhaps there would be little to be added by an external biographer; no biography has yet appeared, though a useful collection of interviews with the author has been edited by Charlotte Templin (2002). None of her books has had quite the impact of *Fear of Flying*, but Jong's oeuvre includes many collections of poetry, essays, and novels, and continues to grow year by year.

74 – *A Star in the Family*

By Irvin Faust

DOUBLEDAY, 1975. 306 PAGES.

Key players in comedy for over a century, Jews have often made their most influential and cutting statements to the American public in the guise of the joke teller. From the Hebrew comedians of the early vaudeville stage to the Borsht Belt *tummlers*, from the Golden Age radio MCs to the pioneering television impresarios, and from Lenny Bruce to Jerry Seinfeld in the modern art of stand-up, Jewish comedians have always held up a funhouse mirror to American society, exaggerating all its joys and absurdities. No wonder, then, that Irvin Faust chose a comedian as his "vehicle" in a novelistic attempt to "show the rise and fall of this nation of the last forty years," from the 1930s to the early 1970s.

Related in snippets of interviews, ex-wives' complaints, friends' recollections, and archival materials, as organized by an unnamed biographer, the novel concerns the life and times of one Bart Goldwine, a Brooklyn-born jokester. Managers, agents, producers, and co-stars describe Goldwine's rise from the Borsht Belt to the Hollywood of the 1950s, where he played the inevitable Jewish character in war movies and eventually landed *The Bart Goldwine Show*, a weekly hit. As this storyline develops, the narration flashes back to Goldwine's childhood, family, and World War II experiences tapping out Morse code in the European theater of operations. A patriot, Goldwine not only serves his country—at one point almost getting himself executed by some Nazis—but, at the height of McCarthyism, he volunteers to "blow the whistle" on any "subversive influences" at his movie studio. A stand-up comic in the 1960s, he makes a splash with his impersonation of John F. Kennedy—but, as happened to the real-life impressionist Vaughn Meader, whose album *The First Family* sold 7.5 million copies by the middle of 1963—the assassination of the president on November 22, 1963, brings his career to a screeching, tragic halt. Traumatized, Goldwine sinks lower and lower; his pathetic stint as a circus clown dead-ends with Robert Kennedy's assassination in 1968, and the book concludes with Goldwine mired in an alcoholic stupor, living with a motherly African American woman in his old neighborhood, Crown Heights, and taking pay to rile up Jewish and African American vigilantes with impressions of Hitler and Theodore Bilbo. Goldwine's terrifying slide represents Faust's take on the comedown from postwar ebullience into the dissent and confusion of the 1960s; as the author told an interviewer, "In my judgment, after 1963 there wasn't a hell of a lot to laugh about in America."

Brilliant in its ventriloquism of various showbiz types, and textured with the detritus of pop culture—slogans, neighborhood gags, dirty jokes, bar mitzvah speeches, and English class assignments as well as the technicalities of seduction among Brooklyn high school kids in the late 1930s—the novel is both a history of comedy and a broader rumination. Goldwine steals bits from his comedic betters—he is described as "the best of Gobel crossed with the best of Sahl, with a touch of Cox and a soupçon of Randall"—but also imagines, as he travels through Europe, that he receives advice directly from Benjamin Disraeli, Alfred Dreyfus, Thomas Mann, and, in Japan, Commodore Matthew Perry. Engaged equally with the serious and the frivolous aspects of history, the tragic and the comic, Faust's novel deserves to be remembered not only as a faux biography of a Lenny Bruce wannabe but also as a thoughtful and successful fictional experiment.

Further reading: Faust worked as a counselor in a New York City high school; his best-known works include the stories collected in *Roar Lion Roar* (1965), and the high-concept and bedazzling novel *Foreign Devils* (1973). Wallace Markfield's *You Could Live If They Let You* (1974) also centers on a Jewish comedian. Gerald Nachman's *Seriously Funny* (2003) offers nonfictional profiles of the stars of comedy in the 1950s and 1960s; *Lenny* (1974), a hagiographic film portrait of Lenny Bruce starring Dustin Hoffman, uses a similar approach to Faust's in sketching its protagonist's life.

- -

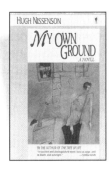

75 – *My Own Ground*
By Hugh Nissenson

FARRAR, STRAUS, AND GIROUX, 1976. 181 PAGES.

In his first two collections of stories, *A Pile of Stones* (1965) and *In the Reign of Peace* (1972), Hugh Nissenson demonstrated a facility for crafting terse, moving fictions as well as a fundamental interest in the intensities of Jewish life outside the United States. Raised in Brooklyn on the stories of his immigrant father, and having spent some years in Israel, Nissenson set the majority of these stories either in the Eastern European past or in the Middle Eastern present, where just being Jewish was often a life-or-death struggle. His first novel, *My Own Ground*, returns to an American setting and manages to find equally exotic and powerful material there. In doing so, the book digs so deeply into the barrel of immigrant history that it scrapes the very bottom.

A harsh story of urban life in 1912 narrated by a 15-year-old orphan named Jake Brody, *My Own Ground* centers on the sexual enslavement of a pretty rabbi's daughter, Hannah Isaacs, by a charismatic Jewish pimp named Schlifka. Jake involves himself first by tipping Schlifka off to the girl's whereabouts after she escapes and later by joining forces with an idealistic communist journalist in an attempt to save Hannah from the pimp's clutches. Narrating this tragedy in taut prose, Nissenson spares the reader few of the bloody or pornographic details. In particular, Hannah narrates explicitly her initiation into prostitution, as Schlifka systematically rapes her so as to addict her to sex. This is not the sepia-toned Lower East Side for which we tend to wax nostalgic.

Nissenson is a consummate researcher—he describes Hannah willowing ostrich feathers for women's hats, and Jake's labor as a presser, in extraordinary detail—and Schlifka is, unfortunately, not an invented nightmare. The scandalous practice of "white slavery," in which Jewish pimps abducted poor girls from their homes, drugged them, and sold them as prostitutes, did actually happen in the early 20th century, though not as commonly as the sensational press, police commissions, and a series of wildly popular movies claimed. Along with his toughs and pimps, Nissenson includes some charitable and well-meaning folk, so the picture is not entirely bleak, and his larger interest, evinced by parallels with Dostoyevsky and with Isaac Bashevis Singer's *Satan in Goray* (1935), is in the various forms messianism takes, from socialist to mystical. Nissenson's razor-sharp prose uses elision and silence expertly ("You have to trim away the fat, achieve more with less," he has said of his technique), and it drives forward what is one of the grimmest novels about American Jews ever written.

Further reading: Nissenson's subsequent novels have ranged wildly in setting, from Ohio in 1811 (1985's *The Tree of Life*) to a dystopian science fiction future (2001's *The Song of the Earth*) to September 11, 2001 (2005's *Days of Awe*). The best general introduction to Nissenson's writing can be found in *The Elephant and My Jewish Problem* (1988), a collection including selections of the author's fiction and nonfiction. On white slavery, see Edward Bristow's *Prostitution and Prejudice* (1982) or Isabel Vincent's *Bodies and Souls* (2005). In Yiddish, the theme was treated in Sholem Asch's play, *God of Vengeance* (1906), and in Sholem Aleichem's short story "The Man from Buenos Aires" (1909). Adele Wiseman's superb *Crackpot* (1974) features a Jewish prostitute in Winnipeg, and Jerome Charyn's memoirs, such as *The Dark Lady from Belorusse* (1997) and *Bronx Boy* (2002), imaginatively recall and recreate a Bronx at times as gritty as Nissenson's Lower East Side.

107

. . . .

76 – *Refiner's Fire: The Life and Adventures of Marshall Pearl, a Foundling*
By Mark Helprin

KNOPF, 1977. 373 PAGES.

Mark Helprin's first novel, *Refiner's Fire*, can be understood as the skillfully articulated fantasy life of a political conservative. Not exactly autobiographical ("if not consistently in fact, then always in spirit," the author observed), the fiction appropriates details of the author's life (an upbringing in New York and the Caribbean, studies at Harvard, service in the Israeli military), expanding and exaggerating them into their most extreme, tender, and stunning possibilities. The book's hero, Marshall Pearl, is a neocon James Bond, the personified ideal of the militaristic and moralistic Jewish culture whose influence has been steadily expanding in the United States for decades.

Marshall is officially an orphan (according to the subtitle, he is a "foundling")—he is born on a refugee ship en route to Palestine in 1947, and his mother dies in a battle with the British—but the kid has at least three father figures. His first protector is Paul Levy, the ship's captain and a navy lifer who eventually rises to the rank of admiral and becomes Marshall's brother-in-law; his adopted father is an eccentric American capitalist, Livingstone (né Lischinsky); and his biological father, unknown to him for most of his life, is an Israeli general whose name, Arieh Ben Barak, like the story of the refugee ship, echoes Leon Uris's *Exodus*. As his role models suggest, Marshall is hardly the pale and intellectual scholar of traditional Ashkenazi Jewish culture; in fact, he is a crack shot, a fantastic horseback rider, a world-class mountain climber, and an all-around manly man. His adventures verge on magic realism, but they also reach back to the romance tradition of chivalric adventures; extremely capacious, the book has time to touch on many causes sacred among right-wing Jews, from the morality of capital punishment to the historical right of the Jews to the Land of Israel. Every woman Marshall encounters is described as stunningly gorgeous, and—once more, as if in a conservative's dream come true—the one he marries publicly denounces feminism on the eve of their wedding. Whether Marshall is tooling around the United States or being inducted brutally into the Israeli military, he is always a model of American masculine dignity, while never denying his Jewish identity. He is the sort of Jewish cowboy that Ronald Reagan would have adored.

Helprin's prose is decorous, lyrical, and often affected—he has cited Dante's *Divine Comedy* and the Bible as his major aesthetic influences—and in the novel the resulting effect is more often comical and endearing than in Helprin's short stories. In addition to his fiction, Helprin has distinguished himself over the years with his political writing (besides newspaper work, he wrote speeches for the Republican presidential candidate Bob Dole, and he is now on the staff of a conservative think tank), and through it all he has consistently followed a piece of advice given to Marshall: "You always got to fight the trends." A contrarian at heart, Helprin writes unusual fiction, and his first novel is nothing less than a literary monument to the rightward swing of Jews in American politics and culture in the years after World War II.

Further reading: Helprin's most renowned novel is a New York fantasia, *Winter's Tale* (1983), and he has been praised for his three volumes of short stories, including a National Jewish Book Award for *Ellis Island and Other Stories* (1981); Jewish themes and interests recur inconsistently throughout his oeuvre. In addition to his widely discussed journalism and political writing, he has also published a number of children's books illustrated by the acclaimed artist Chris Van Allsburg. Irving Kristol's *Neoconservativism* (1995), Murray Friedman's *The Neoconservative Revolution* (2005), and Norman Podhoretz's memoirs, such as *Making It* (1968) and *Ex-Friends* (1999), offer political, personal, and historical perspectives on the cultural shifts that underlie Helprin's fiction.

77 – In Dreams Begin Responsibilities and Other Stories
By Delmore Schwartz

NEW DIRECTIONS, 1978. 202 PAGES.

Delmore Schwartz was a poet first and foremost, and an important one, but his short stories—a valuable selection of which are collected in *In Dreams Begin Responsibilities and Other Stories*—aren't too shabby themselves. Concerned for the most part with sensitive young men at odds with their families, these pieces often hark back to the 1930s, to the Great Depression as it was experienced in New York City and to the philosophical struggle between left-wing ideologies and the desire to earn a solid living that characterized Jewish communities of that era. That conflict has long been more or less resolved, but in Schwartz's telling, it retains a kind of freshness and poignant humor: in a representative moment, one of Schwartz's young intellectuals introduces his mother to a brilliant scholar and tells her, "You have just seen a genius"; without missing a beat, she answers him, "How much money does he make?"

The most famous story here is the title piece, originally printed in *Partisan Review* in 1937, which also, confusingly enough, provided the title for Schwartz's first collection of prose and poetry the following year. In it, a young man in a movie theater watches a film of his parents' courtship, feeling more and more uncomfortable, until at the moment his father proposes marriage, he cries out: "Don't do it. . . . Nothing good will come of it, only remorse, hatred, scandal, and two children whose characters are monstrous." The concern with familial dysfunction and the autobiographical impulse are both typical of Schwartz's fiction. The other stories range from surreal and absurd fables ("The Track Meet" and "The Commencement Day Address") to detailed fictionalized accounts of Schwartz's circles (for example, "The World Is a Wedding"; "New Year's Eve" is based on a party thrown by the *Partisan Review* crowd). They are almost always anchored by a sensitive avatar for the author, sometimes called Shenandoah Fish. Among the strongest of the pieces is "America! America!," which describes a gregarious but troubled immigrant family who find the United States enthralling, if often tragic, and hold tight to their high hopes for it; the mother of this tribe, while spoiling her youngest son, "hoped and expected her grandchildren would be millionaires and grandsons, rabbis, or philosophers like Bergson."

Schwartz received acclaim—he was praised by luminaries from T. S. Eliot to Vladimir Nabokov, and he was handed a plum assistant professorship at Harvard without having finished a Ph.D.—but he was also haunted, paranoid, and dissatisfied in his personal life, in part, at least, because of the failure of his parents' marriage during his childhood. His fiction, an irreplaceable body of work, reflects his extraordinary sensitivity, humor, and insight.

Further reading: *Selected Poems* (1967) provides an introduction to Schwartz's verse. Readers interested in the poet's personal life have a tough choice, between James Atlas's splendid biography (1977) and Saul Bellow's fictionalized treatment, *Humboldt's Gift* (1975). Two collections of the poet's letters have been published (1984, 1993) as well as selections from his notebooks and journals (1986).

109

78 – *A Weave of Women*

By E. M. Broner

HOLT, RINEHART, AND WINSTON, 1978. 296 PAGES.

In recent decades, Jewish ritual has been undergoing a quiet revolution in certain corners of America, led by feminists for whom the traditional ceremonies and prayers are hopelessly marred by anachronistic ideas about women. Whatever one's religious position, it doesn't take a doctor to establish that the rabbis who conceived the laws of *niddah*, or female ritual purity, seem in some cases to have known less about the menstrual cycle than a contemporary 15-year-old girl; and, whatever one's gender, the aggressive violence in traditional texts, like the Book of Esther, can come across as less than an ideal embodiment of Jewish ethics. Redesigning rituals, rewriting stories, reinvigorating the practice of Judaism with new energy through a particular sensitivity to women's concerns—this project is the subject of E. M. Broner's *A Weave of Women.*

Rejecting a novelistic tradition where a single hero (usually male) is the center of every story, Broner's text has no one protagonist. As in the French feminist Monique Wittig's *Les Guérillères* (1969), Broner instead populates her novel with a diverse group of women. Hailing from all over the world (including the United States), and connected to one another through a house in the Old City of Jerusalem, these women range in age, religious affiliation, ethnicity, occupation; their group includes a politician, a singer, a scholar of Shakespeare, and a scientist. A few teenage former prostitutes, residents of the Home for Jewish Wayward Girls across the street, also join the circle. Sympathetic men occasionally appear, but most of the male characters embody the repressive standards of the state or of Orthodoxy. The novel is far from plotless—the women endure murders and sexual assaults, create rituals, and stage performances as reactions to oppression—but the book moves with deliberately biblical rhythms, time shifting forward and backward, stories cycling, repeating, and lapsing occasionally into verse. When the women recite psalms or traditional prayers, which they often do, they feminize them: "O, my Shehena, who shall live in your tent? . . . She that is upright and proud."

It is surprising that *A Weave of Women* is set in the heart of Jerusalem, the seat of ultra-Orthodoxy; today, Israel, with no separation between *shul* and state, often lags behind the American Jewish community in terms of religious pluralism and tolerance of alternative traditions. But the location makes sense: for one thing, Broner's point is that feminists must not be satisfied with a position on the periphery of Jewish life but must stake their claim to the center of the religion and culture. For another, the State of Israel itself is a mammoth latter-day invention, perhaps the largest in the history of the Jews; Zionists have had to concoct new holidays, symbols, prayers, and texts, not to mention an entirely reconstructed vernacular—and if Zionists can do it, why not feminists, too?

Further reading: Broner has written a number of plays, some novels, and—no surprise—a feminist take on the Passover haggadah. That the attitude toward tradition in *A Weave of Women* still resonates today is evident on the website http://ritualwell.org, which offers suggestions for ritual innovation for feminists and Jews of every stripe, and in Vanessa Ochs's *Inventing Jewish Ritual* (2007). Those interested in feminist American Jewish literature can consult Janet Handler Burstein's *Writing Mothers, Writing Daughters* (1996) or Lois Rubin's *Connections and Collisions* (2005).

. . . .

79 – *A Contract with God and Other Tenement Stories*
By Will Eisner

BARONET BOOKS, 1978. 196 PAGES.

Despite what he said and what he might have thought, Will Eisner didn't invent the term "graphic novel," and he didn't invent the form, either. Other comic book artists had produced book-length works that looked like comics, and they called them graphic novels, but what Eisner wanted, pure and simple, was respect. Like the underground comix artists of the late 1960s, he wanted grown-ups to read his work; unlike R. Crumb and Gilbert Shelton, though, he was 60 years old and far from the counterculture (he had been producing instructional comics for the American army for decades). He didn't want to be thought of as a lunatic, a way-out hippie with crazy ideas. So what subjects did he choose for his groundbreaking comics, so as to ensure that adults, and not children, would want to read them? Jewish woe, tragic perversity, and a father's heartbreak.

A Contract with God contains four stories, each rendered in Eisner's schmaltzy brand of comic strip expressionism, each dealing with Jewish life in New York around the time of the author's childhood in the 1930s. Two of the stories have clear autobiographical roots: the most acute of the stories, "Cookalein," concerns the sexual shenanigans at a resort in the Catskills, including the rough initiation of a teenager named Willie (a character Eisner called "essentially autobiographical"). The title story, meanwhile, is more oblique in its relation to Eisner's experience: it concerns an Orthodox orphan in the old country, Frimme Hersh, who makes a bargain with God, presumably to the effect that he will be good and pious (which is what his first name means) if God will, in turn, treat him justly. As part of this spiritual arrangement, an abandoned baby girl turns up on Frimme's doorstep, and the story concerns Frimme's despair and disillusion after this girl, his adopted daughter, dies of unspecified causes. Though not based on a memory of his childhood, this was an intensely personal tale for Eisner: he had lost his only daughter to leukemia in the early 1970s.

The other stories are more schematic, reminiscent of pulpy mid-century magazine fiction, but even they contain complexities worth puzzling over, especially in terms of what we might call interfaith relations. The protagonist of the "The Street Singer," an alcoholic bum who croons for pennies in the street, accedes to the seduction of an over-the-hill soprano calling herself Diva Marta Maria, though her real name is Sylvia Speegel, while "The Super" tells the tragic tale of a "discipline"-loving German building manager utterly undone by his uncontrollable lust for a vicious 10-year-old Jewess named Rosie. Even if Eisner's cartoony illustration and writing can be critiqued as histrionic, the queerness of these narratives—when considered from a Jewish perspective—suggests that it would be a mistake to underestimate his talents as an author.

Further reading: After *Contract* (which, among other translations, has been rendered into Yiddish), Eisner went on to publish many more graphic novels, including *The Plot* (2005), a nonfiction debunking of the *Protocols of the Elders of Zion*; most of his late-career works are in the process of being handsomely reprinted as W. W. Norton's Will Eisner Library. Meanwhile, Eisner's acclaimed newspaper strip, *The Spirit* (1940–52), in which his most innovative graphic design work appeared, has also been reprinted by DC Comics (and is being adapted into film), while his textbook, *Comics and Sequential Art* (1985), remains a must-read for aspiring artists. Eisner's authorized biography, *A Spirited Life* (2005), contains a preface by Michael Chabon, who relied on the artist in his research for *The Amazing Adventures of Kavalier & Clay* (2000). Those interested in Jewish contributions to the development of the graphic novel leading up to the current boom should also seek out *Tantrum* (1980) by Jules Feiffer, who worked with Eisner back in the 1940s, and Art Spiegelman's *Breakdowns* (1977) as well as his famous *Maus* (1986, 1991). Earlier contributions include Milt Gross's wordless novel *He Done Her Wrong* (1930) and Harry Hershfield's *Abie the Agent* strips from the 1910s, about a Jewish car salesman, the first year's run of which was reprinted in 1977 .

· ·

80 – *Good as Gold*

By Joseph Heller

SIMON AND SCHUSTER, 1979. 447 PAGES.

Joseph Heller will always be remembered, first and foremost, for *Catch-22* (1961): it isn't every novel, after all, whose title becomes an enduring American idiom. (It is worth noting that in an early excerpt, Heller's famous satire of World War II was called "Catch-18," but when it came time for book publication his editor thought that title sounded too much like Leon Uris's bestseller, *Mila 18*.) As savage as *Catch-22* is in depicting the insanity of war, and though indispensable as a touchstone of the 1960s, the novel's hero is undeniably an Armenian named Yossarian—albeit an Armenian who sounds Jewish. *Good as Gold*, meanwhile, if not quite as classic, is just as funny as *Catch-22* and as Jewish as it gets.

Well, sort of. Bruce Gold is an insincere and petty neurotic who has achieved middling success as a writer. Always on the lookout for cash with which he can pay his children's tuition at Choate and Yale, he pitches "a study of the contemporary Jewish experience in America" to a couple of his editor buddies, despite admitting, "I don't even know what it is." One of the editors wants "a scholarly, accurate work that will be useful to colleges and libraries"; the other tells him, "Make it sexy and light and you'll have most of what you'll need for a popular book that could turn out to be a big bestseller." Heller provides us with both, in the form of the novel that Gold might have written if he spent a little more time writing and less on his social climbing, his extramarital affairs, and his bickering with his loopy family. In addition to dealing with his ridiculous Jewish family, Gold hopes to land a cushy government job in Washington—ideally, he would like to take over the role of secretary of state from "that *momzer* Henry Kissinger," whom he loathes. In pursuit of his political dreams and personal pleasure, Gold is "secretly engaged" to a well-connected gentile girl, despite already being married.

The plot shrugs along, but ultimately the point of the story is to provide Heller with plenty of opportunities to lampoon Jewish intellectuals, American politics, and anything else he can cram in. His satirical techniques vary, but he is never far from insinuating that Abbott and Costello's "Who's on First?" routine is the example upon which government functionaries and Jewish relatives model their attempts at communication: "Is it always like this?" Bruce asks his friend Ralph, a White House aide, at one point, impressed by the pleasantness of Ralph's office. "Oh, yes," Ralph replies, "It's always like this when it's this way." "How is it when it isn't?" "Isn't what, Bruce?" "This way." "Different." "In what way, Ralph?" "In different ways, Bruce, unless they're the same, in which case, it's this way." Spinning onward like this, Gold's conversations resemble something out of Samuel Beckett, except zanier. Occasionally, Heller quotes real news articles and politicians' statements, and that's when the satire turns bitterest: "Asked about his role in the Cambodian war, in which an estimated five hundred thousand people died, [Kissinger] said: 'I may have a lack of imagination, but I fail to see the moral issue involved.'" Equally harsh, at times, on Protestant anti-Semitism and on Gold himself, Heller's work is not all fun and games, but it does manage to wring a whole lot of comedy from the enduring absurdity of Jewish life in America.

Further reading: Heller published a handful of novels in addition to *Catch-22* and *Good as Gold*—including the somewhat depressing *Something Happened* (1974) and a biblical retelling, *God Knows* (1984)—as well the autobiographical volumes *No Laughing Matter* (1986) and *Now and Then* (1998); a final novel and a collection of his articles and essays appeared after his death in 1999. Critical perspectives on Heller's work can be found in works by Sanford Pinsker and Judith Ruderman, both published in 1991.

81 – *O My America!*

By Johanna Kaplan

HARPER AND ROW, 1980. 286 PAGES.

The New York intellectuals were nothing if not prolific: gazing at bibliographies of works by Paul Goodman or Irving Howe or Susan Sontag, one has to wonder whether these people could type in their sleep. In her character Ezra Slavin—"ICONOCLASTIC SOCIAL CRITIC," as his obituary's headline phrases it—Johanna Kaplan conjures up a man of letters who produces not only essays but also children in impressive quantities. A family tree, of sorts, on the book's endpaper lists Slavin's six offspring, by four women, with birth dates ranging from 1939 to 1970. Just as an author must accept that his ideas belong to his readers, though, Ez, as he is called, is content for his kids to be raised by anyone who feels like raising them. As a result, one, a doctor, won't speak to him; another, a musicologist, is stranded, ill, in India; and a third wants to trade in her adopted father's name for Slavin, even though she is too flighty to read any of Ez's books. In presenting a sharp fictional biography of a irresistible personality, Kaplan also shows us the game of broken telephone through which cultural critique is transmitted to the next generation.

Kaplan's novel begins with Ez's death and ends with a memorial service; in between, the narrative follows his eldest daughter, Merry, as she remembers her father and his ex-wives, colleagues, and children. A journalist herself, Merry isn't at all the bombastic rabble-rouser her father was (among other achievements, Ez managed to become an intellectual guru of the 1960s student movements; teenagers tell him, "My parents have all your books—and I just think you're so *cool!*"). She is the right guide through Ez's life, though, because she is aware of his flaws but not immune to his charms. And Ez certainly made mistakes: he mistreated Merry's mother, a Polish immigrant and writer herself; alienated most of his children through blatant neglect and inattention; and, as he aged, indulged himself more and more in bitterness and nostalgia. But he manages to be attractive, at times—for example, when he is deflating the inane rhetoric of a fawning admirer, or when he gets so fed up with one of his genteel anti-Semitic colleagues from Amherst College (where he teaches American studies as a visiting professor) that, despite being "by nature and temperament an anarchist and pacifist," he punches the ridiculous snob in the chest. As they are taken up by the 1960s generation, though, Ez's ideas about community and cultural critique are watered down into new age platitudes, as personified by Ez's daughter Ffrenchy. Her politics include shunning sofas in favor of "zafus . . . they're these incredible huge like pillows? . . . from like Afghanistan?"

An expert ventriloquist, Kaplan assembles her portrait of Slavin not only through precise and pitch-perfect dialogue—capturing particularly well the banality of insincere liberals—but also through bits of text that she pastiches ingeniously, including period essays, aphorisms, obituaries and marriage announcements in the *New York Times*, editor's notes in academic anthologies, even a synagogue newsletter. These pieces add up to a portrait not just of a man, but of a whole intellectual movement of American Jews, encapsulated by Ez's statement that he has "had a lifelong affair with the idea of America."

Further reading: Like *O My America!*, Kaplan's first book, a collection of stories called *Other People's Lives* (1975) that includes pieces she published in *Commentary* and *Harper's*, won the National Jewish Book Award, among other prizes. Aside from these two works of fiction, Kaplan's writing has appeared mostly in the *New York Times Book Review*, for an autobiographical essay, see Derek Rubin's *Who We Are* (2005). For autobiographies of Slavin-like figures, see Alfred Kazin's *New York Jew* (1978) and Irving Howe's *A Margin of Hope* (1982); and don't miss *Arguing the World* (1998), Joseph Dorman's documentary on Howe, Daniel Bell, Irving Kristol, and Nathan Glazer.

· ·

82 - *The Mind-Body Problem*
By Rebecca Goldstein

RANDOM HOUSE, 1983. 275 PAGES.

One of the paradoxes of modern fiction is that it trades both on the loftiest of philosophical and aesthetic ideas, and, at the same time, on the most debased sensational and voyeuristic impulses: a great novel aspires to speak to the weighty ideas of life and meaning, and, equally, to the pettiest of our cravings, lusts, and anxieties (whodunit? will they kiss? what's going to *happen*?). This paradox is the subject, and the method, of Rebecca Goldstein's intelligent and yet breezy first novel, *The Mind-Body Problem*.

Goldstein's protagonist, Renee Feuer, having grown up in a Modern Orthodox home and excelled in her philosophy classes at Barnard, arrives at Princeton as a graduate student ready to tackle the headiest mysteries of human thought; unfortunately, she finds her professors in the grip of the "linguistic turn"—following the lead of Ludwig Wittgenstein, a baptized Roman Catholic of mostly Jewish descent—examining topics like "the metaphysics of adverbs," which she finds bafflingly mundane. Instead of studying, she devotes herself to seduction, and soon finds herself marrying a certified genius: Noam Himmel, who stunned the mathematical world at the age of 12 by discovering an entire category of numbers, the "supernaturals." (American history is full of such Jewish prodigies: one example is the mathematician Noam Elkies, who was granted a tenured professorship at Harvard in 1993 at the age of 26, the youngest person ever to have been so honored.) Using Renee's and Noam's social interactions as a spur, the book dabbles learnedly not only in the philosophical tradition—Goldstein, unlike her character, did receive a Princeton Ph.D. in the subject and has gone on to teach it—but also higher math, formal logic, and other such intellectual fare.

Yet the driving force of the book is the marriage, with its disappointments and frustrations and infidelities, as well as Goldstein's wit.

Part of Renee's personal challenge is that because she is an attractive woman, people do not take her seriously as a major intellect. One of her friends remarks that according to the culture at large, "feminine is dumb." Whether this was ever the case is up for debate, but Renee believes it, a perspective colored by the gender norms imposed in her Orthodox childhood; her mother hid her report cards so that her brother "wouldn't have to see how much better than him his sister had done." Yet Renee has positive feelings toward Jewish tradition and is valuable as a representative of the many Modern Orthodox men and women who pursue brilliant careers in physics or chemistry, still praying three times a day and believing in the Torah and its teachings.

Further reading: Goldstein is the recipient of a prestigious MacArthur Fellowship and has published many novels; *Mazel* (1995) won both the National Jewish Book Award and the Edward Lewis Wallant Award. More recently she has turned to nonfiction work on great intellects, such as *Gödel* (2005) and *Spinoza* (2006). She is frequently interviewed and maintains a website—http://rebeccagoldstein.com—with links to articles and autobiographical essays. Fans of Goldstein might also enjoy Aryeh Lev Stollman's exceptional short stories, collected in *The Dialogue of Time and Entropy* (2003), which explore the lives of Jewish prodigies in science and music.

116

. . . .

83 – *Hungry Hearts*

By Francine Prose

PANTHEON, 1983. 213 PAGES.

Francine Prose's playful sixth novel, published in the 1980s, shares its title with Anzia Yezierska's debut collection of short stories, which appeared and was adapted into a movie some 60 years earlier. Though there is nothing to indicate that Prose's title alludes deliberately to Yezierska's work, the two books called *Hungry Hearts* also happen to have coincident settings, at least at first: as in Yezierska's tales of willful Jewish immigrants, Prose's novel begins in the teeming ghettos of the Lower East Side. For Prose, the title refers to Yiddish theater audiences, starving for drama, for sentiment, and for corned beef. Her novel's heroes are the stars of the stage, circa 1921—not the heroes and villains of mawkish Second Avenue melodramas, but the ensemble casts, immersed in Stanislavski's theories, of the high-minded Yiddish Art Theater.

Dinah Rappoport narrates the novel, reliving the glory days of her first major role, her first international tour, and the twists of fate that lead her to the wedding canopy three times in one year—all with the same man. Dinah stars in S. Anski's legendary ghost story, *The Dybbuk*. In it, Leah and Chonon are betrothed to each other even before birth; when they grow up, Leah's father decides to marry her off to a richer man. Chonon dies, heartbroken, and his spirit returns to earth to possess Leah's body. Dinah plays Leah, of course, and the man she marries so often, Benno Brownstein, plays Chonon. The two actors fall in love in rehearsals and sneak off to a justice of the peace—but when they announce the good news to their director, Dalashinsky (Prose's affectionate caricature of the great Maurice Schwartz), he orders them to hush it up. It will distract audiences, he proclaims, if anyone discovers that the fatefully separated lovers of the play "can run home" after the final curtain "and hop into bed." Dalashinsky is worshiped by his actors, and Dinah and Benno cheerfully comply with this request, just as they agree to the "preparation" Dalashinsky assigns to bring them closer to their characters—Dinah sits "for hours in overgrown cemeteries," while Benno studies Kabbalah.

The play is an opening night smash, and after a run in New York, the whole company departs for a South American tour; in Buenos Aires the audiences consist of "haggling pimps, squealing babies, and their sandwich-eating mamas." As they attempt to bring their version of modern Jewish culture to the Southern Hemisphere, they encounter a number of more or less magical circumstances, including an Argentine dybbuk that possesses Dinah, spewing Spanish when she is on stage ("it was a prima donna's prerogative to go nuts from time to time"), as well as a Uruguayan Hasid, by way of Budapest, whose claims to fame are his vast collection of copper pots and the delicious omelets he cooks up on Friday nights for his followers. Everything turns out fine, with a final, joyous wedding—on stage, as was often done to bring in the crowds. A sweet and charming book, the winner of the Edward Lewis Wallant award, *Hungry Hearts* winningly brings to life the long-forgotten golden age of the American Yiddish stage.

Further reading: Prose's many fictions are set in a diverse range of locales and periods; a few, such as *Judah the Pious* (1973), *Guided Tours of Hell* (1997), and *A Changed Man* (2005), deal with Jewish themes and characters. Prose is also well-known as an essayist and a children's author (in 1996, she published a version of *The Dybbuk* for kids), and she has translated the work of Ida Fink. The dybbuk folktale has inspired many modern Jewish writers and artists, from Leonard Bernstein and Jerome Robbins, who produced a ballet adaptation, to the playwright Tony Kushner, who offered his own version (1997). Those interested in American Yiddish theater can consult Stefan Kanfer's history *Stardust Lost* (2006) or enjoy Sholem Aleichem's novel of the Yiddish stage *Wandering Stars*, first translated in 1952 and slated to appear in a new translation from Penguin Classics in 2009.

84 – *Disturbances in the Field*

By Lynne Sharon Schwartz

HARPER AND ROW, 1983. 368 PAGES.

Lynne Sharon Schwartz's fiction might be described as psychological realism: without high modernist stream of consciousness or the stylization of typical realism, Schwartz presents a protagonist whose relationships, emotions, likes and dislikes, and patterns of thought and behavior are extraordinarily subtle and textured. The title of her third novel, *Disturbances in the Field*, is psychiatric jargon—the idea, drawing on physics, being that the source of many people's psychological problems is that "something intrudes between the expressed need on the one hand and the response of the other"—but Schwartz herself, and her protagonist, Lydia, have no investment in dogma, psychoanalytic or otherwise.

The novel describes Lydia's busy life on the Upper West Side of New York: she maintains close friendships with a group of women she knew in college at Barnard, who bonded over an introduction to philosophy course, and she is married to a painter, Victor, with whom she has four children. The size and number of her social groups suit her well: as a professional musician and music teacher, she prefers to play in ensembles, enjoying trios and quintets in which "nothing individual is accomplished without the deferential support of the rest"—a statement that could also describe many families, happy and otherwise. With extraordinary precision and empathy, and in a narrative that gracefully swings between the past and the present, Schwartz describes the personalities of each of Lydia's friends, lovers, and kids, down to the songs they sing and their thoughts about the ancient philosophers. When tragedy strikes Lydia's family, and she begins, understandably enough, to falter, the responses of each of her loved ones reflect their personalities and positions relative to her, providing a vibrant sense of the fullness of Lydia's experience.

Lydia is a modern Jewish woman, unself-consciously; the family holds a Passover seder not out of obligation but because they want to. In an almost proto-*Seinfeld* dilemma that sharply evokes what life can be like on the Upper West Side, Lydia struggles over whether to buy fruit from the new Korean grocery or continue to patronize her current fruit man, a Holocaust survivor whose rudeness and paranoia bother her, but who addresses her, because she is Jewish, as one of his "*landsleute*" (that is, countrymen). Lydia's thinking owes more to the Greek philosophers than to the Talmud, but even the psychological perspective she brings to her experiences could be said to be Jewish; it is not coincidental that the title phrase itself is taught to her by a psychiatrist who is the son and grandson of rabbis. A heartbreaking novel that captures the small world of one woman in good times and bad, *Disturbances in the Field* is at once both intellectually stimulating and emotionally riveting, a quiet tour de force of family, love, and loss.

Further reading: Schwartz did not begin to write until dropping out of graduate school in her early 30s and has since published many novels and short story collections: *Leaving Brooklyn* (1989) and *Referred Pain* (2004) touch on Jewish themes more directly than most of the others. In a memoir and essay, *Ruined by Reading* (1996), Schwartz describes how she learned to read at the precocious age of three; she also won a major prize for her translation, from the Italian, of Liana Millu's Holocaust testimony *Smoke Over Birkenau* (1991).

· ·

85 – *Heartburn*

By Nora Ephron

KNOPF, 1983. 224 PAGES.

Not the world's first novel to include recipes (the Brazilian author Jorge Amado, for one, did it in his novel of 1966, *Dora Flor and Her Two Husbands*), Nora Ephron's *Heartburn* nonetheless predated the mainstreaming of the practice in bestsellers such as *Fried Green Tomatoes at the Whistlestop Café* (1987) and *Like Water for Chocolate* (1989), both of which followed in Ephron's book's footsteps, too, in being adapted into hit movies. The conjunction of food and narrative isn't surprising, as gourmands and litterateurs have had much in common for centuries. What is more shocking about Ephron's witty roman à clef is how bravely it tells the story of the author's own divorce.

The novel concerns one Rachel Samstat, who is seven months pregnant and already the mother of a two-year-old when she discovers that her husband has been sleeping with another woman. The louse, Mark, is a syndicated columnist for whom Rachel—a New Yorker at heart—has relocated to Washington, D.C. ("Listen, even the Jews there are sort of Gentile"); according to gossip, the sordid details resemble those precipitating Ephron's divorce from the journalist Carl Bernstein, widely known for breaking the Watergate scandal and for having been played by Dustin Hoffman in the movie *All the President's Men* (1976). Herself an author of "personal and chatty" cookbooks, Rachel peppers her tale of woe with jokes as well as cooking tips, and likewise dishes on the affairs and peccadilloes of her friends in D.C. and Manhattan. Therapists abound; Rachel, back in New York, attends her old therapy group, which is promptly—and typically, given that this is the gritty pre-Giuliani city—robbed at gunpoint by an armed bandit.

Aside from the voyeuristic pleasures of sorting out fact from fiction (which was also done by lawyers in the trials surrounding the movie adaptation in 1986 starring Meryl Streep and Jack Nicholson), the novel provides an insightful take on the social and culinary habits of ambitious, well-to-do Jews in what Tom Wolfe labeled the "Me Decade." Though her shtick is to publish cookbooks of family recipes (with titles like *My Grandmother's Cookies* and *Uncle Seymour's Beef Borscht*),

Rachel is far from kosher—she treats depression with shrimp fried rice and bacon hash. Still, she is deeply connected to Jewish culture of one sort or another. The riff on Jewish Princes (Ephron's riposte to the ridiculous stereotype of the Jewish American Princess) is an exemplary statement not only on gender relations and the fate of second-wave feminism but also on the trajectory of Jewish comedy. Ephron's one-liners, meanwhile, speak for themselves: "If pregnancy were a book, they would cut the last two chapters." "The major concrete achievement of the women's movement in the 1970s was the Dutch treat." "'I think we'd better have a talk' are the seven worst words in the English language."

Further reading: Ephron has written and/or directed a few of the definitive contemporary romantic comedies, including *When Harry Met Sally* (1989) and *Sleepless in Seattle* (1993). Her many collections of light-hearted essays include *Scribble, Scribble* (1979) and *I Feel Bad about My Neck* (2006). Meanwhile, for further background and personal details, Ephron's parents, Henry and Phoebe, describe their lives as a Hollywood screen-writing team in *We Thought We Could Do Anything* (1977), while their play and movie, *Take Her, She's Mine* (1963) was based in part on the letters young Nora sent home when she was a student at Wellesley College.

· ·

86 – *Mainland*

By Susan Fromberg Schaeffer

LINDEN PRESS, 1985. 285 PAGES.

For a 40-year-old Jewish Brooklynite, the heroine of Susan Fromberg Schaeffer's *Mainland* has typical problems: her mother and grandmother give her constant grief, her eyes bother her ("You brought this on yourself . . . all that reading in the dark," her mother tells her), and she is alienated from domestic life: "They seem unreal, her husband, her two children, mythical animals about whom she hears frequent reports." She feels that she is drifting away. ("'Then stop drifting,' says her grandmother. 'What are you? A rowboat?'") Not everything about Eleanor is conventional, though; for one thing, her chatty mother and grandmother are both dead; for another, her solution to her malaise is a romantic affair with a 27-year-old chemistry student from Peking.

This delightful novel focuses on that relationship and on whether Eleanor will screw up her enviable life—as a respected writer and professor, she has fame and fortune—as well as her marriage to "a nice Jewish man," a computer entrepreneur who stands 6'3" tall. Toh enters Eleanor's life as her chauffeur, ferrying her around to appointments before and after her cataract surgery, but soon she is teaching him English ("You tell me when I wrong," he requests) and he is cooking Chinese delicacies for her family. Thanks to the historic visit of the Chinese leader Deng Xiaoping to the United States in 1979, and a few fortuitous car accidents, soon

Eleanor and Toh are spending afternoons in "a one-room apartment in Chinatown he has borrowed from a friend." What's the attraction? Eleanor offers the lonely immigrant a sense of belonging in a strange land, while he provides her exotic but nonthreatening charm, as in Marguerite Duras's contemporaneous bestseller *The Lover* (1984). When she first kisses Toh, Eleanor notes that "he tastes of ginger."

Mainland is suggestive, even playful with autobiographical hints. Eleanor's life mirrors the author's in some respects, but who knows—or even wants to speculate—whether or not Schaeffer has cheated on her husband? Whatever happened in real life, Schaeffer's novel affirms Eleanor's infidelity: not only does the affair inspire her to reconnect with long-lost friends but it also makes her a better mother to her kids and a better wife to her husband. *Mainland* also subtly engages with the frequently discussed notion that Jews and the overseas Chinese have something significant in common—"They say the Chinese are the sixth lost tribe of Israel," Eleanor jokes—but more important than that, perhaps, *Mainland* reflects the way that by the 1980s American Jews could confidently, and unremarkably, represent the promise of America to new immigrants.

Further reading: Schaeffer has published many novels—only some of which, like *Falling* (1973), her well-received debut, and *Anya* (1974), a story of the Holocaust, take up Jewish themes—as well as collections of poetry and short stories; as a budding literary scholar, she wrote the first ever dissertation on Vladimir Nabokov. Daniel Chirot and Anthony Reid edited a collection of essays, *Essential Outsiders* (1997), that ponders the commonalities of the Jews and the overseas Chinese; the literary relationships between Asian Americans and Jews is also studied in Judith Oster's *Crossing Cultures* (2003) and two chapters of Jonathan Freedman's *Klezmer America* (2007).

121

. . . .

87 – *Her First American*
By Lore Segal

KNOPF, 1985. 320 PAGES.

At the end of Lore Segal's first, autobiographical novel, *Other People's Houses* (1964), the heroine, who goes by the name Lore Segal and who has finally made it to the United States after being rescued from her hometown of Vienna during World War II, encounters a dazzling, middle-aged African American named Carter Bayoux in a creative writing class. In Segal's third book, *Her First American*, the heroine is now named Ilka Weissnix, though she is more or less the same person, and she meets Carter again; this time she comes across him in a saloon in a western state, where she is traveling by train in the hopes of meeting some genuine Americans (as opposed to the mélange of refugees, immigrants, and foreigners that surround her in New York City).

A precocious and sweet-tempered refugee, all 21-year-old Ilka wants is a native friend to help her improve her speech—the only people she has met so far are the students in her English class "which," she says, "are yet other outlanders, which know always only other outlanders, which know yet lesser English as I!" Carter turns out to be the perfect teacher, and much more. A alumnus of Yale and a columnist for the *Harlem Herald*, he carries the weighty title of "Special Adviser on Race Relations to the U.S. Ambassador to the United Nations"; he is also a terrible drunk. No stranger to Jews (his first job was organizing a chapter of the Anti-Defamation League in New Haven), he woos Ilka, all the while shepherding her through the byways of American culture. He decodes baffling newspaper headlines, introduces her to celebrities, parses idioms, and presents her with novels to read; they spend a pleasant summer in Connecticut with an interracial group of his friends. Through all of this, Ilka's English improves by leaps and bounds, but she also begins to understand the intricacies of race relations in the United States. Soon enough, everyone—Carter, Ilka's cousin and mother, and a cast of minor characters—finds his or her life unexpectedly enriched through Ilka's and Carter's surprising relationship.

Segal's prose is charming and assured, and her satirical touch gentle—none of her characters, no matter how misguided or foolish, is denied the author's sympathy. Yet the book handles thorny and emotionally fraught issues, including the comparative sufferings of Jews and African Americans, the hypocrisies and inanities of well-meaning liberals, and the tragic slide of a formerly powerful alcoholic into sickness and despair. The recipient of an award from the American Academy of Arts and Letters, *Her First American* still feels fresh a couple of decades after its first appearance, and it is one of the most sympathetic fictional accounts of the potential for warm relations between Jews and African Americans.

Further reading: Like much of Segal's fiction for adults, parts of *Her First American* appeared in the *New Yorker*, and Ilka has lived on in a series of stories in that magazine that have been gathered into a collection called *Shakespeare's Kitchen* (2007). Apart from that, Segal has concentrated her talents on writing award-winning children's books and occasional essays and reviews. Scholars have spilled a great deal of ink on the relations between American Jews and African Americans in literature; see, for starters, Eric Sundquist's *Strangers in the Land* (2005) and Emily Budick Miller's *Blacks and Jews in Literary Conversation* (1998).

88 – *Lazar Malkin Enters Heaven*

By Steve Stern

VIKING, 1986. 250 PAGES.

The term "magic realism" came into vogue during the Latin American boom of the 1950s and 1960s, as writers such as Gabriel García Marquez and Jorge Luis Borges rocketed to international fame. But magic realism is nothing new in Jewish narratives. What is the biblical book of Bereshit [Genesis], after all, if not an extended saga of family relations punctuated with appearances by angels, miracles, and prophetic dreams? In Yiddish, meanwhile, early-20th-century writers such as I. L. Peretz and S. Anski built upon research in folklore and mysticism to craft modernist literary fables about golems and dybbuks. A descendant of all of these traditions, Steve Stern has winningly brought Jewish magic realism to an unlikely home, Memphis, Tennessee, beginning with his first widely circulated collection of stories, *Lazar Malkin Enters Heaven*.

In one of Stern's typical tales, an old man bickers with the Angel of Death, who would like to cart him off to Paradise: "Don't make me laugh," the man retorts. "There ain't no such place." In another, a young boy conjures up an unearthly suitor for his spinster aunt, while, in a third, a wealthy Laundromat tycoon receives, and attempts Jonah-like to reject, the call to prophecy. All of these magical circumstances occur in one place: the Pinch, an immigrant neighborhood in Memphis where Jews, like the Germans and Irish before them, settled and plied their trades in the early 20th century, before the community moved on up and out to more comfortable suburbs. Stern transforms this real-life neighborhood into the locus of powerful Jewish magic, but the Pinch is not an American version of the ideal or nostalgic shtetl. Crucially, Stern's miracles take place in a Jewish community on the verge of dissolution (the Pinch has "been dead since the War," one of Stern's characters says). Stern's stories were inspired not only by his readings in folklore and mysticism but also by a job at Memphis's Center for Southern Folklore, where he was responsible for recording the memories of the former residents of the Pinch before the last of them succumbed to old age.

With this in mind, the collection's first story, "Moishe the Just," can be read as a metaphor for Stern's project. It concerns an imaginative boy eager to hold the attention of his friends, who believe their "neighborhood held no particular secrets" and who are more interested in "life outside the Pinch." To do so, he shares with them every intriguing factoid he can dig up in what they refer to as their "exotic heritage" (eventually, he tries to convince them that an old disheveled man is a *lamed-vavnik*, one of the world's 36 holiest Jews). In a sense, this is Stern's mission, too, one that he articulates, to some degree, in the collection's finale, which takes place at a writer's colony: to add miracles and magic to stories about the quotidian details of Jewish life, and thereby to make them alluring to Jewish readers who might otherwise be more concerned with the conflicts and dramas of the wider, non-Jewish world. Stern's achievement with these witty and well-crafted stories, in other words, is rescuing from irrelevancy the desires and tragedies of one specific Jewish community through the magic of literary invention.

Further reading: In addition to *Lazar Malkin Enters Heaven*, which won the Edward Lewis Wallant Award, Stern has published short story collections, children's books, novellas—three of which are collected in *A Plague of Dreamers* (1994)—and a few novels, the most recent and noteworthy of which is *The Angel of Forgetfulness* (2005), a winner of the National Jewish Book Award. Many contemporary Jewish writers—from the Brazilian Moacyr Scliar to the Israeli Meir Shalev—employ techniques of magic realism to some degree; Daniel Jaffe's anthology, *With Signs and Wonders* (2003), would be a useful place to start exploring this new Jewish fabulism.

. . . .

89 – *The Ritual Bath*

By Faye Kellerman

ARBOR HOUSE, 1986. 277 PAGES.

Faye Kellerman's first novel, *The Ritual Bath*, trades on a fascination with extremes of human behavior, from the piety and rigidity of ultra-Orthodox Jews to the brutality of rapists and drugged-out anti-Semitic gangbangers. Set primarily at a cloistered yeshivah in the gritty hills outside of Los Angeles, the novel employs some, but not all, of the conventions of the mystery novel formula: for one thing, it begins with a violent rape rather than a murder and, for another, instead of a solitary sleuth, Kellerman serves up an unexpected pair of crime solvers, Peter Decker, a cynical police detective, and Rina Lazarus, a young and open-minded ultra-Orthodox widow. Though at first the oddest of confederates, brought together because Rina was on hand at the *mikveh* when the rape occurred and is the only person willing to explain the peculiarities of yeshivish culture to Detective Decker, these two turn out to have more in common than they, or the reader, could have expected.

Weaving in Peter's and Rina's growing intimacy with the search for the rapist, Kellerman keeps the tension high and the violence harsh. Before long the reader is privy not only to the rape but to murder and an anti-Semitic attack. To her credit, Kellerman does not shy away from the representation of obscene speech, racist taunts, or physical violence, making the novel every bit as graphic and disturbing as other thrillers of the period, like Thomas Harris's *The Silence of the Lambs* (1988). At the same time, as Rina both practices and explains to Peter the ins and outs of Orthodox ritual, including the laws of *kashrut*, feminine modesty, and "*Taharat Hamishpacha*" or family purity, peculiar situations arise. Long before Rina has ever allowed Peter to touch her hand or see her with her hair uncovered, for example, the pair has discussed, apropos of the rape investigation, subjects including anal penetration and the analysis of seminal fluid.

Kellerman's novel dramatizes the ways in which even a cloistered and relatively self-contained religious community grapples with and fends off the temptations and threats of the mainstream culture, whether they come in the form of baseball games and children's toys or criminal attacks. She treats her pious Jewish characters with respect, too—carefully showing that they are just as good and bad, just as admirable and flawed, as anybody else—and devotes considerable space to explaining and justifying Orthodox beliefs and practices that are likely unfamiliar to many of her readers. Throughout a long series of novels featuring the same characters, Kellerman has built upon these explorations as Rina and Peter reevaluate their relationships to Jewish practice and to each other. Driven forward by suspense plots and by seamless prose, Kellerman's novels engage with the changing possibilities of traditional Jewish culture in late-20th-century America, making them a remarkably successful hybrid of popular and traditional textual practices.

Further reading: Though many readers feel that Kellerman's first novel is her strongest, she has published more than 10 books to date featuring the same characters as well as a mystical mystery, *Moon Music* (1998), and a historical romance novel, *The Quality of Mercy* (1988). Kellerman's husband, Jonathan, and son Jesse are also successful mass-market novelists, though their books have not treated Jewish themes as centrally as the Lazarus/Decker novels. Jewish-themed mysteries and suspense novels are extremely common, ranging widely in their interests and settings; some notable contributors to the genre include Rochelle Krich, Rabbi Joseph Telushkin, and country-musician-cum-politician Kinky Friedman. Worthwhile anthologies of Jewish mystery and crime fiction include *Murder Is No Mitzvah* (2004), *Mystery Midrash* (1999), and *Criminal Kabbalah* (2001), and the editor of the latter two books, Rabbi Larry Raphael, provides an extensive if not exhaustive bibliography of the field on his website, http://www.jewishmysteries.net.

90 – *The Shawl*
By Cynthia Ozick

KNOPF, 1989. 70 PAGES.

Separately, "The Shawl" and "Rosa" were judged the best stories published in America in the years 1980 and 1983. Brought together in a slim volume titled *The Shawl*, they are even more powerful. Many writers have spun out thick novels and massive histories, such as André Schwarz-Bart's *The Last of the Just* (1959) and William Shirer's *The Rise and Fall of the Third Reich* (1960), that grapple with the enormity of the Holocaust's devastation through the accumulation of detail. In these stories, Ozick takes the opposite tack, nailing an infinite expanse of sorrow and pain to the smallest of objects and briefest of experiences. The result is as moving as anything in the vast and ever-expanding canon of post-Holocaust fiction.

The title story begins as Rosa; her daughter, Magda; and her niece, Stella, march to a Nazi concentration camp. Weakened by malnutrition, Rosa can no longer nurse Magda, but the baby continues to live, sustained somehow by a shawl, a small scrap of fabric on which she sucks. They are in "a place without pity," though, and this small consolation is taken from Magda. Later, when Rosa watches a guard hurl her baby at the camp's electrified fence, the shawl serves to muffle her agonized screams. Thirty years later, in "Rosa," the title character has relocated to Miami, where she lives on Stella's money, surrounded by nostalgic Jewish kitsch that repulses her. She composes letters, "in the most excellent literary Polish," to the dead Magda—still the most important person in Rosa's world. Everyone, including Stella, a genial suitor named Persky, and a Midwestern pathologist named Dr. Tree, thinks Rosa should move on; as Stella says, "It's thirty years, forty . . . give it a rest." Rosa writes off all of these well-meaning parties as morons and worse, rejecting, most of all, the word that they use to describe her: "It used to be *refugee*, but by now there was no such creature . . . only survivors," Rosa rails. "Survivor and survivor and survivor; always and always. Who made up these words, parasites on the throat of suffering!" (This, by the way, was well before the advent of the reality television show *Survivor*, which would add yet another layer to the word's connotations—a development exploited hilariously by Larry David on *Curb Your Enthusiasm*.)

The achievement of *The Shawl* lies in its careful portrait of an understandably bitter woman, and in its refraction of her tortured Polish consciousness through Ozick's sinuous and brilliantly textured English prose. Unlike most of the novelists who treat the subject without thinking twice, Ozick has noted she is profoundly uneasy about the idea of "making art out of the Holocaust," aware that "this subject is corrupted by fiction and that fiction in general corrupts history"—a worthwhile caution, and one that complements the devastating force of Ozick's fictional efforts.

Further reading: Tova Reich's scathing satire, *My Holocaust* (2007), takes Ozick's critique of the exploitation of Holocaust survivors even further, while Paula Marantz Cohen's *Jane Austen in Boca* (2002) treats the life of elderly Jews in Florida sweetly.

91 – *The Great Letter E*

By Sandra Schor

NORTH POINT PRESS, 1990. 204 PAGES.

If being Jewish were simply a matter of practicing Judaism, there would be a lot less to say about it. Modern Jewish literature had tended to focus on the outsiders, the rebels, and the eccentrics. Perhaps this explains why so many literary works have been inspired, like Sandra Schor's *The Great Letter E*, by the apostate philosopher Baruch Spinoza.

Schor's protagonist, Barry Glassman, practices optometry, and his work with lenses is one of the many ways in which his life, at least as he sees it, runs parallel to Spinoza's. Like his hero, Barry is something of a *luftmensch*: he neglects his shop, his wife, and his son in favor of pondering the *Ethics* and toiling away at an essay on rainbows, pollution, and the retention of contact lenses, hoping finally to recover from the B+ he received in a college seminar on Spinoza. He annoys his rabbi and synagogue president with his rationalist version of Judaism: on his son's bar mitzvah invitation, he explains that "the Torah does not represent revelation but the high thought of reasonable people." As the novel progresses, Glassman's life disintegrates: he separates from his wife, moves to Brooklyn, and loses touch with his son—who starts getting into, of all things, religious Judaism. Imagining his marital separation as a version of the *herem*, or excommunication, placed on Spinoza, Barry befriends a blind man, reconnects (rather intensely) with his brainy cousin Enid, and learns as his horizons shrink that "life is compromise, not paradise." Bitter ironies abound: among other things, his shop suddenly starts turning a profit after a tragic accident kills many of Barry's colleagues en route to an optometry conference.

Schor establishes in Glassman an intricate psychology—he is a faithful, unorthodox believer, and an inconsistently good person overall—and interweaves his story with quotations from and musings on Spinoza that reflect the wider influence of this figure in contemporary Jewish life: a legacy of stubbornness and intellectual courage borne proudly by many contemporary Jews. Philosophic, slapstick, and weird, *The Great Letter E* offers a touching portrait of the philosopher manqué and of a Jew, unsatisfied both by the traditional denominations and the new spiritualism, who desires a theological but reasonable way to remain Jewish.

Further reading: *The Great Letter E* appeared in 1990—the same year that Schor died, at the age of 58—and won Hadassah's Harold U. Ribalow Award. Schor also published short stories, poetry, and guide books in the field of English composition, much of which can be found, along with biographical materials, on a website created by the author's daughter, Esther Schor (herself a distinguished poet, professor, and biographer of Emma Lazarus). See http://www.princeton.edu/~eschor/sandra. Other works inspired by Spinoza include a German novel of 1837 by Berthold Auerbach (translated into English in 1882), stories by Israel Zangwill ("The Lens Grinder") and I. B. Singer ("The Spinoza of Market Street"), and Goce Smilevski's Macedonian novel, *Conversations with Spinoza* (2002, translated in 2006). Those desiring a lively nonfictional approach to the iconoclastic thinker can seek out Rebecca Goldstein's *Betraying Spinoza* (2006), while others interested in Jewish rebellion and heresy more broadly should consult Isaac Deutscher's provocative essay, "The Non-Jewish Jew," in a collection of the same name (1968).

. . . .

92 – *He, She, and It*

By Marge Piercy

Knopf, 1991. 429 pages.

Jewish communities have endured for millennia despite extraordinary challenges. It shouldn't be surprising, then, to find them persisting in the futures imagined by science fiction authors (especially considering that some of the giants in the field of sci-fi, like Isaac Asimov, were themselves Jewish). In Marge Piercy's dystopic *He, She, and It*—also published under the title *Body of Glass* outside the United States—Israel and the rest of the Middle East have been obliterated by a nuclear holocaust, and by 2059 the planet's governing bodies are corporations and roving gangs, not nations. Yet fragile Jewish communities manage to endure, like Tikva, a settlement somewhere on the Atlantic coast of what used to be the United States, not far, one suspects, from Piercy's adopted home of Cape Cod.

While the world around it crumbles, Tikva is Piercy's utopia: Jewish, democratic, feminist, and individualistic, it offers a counterpoint to the corporate blandness imposed outside and survives by selling homegrown technologies and produce in exchange for its freedom. The novel's plot centers on Shira, who was raised in the town but left for college and ended up at a corporation near what used to be Nebraska. She returns to live with her grandmother, Malka, after losing custody of her son and begins to participate in a secret and illegal project in one of Tikva's labs: the socialization of a humanoid robot that has been programmed not only to kill and defend but also to crave human interaction. This creature is named Yod after the 10th letter of the Hebrew alphabet (his nine predecessors all malfunctioned in one way or another). Chapters describing Shira's and Yod's growing intimacy, as well as their attempts to defend the town and reclaim Shira's child, alternate with chapters in which Malka tells a story of her own about the Golem of Prague and his creator, Rabbi Judah Loew, the Maharal. Piercy thus links her speculative version of the future to the mystical mysteries of the past.

Drawing upon William Gibson and other cyberpunk writers, Piercy shares with them occasional flashes of prescience: the Net, one of the features of Piercy's imagined world, is more or less the Internet that we have come to know.

At its best, by thoughtfully envisioning future possibilities and exaggerating current trends—like plastic surgery and movies—the novel forces us to acknowledge how far our own world is from perfection. It also encourages us to consider how differently people express their sense of Jewishness today than they did a century or two ago and to speculate about how Jewishness might be totally different, once again, in our grandchildren's era.

Further reading: Piercy's vast oeuvre includes more than a dozen novels and as many collections of poetry, ranging wildly in setting and subject matter. She describes the challenges and triumphs of her life in *Sleeping with Cats* (2002). Readers desiring more Jewish-themed science fiction should begin with the anthologies *Wandering Stars* (1974) and *More Wandering Stars* (1981); a useful list of relevant titles can also be found at http://www.sfsite.com/~silverag/jewishsf.html. Pearl Abraham's *The Seventh Beggar* (2005) connects science with Jewish mysticism like *He, She, and It*, although Abraham's chosen sage is Nachman of Bratslav, rather than the Maharal.

. . . .

93 – *Operation Shylock: A Confession*
By Philip Roth

SIMON AND SCHUSTER, 1993. 398 PAGES.

Philip Roth's rebellious spirit, extraordinary self-consciousness, and prodigious talents as a novelist position him perfectly to produce books that turn the concept of fiction on its ear. In *The Ghostwriter* (1979), *The Counterlife* (1986), *The Facts* (1988), and *The Plot against America* (2004), Roth does exactly that, calling into question the conventions of his own writing and joyfully subverting his readers' unexamined expectations. Critics like to label such books metafiction (that is, fiction about fiction) or autofiction (fiction that plays with the conventions of autobiography), but the crucial point about them is that they jolt us out of our comfortable sense of what a novel should be and do. *Operation Shylock* is Roth's masterpiece in this field, and it is also his most wide-ranging, incisive, and befuddling analysis of Jewish identity in the late 20th century.

Purporting to be true, the book features Roth telling a story in the first person about "actual occurrences that [he] lived through" in the 1980s. After a bout of suicidal depression brought on by prescription pain medication, Roth travels to Israel to interview the novelist and Holocaust survivor Aharon Appelfeld for the *New York Times Book Review*. Before leaving, he hears that someone calling himself Philip Roth is already in Israel and has been sighted at the trial of John Demjanjuk, who may or may not have been a cruel Nazi functionary at Treblinka. When Roth arrives in the Holy Land, things become considerably more complicated. The fake Philip Roth—whom the author refers to as Moishe Pipik ("belly button"), in a nod to all the navel-gazing at the center of this narrative—has been running around, making a name for himself (and, consequently, for the author) as a proponent of a political movement called Diasporism, the belief that the Jews of Israel should be transferred back to the European lands of their extraction. As if all this weren't enough to keep him busy, Roth also encounters Pipik's girlfriend, a member of Anti-Semites Anonymous; George Ziad, a former classmate who has become a supporter of the PLO; and the mysterious Lewis B. Smilesburger, who turns out to be a Mossad commander and would like to hire Roth for a secret mission.

Willfully confusing fact and fiction (a preface asserts the book is true; a "Note to the Reader" assures us it is false), and going so far as to cast doubt on aspects of the Holocaust and of the Zionist project, *Operation Shylock* remains resolute in its affirmation of one element of the Jewish tradition: the notion, ascribed by some to the dialectic methods of the Talmud, that everything— everything—is a question. Hilarious, deadly serious, disrespectful, and brilliant as it weaves in testimony from the John Demjanjuk trial and from Roth's interview of Appelfeld, the book captures the confusion and absurdities of modern Jewish identity with consummate style and intelligence.

Further reading: Roth's novel is best appreciated in the context of his other playful experiments in metafiction and autofiction, mentioned earlier; the identity games Roth plays can also be compared to the oeuvres of Paul Auster and Jonathan Safran Foer, as well as Gary Shteyngart's *Absurdistan* (2006). Roth's novel can be understood as a riposte to the many worthwhile, and earnest, novels about Israel and Israeli identity written by American Jews, ranging from Meyer Levin's novel of kibbutz life, *Yehuda* (1931), to Rachel Kadish's *From a Sealed Room* (1998); and Roth may also have been responding to the genre of nonfiction accounts of North American authors' visits to Israel, such as Saul Bellow's *To Jerusalem and Back* (1976) and Mordecai Richler's *This Year in Jerusalem* (1994).

. . . .

94 – *The Prince of West End Avenue*
By Alan Isler

BRIDGE WORKS, 1994. 246 PAGES.

T hose born at the end of the 19th century didn't have it easy. To make it to their old age, they had to persist through two global wars and any number of revolutions; they saw their world transformed again and again by automobiles, radio, television, and computers. Any of them who have survived into their 80s with half as much aplomb and humor as Otto Korner, the hero of Alan Isler's *The Prince of West End Avenue*, deserve not only our respect but also frank admiration.

Korner narrates his tale from a seniors' residence on New York's Upper West Side named for the American Jewish poetess Emma Lazarus, which offers "first-class medical treatment, twenty-four hours," "excellent kosher food," not to mention that "every door has a mezuzah, except of course the toilets." Korner shares both the daily intrigues of this retirement community and the exploits from his own European past. The big news in Otto's life at present, in 1978, is a production of *Hamlet* being put on by a group of his peers; as in any theater troupe, egos collide, passions flare, and artistic visions diverge—though this is one of the few performances of Shakespeare, one assumes, that needs three intermissions to accommodate "weak bladders on both sides of the proscenium." By the time he was 19, meanwhile, the German-born Korner had already published a volume of poems that had been praised in a friendly note from Rilke, and in Zurich during World War I, he bumped into personalities on every corner: he drank at the same bar as Joyce, had a heart-to-heart with Lenin, and buddied up to Tristan Tzara and his coterie of wacky absurdists—even managing, he claims, to name their incipient anti-art movement, Dada. Korner is less proud of his romantic experiences; as a youth, he pined after a woman who never gave him the time of day, and then he settled into two loveless and sexless marriages. The first of these, in interwar Berlin, left him with guilt and grief so powerful that he can barely mention them.

Instead, Korner's "memoir" brims with quips, mysteries, and canny observations on the peccadilloes of his fellow residents (who represent a full range of 20th-century Jewish ideologies from communist to Zionist to obscene humorist) as well as enchanting trivia apropos of almost nothing, all conveyed in a voice more charming and less bitter than most men of his age—even those lucky enough not to have shared his trying experiences. All of this is deftly brought to life by the gifted Isler, who, at 60, was no spring chicken himself when this book, his first novel, appeared.

Further reading: Isler has gone on to publish a couple more novels and a well-received collection of short fiction titled *The Bacon Fancier* (1997); one hopes he will, like his character, be writing well into his 80s at least. Another endearing portrait of an older Jewish New Yorker can be found in Nicole Krauss's *The History of Love* (2005), and Isler's fans might also enjoy the novels and stories of Jonathan Wilson, who, like Isler, spent his childhood in England before settling into American academia.

95 – *The Collected Stories*

By Grace Paley

FARRAR, STRAUS, AND GIROUX, 1994. 386 PAGES.

Calling this volume the "collected" stories of Grace Paley is a little silly: it couldn't have been too hard to collect them. These 45 stories previously appeared, in the same order, in just three books—published in 1959, 1974, and 1985—and are the author's only works of fiction. Perhaps a more apt title would have been *The Celebrated Stories of Grace Paley*, as that was the point of bringing them together in this format: to celebrate them as masterworks of 20th-century American fiction, and to introduce them to any unlucky readers who haven't yet had the delight of tripping over a Paley sentence.

In "Goodbye, and Good Luck," the elderly Aunt Rose describes her girlhood as a ticket seller for the Yiddish theater and her unconventional but finally satisfying relationship with the company's heartthrob. As passionate as her affair may have been, what the reader falls in love with here is Rose's voice: her language brims with surprising locutions and images as Paley recreates a Yiddish-inflected English bursting with vitality. Another jewel, "The Loudest Voice," centers on young Shirley, whose loud Jewish mouth comes in handy when her school needs a narrator for the Christmas pageant. Her mother, Clara, blanches at the prospect of her daughter playing Christ, but Shirley's father has a wider perspective, attuned to the choices they have faced: "You're in America! Clara, you wanted to come here. In Palestine the Arabs would be eating you alive. Europe you had pogroms. Argentina is full of Indians. Here you got Christmas . . . some joke, ha?"

Many of Paley's stories feature the semi-autobiographical Faith Darwin (whose name may be Paley's joke on her own: Faith isn't far from Grace, and part of Charles Darwin's legacy was the challenge his notions of evolution presented to his predecessor William Paley's creationist "natural theology"). These largely plotless stories reflect the diversity of New York, which includes African American and Hispanic voices—see particularly the surreal fable, "The Long Distance Runner"—as well as those of Faith's aging parents in the Children of Judea, a Jewish senior citizens' home. Of the handful of excellent stories that follow Faith's visits to her folks, perhaps the most useful is "A Conversation with My Father," which articulates the author's theories about writing. If a story's wandering aimlessness confounds you, refer back to this "Conversation," in which Faith explains that she despises "plot, the absolute line between two points. . . . Not for literary reasons, but because it takes all hope away. Everyone, real or invented, deserves the open destiny of life." Suffused with this spirit of openness and tolerance, Paley's utopian, left-wing beliefs do not blind her to the struggles and hardships of contemporary life, but rather allow her to treat the experiences of those around her with the utmost sensitivity and kindness.

Further reading: Although this book collects all of Paley's stories, she has also written several volumes of poetry, and in 1998, she published *Just As I Thought*, a collection of poems, essays, and political speeches. Judith Arcana's *Grace Paley's Life Stories: A Literary Biography* (1993) and a volume of *Conversations with Grace Paley* (1997) provide insight into the author's personal life and opinions. Those enchanted by Paley should look back to the novels of Anzia Yezierska, whose Yiddish-inflected English prose and leftist politics both prefigure aspects of Paley's work.

. . . .

96 – Mr. Vertigo

By Paul Auster

VIKING, 1994. 293 PAGES.

However you choose to define postmodern American fiction, it ends up having something to do with the Jews, wrapped up as it is with pop culture, slapstick, irreverence toward history, irony, and heavy doses of authorial self-consciousness. It is not surprising that, Jewish characters feature prominently in the best-known examples of the genre, such as Thomas Pynchon's *The Crying of Lot 49* (1966) and Don DeLillo's *White Noise* (1985), even when written by non-Jewish authors—and, in the works of Jewish postmodernists, such as Paul Auster, Jewishness also crops up in unexpected ways.

Auster's eighth novel offers an example of this tendency, in addition to being a delightful read. The story of Walter Claireborne Rawley, a non-Jewish orphan native to St. Louis, Missouri, *Mr. Vertigo*'s animating presence goes by the name of Master Yehudi and is the son and grandson of Hungarian rabbis, a former Brooklyn resident, and a devotee of Spinoza. Young Walt calls this man master, as he has been instructed "never, under any circumstances . . . to call [him] Yehudi"—which means, literally, "Jew." It is 1927, and the master rescues young Walt from the clutches of his cruel uncle and aunt, whisking him away to a farm in Kansas to begin the 33 stages of his training. Soon, thanks to the master's guidance, Walt has learned to levitate—rising off the ground and floating, with no strings attached. Walt the Wonder Boy, as he is christened, proceeds to wow small-town audiences across the United States with displays of aerial acrobatics, stealing headlines from figures such as Charles Lindbergh and Babe Ruth. Money pours in, but trouble finds them, too, in the form of the newly vigorous Ku Klux Klan, which murders a couple of their housemates, and in Walt's villainous uncle Slim, who wants a cut of the boy's box office receipts. Walt's relationship with the master develops into a sweet surrogate father–son arrangement, whether times are good (when Walt is "the hottest child star since David loaded up his slingshot") or bad. Narrated by Walt in filthy, bouncy, slang-filled heartland dialect, this fantastic, simply told story turns into a broad, winning meditation on art and life, a loopy version of *Huckleberry Finn* with the Jewish mystic and showman as a "gentle, munificent guide" and boon companion.

Though loyal to Brooklyn, Auster is one of the few American writers more famous internationally than in his homeland. His works have been translated into 20 languages and are particularly prized in Israel; his novel *Brooklyn Follies* (2006) is reported to have sold more than twice as many copies in France as in the United States. It isn't clear whether his international fans read him as Jewish, American, or neither, but in *Mr. Vertigo*, at least, the centrality of Jewishness is clear: "Without the master I was no one," Walt says. "Everything I was flowed directly from him."

Further reading: Among about a dozen novels, Auster's most famous works remain *City of Glass* (1985), *Ghosts* (1986), and *The Locked Room* (1987), postmodern detective stories known collectively as the New York trilogy. He has also published a great deal of poetry, memoirs, and essays, and in the 1990s he was involved with a couple of movies, *Smoke* and *Blue in the Face*—http://paulauster.co.uk provides useful bibliographies. A scholarly collection, *Beyond the Red Notebook* (1995), contains essays on Auster's work, and given the attention Auster has been receiving in academic circles lately, one can expect many more studies to appear as his oeuvre continues to grow.

. . . .

97 – *A Disturbance in One Place*
By Binnie Kirshenbaum

FROMM INTERNATIONAL, 1994. 190 PAGES.

"Vestigial" is not a bad description for a particular strain of Jewishness found in late 20th-century America: like an ostrich's wings, this sense of Jewish identity persists long after its original purposefulness has passed. Such vestigial Judaism is not entirely unique to any time and place— crypto-Jews lighting candles on Fridays without knowing why have a powerful claim to embodying vestigial Judaism—but Binnie Kirshenbaum's *A Disturbance in One Place* dramatizes the odd contemporary experience of remaining Jewish without knowing why, or even what it means. As Kirshenbaum's protagonist puts it, "My Jewishness, about which I sometimes make a great fuss, is ersatz. As fake as paste." No kasha or kugel for her growing up: "The food we ate was from the A&P: Oscar Mayer hot dogs, Shake 'N Bake, Tater Tots."

She claims to have "never been on the inside of any synagogue" except for two bar mitzvahs—a stunning achievement, given that she has lived mostly in New York City, where it can be hard to find a block *without* a *shul*. A sinner and a hedonist, she cheats on her Anglo-Saxon husband unremorsefully with not one but two lovers, the first a Sicilian history professor whom she calls the hit man, and the second a repulsive, vaguely Jewish, multimedia artist. "I have broken seven of the Ten Commandments," she announces with pride. It is astonishing that, though, this young woman remains faithful in odd, inconsistent, and revealing ways. For one thing, she loathes Germans unconditionally and vehemently (so vehement is this prejudice that she refers to Ludwig Wittgenstein as an example of "Aryan intellectualism"); for another, she eats only vegetarian food and refuses the osso buco the hit man prepares as part of one of the Italian feasts he whips up. She may not know it, but her culinary practices signal something more profound than taste: in the fight that emerges from her refusal, she screams at the proud Sicilian, "This heritage of yours eats people, swallows them whole. . . . Do you know what I want? I want a fucking grilled cheese sandwich on Wonderbread." She wants, in other words, to be American. Her greatest loyalty, meanwhile, is to "the love of her life," who not incidentally happens to be a Holocaust survivor who does not requite her devotion.

The pulse of the novel is sex, throbbing and passionate and dispassionate and everyday and kinky: Kirshenbaum describes, in more detail than Erica Jong, with more variety than *Portnoy's Complaint* (1969), the wild specifics of her characters' sexual practices and history, ranging from childhood discoveries to adult explorations. Not many writers can wring out a compliment from Norman Mailer on the topic of frank treatment of sex, but Kirshenbaum did. Might this obsession with sex in and of itself be a component of the Jewish affiliation Kirshenbaum is invested in documenting? Sexy, mordant, and cynical, *A Disturbance in One Place* manages, with its string of unusually short chapters and its tense, disorienting flashbacks, to provide glimpses into the dangerous, sometimes depressing, often frightening world of the 1990s' cutthroat sexual politics that *Sex in the City*, some years later, would treat as good clean fun.

Further reading: Similar motifs recur in many of Kirshenbaum's various fictions; *Hester among the Ruins* (2002), for example, presses harder on her feelings for Germans. Reading guides to most of her books can be found at the author's personal website, http://www.binniekirshenbaum.com. Though it is unclear, as yet, how influential her writing will be, Kirshenbaum is making a definite impact as a teacher: through her position at Columbia's M.F.A. program in creative writing, she has shepherded many young writers—including Tova Mirvis, Aaron Hamburger, and Elisa Albert—into print.

135

· ·

98 – *The Romance Reader*

By Pearl Abraham

RIVERHEAD, 1995. 296 PAGES.

A type of Judaism that developed in the 18th century in Eastern and Central Europe, Hasidism involves extreme piety and ecstatic prayer; while one Hasidic sect, Lubavitch, seeks out non-Hasidic Jews (they're the ones who will find you on a street corner, ask you if you're Jewish, and sweetly request that you perform a religious ritual), many strenuously resist modern life and secular society. The Satmar sect is particularly cloistered; unlike the Amish they do not shun technology, but Satmarers speak Yiddish rather than English in order to guard themselves and their children from the social temptations of the non-Jewish world. (Yiddish students often enjoy a round of *Handl Erlikh*—"Deal Honestly"—a Yiddish-language version of *Monopoly*, marketed to Satmar families.) One might suspect that such a position is difficult to maintain, but it is estimated that more than 100,000 Satmarers live in either New York or Israel. Pearl Abraham's debut novel, *The Romance Reader*, details the challenges faced by a teenage girl growing up in a Satmar family in the 1970s. Rachel Benjamin is the oldest of seven children (Abraham herself was the third of nine), and her childhood environment is even more intense than the average ultra-Orthodox home. Her father, an aspiring scholar and rabbi, has the family living in a rural summer hotel that has fallen into disuse, rather than in Williamsburg, Brooklyn—where they would at least have a community of people like them. The good news for Rachel is that because there aren't other Satmarers around, she can slip away to the public library to check out English-language books, which are forbidden as secular foolishness by her father. Rachel's taste runs to romances like Victoria Holt's, though she also enjoys English classics; on a couple of occasions Abraham's otherwise straightforward narrative follows along as Rachel's fantasies of love, based on what she has been reading, unfurl. Throughout the book, Rachel struggles to compromise with her father's demands—she manages to become a lifeguard at an all-female pool, but she never obtains permission to wear less-obtrusive stockings—but when she is pressed, at 18, into an arranged marriage, she finds the courage to break away and pursue a different life.

According to its marketing, at least, *The Romance Reader* was highly autobiographical, as well as unprecedented—the book "lifts the veil from a sealed-off world," as one of its back cover blurbs puts it. Given the large size of the Satmar and other Hasidic communities that persist in the United States, we can expect many more storytellers to emerge from these groups as time goes on. (Intending to appeal to that demographic, the first all-Yiddish film in years, a moralistic thriller called *A Gesheft*, garnered press in 2006.) While not distinguished by its prose or plotting, *The Romance Reader* is noteworthy for the thoughtfulness and tenderness of Rachel's perspective. Even in difficult circumstances, she manages to provide a fair view of not only the anachronistic elements of Hasidism but also the faith and love that inspire it.

Further reading: Abraham has published two further novels, *Giving Up America* (1998) and the ambitious *The Seventh Beggar* (2005). A handful of interviews with and essays by the author, many of which are available online, provide a sense of Abraham's personal life as it relates to her fiction as well as to her artistic aims. For those interested in learning more about Hasidism, a useful documentary, *A Life Apart: Hasidism in America* (1997), offers an introduction to the histories and practices of various Hasidic sects.

99 – *While the Messiah Tarries*

By Melvin Jules Bukiet

HARCOURT BRACE AND CO., 1995. 197 PAGES.

A sarcastic, sharp-tongued Holocaust survivor in one of Melvin Jules Bukiet's stories asserts, somewhat cryptically, that "there are two separate, inviolate realms": memory and theology. Whether these are indeed separate and inviolate, they are certainly the two primary wellsprings of Bukiet's fiction. In books such as *Stories of an Imaginary Childhood* (1992) and *After* (1996), the author imagines himself into places and times made poignant by the memory of the Holocaust, whether or not it has occurred yet in the world of the fiction; and in the tales of *While the Messiah Tarries*, set mostly in the United States, he pairs the weight of Jewish memory with the wonders of messianism. It is no coincidence that the first story in the book alludes to Walter Benjamin, Gershom Scholem, and Jorge Luis Borges, three great modern mystics.

Bukiet aims for playfulness rather than realism in his plots: in one story, a Kabbalah-influenced murderer targets Jewish gem merchants in New York's Diamond District, while another tale describes a kosher butcher tempted into selling bacon by a sexy redhead. The devil himself pops up, complete with a name tag reading "Lucifer," and, in a story about the frenzied rush to exploit post-Soviet markets and immigrants, two brothers turn out to be the same person. These au courant fabulist gestures coexist with an older sense of humor, with its roots in the Borsht Belt; Bukiet can't resist a pun, a wisecrack, or a morbid laugh-line like, "Cemeteries are the best business in the world. . . . You buy by the acre and sell by the foot." Tying the volume together is Bukiet's concern with the ever-fading diasporic Jewish dream of Messiah, tainted as it is by the gruesome events of the 20th century. In one of the sharpest of these offbeat stories, "Postscript to a Dead Language," a student at the University of Minnesota named Ira Kepler builds a scale model of the Temple Mount, as it existed before the Babylonian Exile, in an unused gymnasium. His aim is to capture some of the magic of Jerusalem, but it turns out that both his faculty adviser and his girlfriend are Jesus-freaks who need Ira's model as part of an insane, violent gambit to bring about the second coming. A sharper metaphor for the distressing contemporary alliance between American Zionists and evangelical Christians would be hard to find.

Prolific in his own right—to date, he has published four novels and three story collections—Bukiet is also noteworthy as a promoter of contemporary Jewish writing and the editor of the anthologies *Neurotica: Jewish Writers on Sex* (1999), *Scribblers on the Roof* (2006), and *Nothing Makes You Free* (2002). The topic of the latter, a collection of memoirs and fiction by children and grandchildren of Holocaust survivors, has been central in all of Bukiet's publications, which deploy humor, sex, mysticism, and whimsy in their attempts to grapple with the meanings and lasting consequences of the Nazi genocide.

Further reading: Bukiet's most recent novel, *Strange Fire* (2001), is a cockeyed political thriller set in Israel. He contributes acerbic essays and book reviews to various magazines and newspapers. Bukiet's admirers will enjoy the mordant humor of his student, Jon Papernick, on display in the story collection *The Ascent of Eli Israel* (2002).

. . . .

100 – *Tales Out of School*
By Benjamin Taylor

TURTLE POINT PRESS, 1995. 283 PAGES.

Despite the central position Ellis Island occupies in the memories of American Jews—as the physical spot on the continent in which the vast majority of their European ancestors first set foot, and in many cases acquired the names their families still carry—some immigrants arrived elsewhere. Galveston, Texas, for example. During the peak years of immigration around the beginning of the 20th century, in the hopes of not piling more Jews into the ghettos of New York, Jewish agencies arranged for immigration through Texas to less saturated southern and western cities. It is still possible to find Jews, particularly in the South, for whom Galveston resonates more powerfully than the Lower East Side. Benjamin Taylor's *Tales Out of School* situates itself in this milieu, presenting a lyrical and engrossing tale of a boy's maturation and a family's dissipation.

Taylor's protagonist, Felix Mehmel, hails from the sort of wealthy German Jewish stock that is familiar from the works of Ludwig Lewisohn. His grandfather, Gerson, earned a fortune brewing "the finest beer in Texas," and his father, Aharon, like Lewisohn's Arthur Levy before him, charms and marries a non-Jewish woman—in this case, a Catholic from New Orleans. Aharon is not around to watch his son grow up, unfortunately, as the great hurricane of 1900 washes him out to sea. Felix's uncle is an eccentric bachelor, his grieving mother isn't much interested in childcare, and the local rabbi, though well-meaning, is occupied with his own crises of faith, so the precociously intelligent boy is mostly left to his own devices. In 1907, at the age of 14, he is watched over by his mother's African American servant, Neevah, and a kindly couple of what would be called, at that time, spinsters. Felix's curiosity leads him to befriend a bully and engage in sexual experimentation with him; to seek out a father figure in a newly arrived and mysterious mute Russian, Yankel Schmulowicz; and, eventually, to meddle in the plans of a couple of local "aeronauts" who aspire to improve upon the achievements of the Wright brothers. Schmulowicz turns out to be a preternaturally talented puppeteer who may or may not be Elijah the Prophet; as in tales by Lewisohn, Malamud, Ozick, and Philip Roth, the Eastern European Jew functions here as a redeemer of an assimilated American whose world has collapsed. By the novel's end Felix isn't living with his mother anymore, for, as Neevah says, "It ain't no home left here."

Taylor loops this narrative together through the perspectives of all of these characters with a Faulknerian sense for the speech patterns, vocabularies, and unarticulated desires of each one of them. He writes extraordinarily decorous prose—he cherishes neglected and unfamiliar words, and he has hunted down precise historical details, down to the proper terms for the components of a draught horse's collar. Occasionally the elevated diction isn't justified (one extreme example: instead of getting drunk, someone "relinquishe[s] his sobriety")—and it is odd that German Jews of this period would observe *kashrut* as Taylor's characters do—but mostly the mannered syntax and diction capture the spirit of these highly educated, pretentious people. This exquisite novel proves that there are still new stories of Jewish life in America yet to be told.

Further reading: *Tales Out of School* won the Harold Ribalow Prize but quickly went out of print; a paperback edition (2008) has made the novel more widely accessible. Taylor teaches at the New School in New York, and his other books include a critical study of genius, *Into the Open* (1995), and a second bildungsroman, set in the 1970s, *The Book of Getting Even* (2008). A collection of Saul Bellow's letters, edited by Taylor, is scheduled for publication in 2010. Those seeking a history of the Galveston immigration should seek out a copy of Bernard Marinbach's *Galveston: Ellis Island of the West* (1983), one of Taylor's sources, or *Kindler of Souls* (2007), a profile of Rabbi Henry Cohen—who helped organize the Galveston immigration—written by the rabbi's grandson.

· ·

101 – *Mona in the Promised Land*
By Gish Jen

KNOPF, 1996. 304 PAGES

Gish Jen isn't Jewish, and neither is Mona, the hero of her second novel— at first. Mona, like her creator, is the Chinese American daughter of immigrants who grows up in an overwhelmingly Jewish suburb of New York City. The town of Scarshill (a fictionalized version of Jen's hometown, Scarsdale) is chock full of Jews—"the New Jews . . . a model minority and Great American Success"—when the Changs move in, in 1968. Though teenage Mona was confirmed as a Catholic, her best friends in high school are Jewish, and she hangs out with them in their temple youth group so much that people start calling her Changowitz. Soon she is talking theology with the hip young Rabbi Horowitz.

While her sister Callie, a Harvard freshman, rediscovers her Asian heritage and studies Chinese, Mona opts for a new tradition: she converts to Judaism. Jen's interest here, of course, is in the rise of identity politics in the 1960s, at which point it became not only acceptable but also cool for American teenagers to identify themselves as ethnic minorities. Such newfound identifications weren't always about connecting with one's genetic great-grandparents, as Mona demonstrates, and it didn't take long before Jews, African Americans, and others were sampling each other's styles.

While Mona and her Jewish friends fret about black rights and the war in Vietnam, they spend at least as much time falling in and out of love (and bed) with one another. As such, they find themselves crossing and blurring the newly erected ethnic boundaries, suggesting the degree to which, in America, minority identity can be as changeable as fashion—for some lucky people, if not for everyone. While it takes on weighty issues, Jen's novel is an easygoing comic romp and a worthwhile read for anyone who has marveled at the affinities between Jewish and Asian communities in America.

Further reading: Though Jen's other books—two novels and a collection of short stories, to date—make for entertaining reads, they don't focus on Jews as *Mona* does. There hasn't yet been a full-length biography or study of her works, but Jen is frequently featured in the press and on the Internet. A handful of other literary works by Asian Americans incorporate Jewish characters in major or minor roles, such as the title story in Bharati Mukherjee's collection *The Middleman* (1988) and Han Ong's *Fixer Chao* (2001).

. . . .

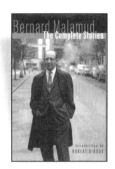

102 – *The Complete Stories*
By Bernard Malamud

FARRAR, STRAUS, AND GIROUX, 1997. 634 PAGES.

Praising Bernard Malamud as a short story writer is like praising the sun for giving light. He was the greatest, and that's all there is to it.

Malamud's novels are nothing to sneeze at, but the stories—absolutely all of which you can find in a single convenient paperback—are masterpieces. One of the pleasures of this collection, in addition to its inclusion of previously unavailable works, is the perspective it provides on Malamud's incredible range. Written between 1940 and 1984, his stories manage to deal with everything from the failure of a Brooklyn grocery store to the situation in the Soviet Union to the travails of a talking horse, while remaining steadfastly Malamudian and even, for lack of a better term, *heymish*.

Everyone who has read Malamud's stories has a personal favorite. Many choose "The Jewbird," which is about just what the title says—a Yiddish-speaking black bird named Schwartz who flies into Harry Cohen's apartment one day. This wacky premise Malamud transforms into an enormously moving tale that can be read as an allegory or as a fable, and it really needs no analysis. "Talking Horse" mines a similar vein, and equally fabulous (in both senses) is "The Angel Levine," an early piece about an African American angel. Some prefer Malamud's detailed miniatures of Jewish immigrant struggles, like "The Loan"; others still would select the Fidelman stories, which treat the experience of a life lived for art (and provide their protagonist with Malamud's mother's maiden name). And then there is "The Magic Barrel," which takes the ridiculous interactions of a rabbinical student and a marriage broker and transforms them into art. Part of the author's genius was his ability to start with the rhythms of Yiddish-inflected English, polish them, and transform them into a prose style that could hit notes of unbridled hilarity and quiet intensity.

Malamud's first collection won the National Book Award in 1959, but more impressive than any prize are the plaudits he received from his peers. The great Flannery O'Connor—herself a master of the form—wrote, in a letter to a friend, that Malamud was "a short story writer who is better than any of them, including myself." Cynthia Ozick answered her own question, "Is he an American Master?" with an assured "Of course." While any one of his collections, or the *Stories of Bernard Malamud* (1983), make for exceptional reading, *The Complete Stories* is a treasure, as worthwhile an investment as one can make in the field of American Jewish letters.

Further reading: Snippets of Malamud's life can be found in *Talking Horse* (1996), which collects many interesting examples from the author's notes, lectures, and essays. Fans will not be able to resist Malamud's authorized biography, by Philip Davis (2007) or a memoir by his daughter, Janna Malamud Smith, called *My Father Is a Book* (2006); there is also *Conversations* with the author, edited by Lawrence Lasher (1991). His brilliant novels include *The Fixer* (1966) and *The Tenants* (1971), both of which are worthy of sustained attention.

103 – *The Puttermesser Papers*
By Cynthia Ozick

Knopf, 1997. 236 pages.

Ruth Puttermesser runs the gamut. In five stories, written over three decades and knitted together into a disjointed but coherent novel, Ruth creates a female golem, unwittingly reenacts an episode from the life of George Eliot, and finally arrives in Paradise, where she encounters a handful of celebrities as well as her own lost love. Since Ruth aged more or less alongside her creator, these stories offer a window into the ways Cynthia Ozick's concerns and techniques have changed, and stayed the same, over time.

The pleasures of this collection are various, and variety itself is primary among them. The first chapter introduces the protagonist, whose last name in Yiddish means "butterknife": she is a lonely 30-something New Yorker, trained as a lawyer but lately departed from a "blueblood Wall Street firm." Not sure where to turn in her career, she also despairs that she has lost connection with her ancestry, and the story ends with a metafictional statement of her confusion: "Hey! Puttermesser's biographer! What will you do with her now?" Next up: magic realism. Ruth, frustrated in work and love, sculpts a female golem out of the dirt in her potted plants and, with mystical knowledge cribbed from Gershom Scholem, brings her to life. Named Xanthippe, after Socrates' wife, the golem cleans up Ruth's messes so effectively that she is soon elected mayor of New York; unfortunately, though, like all golems, Xanthippe becomes uncontrollable (in this case, she has an overzealous sex drive). The third section treats literary history, as Ruth, now in her 50s, introduces her new flame to the pleasures of George Eliot, the author of the great *Daniel Deronda*. Chapter 4 retreats to satirical realism in the era of perestroika, as Ruth hosts a cousin from the Soviet Union who shatters all of the idealistic expectations the Americans have of suffering Russian Jews by hocking tchotchkes at a sporting goods store. At the same time, Ozick lampoons a squishy left-wing Jewish magazine and its founder—a "ferocious entrepreneur" and self-described "sucker for red hair"— who bears more than a passing resemblance to Michael Lerner of *Tikkun*. After a grisly death, the last story sends Puttermesser to heaven, where she makes up for lost time on earth with an old crush and witnesses the notoriously inept dramatist Henry James "growing rich on the triumph of a play." Talk about fantasy!

Ozick is an acknowledged master of short fiction; she has taken first place in the O. Henry Prizes—one of two prestigious annual American awards for stories—an astounding and unequaled four times (once for "Puttermesser Paired," the second chapter in this volume). The short form, massaged here into the shape of a novel, suits her: her wild and elaborate diction, broad erudition, and flights of fancy play best in miniature.

Further reading: In addition to a handful of story collections and a number of excellent novels—including *Heir to the Glimmering World* (2005) and *The Cannibal Galaxy* (1983)—Ozick is well-known for her prize-winning essay collections, in which she can be cranky and obtuse but always witty and fiercely intelligent.

· ·

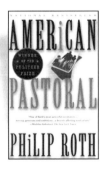

104 – *American Pastoral*
By Philip Roth

HOUGHTON MIFFLIN, 1997. 423 PAGES.

The 1960s changed America with—literally—explosive force, and Philip Roth's extraordinary *American Pastoral* hinges on the destructive power of one little bomb. The explosion in question, in a post office in a small town in New Jersey, kills a local doctor, but Roth's main concern is with another, indirect, victim: the bomber's father.

There is nothing wrong with Swede Levov: nicknamed for his blond hair (he's "a boy as close to a goy as we were going to get"), he is a childhood athletic champ who inherits his father's glove-making business, marries the non-Jewish Miss New Jersey, and raises his daughter, Merry, in suburban splendor. Somehow, for reasons he can't divine, Merry grows into a stuttering, hate-filled teen, enraged by the war in Vietnam. Still in high school, she involves herself with radicals—like the real-life teenage Jews who founded groups such as the Weather Underground—and, through an act of unforgivable violence, transforms herself into the infamous Rimrock bomber. The Swede's life is torn to shreds, and his personal descent into confusion and chaos mirrors that of the city of Newark, where he has his glove factory, and of American idealism as a whole.

The first volume of a powerful trilogy of novels focusing on social and cultural phenomena of America in the aftermath of World War II that Roth published late in his career, *American Pastoral* is nothing short of a masterpiece; it won the author a Pulitzer Prize, among other honors. Much more than a story of radicalism in the 1960s, it is a masterful meditation on the unbridgeable gaps between people, even parents and their children; a lush social history of the glove-making industry; and perhaps the most technically brilliant of Roth's many impressive fictions. His prose winds through labyrinthine sentences, linking cerebral insights to the expressiveness of vernacular speech, and Roth delves deep into the consciousnesses of his many characters, refracted through the perceptions of his narrative alter ego, Nathan Zuckerman. The novel's various elements—which include a long introductory section set at Zuckerman's 50th high school reunion, and a 100-page, sublimely awkward dinner party—fit together in fascinating ways. Critics have pointed out, for example, that the interest in glove making is paralleled throughout the text in Roth's interest in surfaces, skins, and outward appearances. This is one novel that grows richer and more complex with rereading.

Further reading: Many other novels contemplate the Jewish involvement in the radicalism of the 1960s, including Alan Lelchuk's *American Mischief* (1973), Roger Simon's *The Big Fix* (1973), and Jay Cantor's *Great Neck* (2003). The works that followed *American Pastoral* in Roth's American trilogy—*I Married a Communist* (1998) and *The Human Stain* (2000)—are, in many ways, equally stunning productions of the late phase of Roth's career.

143

. . . .

105 – *Like Never Before*
By Ehud Havazelet

FARRAR, STRAUS, AND GIROUX, 1998. 268 PAGES.

Ehud Havazelet's second book, *Like Never Before*, consists of 10 distinct short stories about a single family that bears a strong, if not total, resemblance to that of the book's author. Like Havazelet himself, the collection's central character rejects his position as the heir to an Orthodox rabbinic dynasty in Brooklyn and Queens; marries out of the faith, twice; and winds up in Oregon, far from his father's sphere of influence. Several of the details diverge, of course: for one thing, Havazelet's stand-in has a remarkably unremarkable American Jewish name, David Birnbaum; for another, David's father, Max, doesn't achieve nearly the success of Havazelet's father, a professor at Yeshiva University. The number of David's siblings is off, and so is his vocation: he is an architect by training, and landscaper by necessity, but not a short story writer.

The point, is not to determine which of the details from the book—the strained father–son relationship, the childhood rebellion, a charming sister still single at 40, an episode of narrow escape during the Holocaust—line up with Havazelet's family history. More interesting are the ways that the book exemplifies the stylistic trends of the short story in the 1990s. For one thing, as has been common in fiction produced in M.F.A. programs—Havazelet studied at the venerable Iowa Writers' Workshop and now teaches at a similar program in Oregon—each story builds in emotional intensity and concludes with an ambiguous, pregnant moment. For another, conventional wisdom has it that story collections are hard to sell, but novels often take forever to write; producing a "novel-in-stories," of which nascent genre Havazelet's book is an exceptional example, a writer can work piecemeal, but still offer the reader a cohesive and thoughtfully structured narrative. The gambit works in *Like Never Before* because Havazelet commits so intensely to capturing the emotions and voices of David, his father, his sister, and his first wife. Thanks to the multiplicity of perspectives we see a second side to everything: at times David is a sympathetic rebel, at others a petulant child; Orthodox religion comes across sometimes as a straightjacket, and, alternatively, as in "Leah," as a substantial comfort. Family itself, a burden and a curse to David in the title story, recurs as spiritual destiny in the book's final, magical realist, piece, "Eight Rabbis on the Roof."

Ranging from Hebrew school hijinks to the death of a parent, the stories ambitiously aim to capture the changing texture of a family. Though they can be critiqued, at times, for sentimentality, or for begging off at the crucial moment, in their subtle and oblique treatment of common themes—the attenuation of Orthodox beliefs over time, the scandal of interfaith marriage, the conflict between generations—Havazelet's fictions attest to a notion of David's: "Maybe," he thinks, "that's as close as you could come to knowing anyone . . . hearing their stories."

Further reading: Havazelet has also published an earlier collection of stories, *What Is It Then Between Us?* (1988), and his widely praised, first bona fide novel, *Bearing the Body* (2007). The current enfant terrible of online Jewish journalism, Luke Ford, conducted an in-depth interview with Havazelet in 2006, which can be read at http://www.lukeford.net. Shalom Auslander's stories in *Beware of God* (2005), as well as his memoir *Foreskin's Lament* (2007), are even more fiercely bitter about Orthodoxy than Havazelet's writing. Similar to those in *Like Never Before*, the separate stories in David Shields's *A Handbook for Drowning* (1992), David Bezmozgis's *Natasha and Other Stories* (2004) and David Evanier's *The Great Kisser* (2007) can, or should, be read as the components of fragmented novels.

106 – *Paradise, New York*
By Eileen Pollack

TEMPLE UNIVERSITY PRESS, 1998. 251 PAGES.

The heyday of the Jewish resort hotels is long past, but the Borsht Belt lives on as a site of nostalgia for a thickly Jewish leisure culture unique to the United States. Sure, Jewish resorts existed in various locales in Europe and Canada, as well as Las Vegas and Miami Beach, but nothing compares to the Catskills in their prime, probably because they were always just a short drive or train ride away for the millions of Jews of New York City. Starting with *cookaleins*—bungalows with attached kitchens—and flowering into luxurious full-service pleasure palaces, owners built their hotels up until they were the ne plus ultra of schmaltzy, *heymish* relaxation, and in the process they provided the first gigs to a generation of performers who would leave an indelible mark on American comedy.

Eileen Pollack's first novel, *Paradise, New York*, picks up this story toward its conclusion: it is the late 1970s, and most of the resorts have already folded or been sold to Hasids. Lucy Appelbaum, the dutiful heir of the family-owned Garden of Eden ("no one could miss the pun at the core of the owners' name"), is less than sanguine about the thought of the hotel closing down and depriving the few remaining guests of their "THREE MEALS A DAY, VERY STRICT KOSHER," and their "SHUFFLEBOARD, BASEBALL, HEALTHFUL POOL . . . and NITELY AMUSEMENT." More than a commitment to hospitality, Lucy's resistance comes from her need for an identity: as a student at New York University, she realizes that "there were so many clubs for Jews it was hard to feel distinction for being a Jew"—but that she *is* special, because she is "the only student whose family owned an authentic Borsht Belt hotel." That realization, and her childhood memories, are enough reason for her to try to save the Eden, even if that means having to scrimp, cut corners, and do everything else that everyone else in the hotel business does on a regular basis.

It is a lost cause, but one that Lucy devotes herself to with wit, energy, and a sense of humor. In outlining her efforts to save the resort, she remembers happier days there and introduces a cast of characters that helps to keep the place running, including her love interest, the hotel's African American handyman, who quotes Jewish sages as well as the Bible. Reflecting on the relationship, and on the fate of the Eden, Lucy confronts racism and issues of family continuity; as the author herself has said, "the novel is about the mistake of treating someone's ethnic identity as a commodity." Though dark, the book retains its comic flair, and if Pollack's humor can be a little zany, that's only fitting: the stars of the Borsht Belt stages, guys like Milton Berle, Rodney Dangerfield, and Henny Youngman, were no more subtle.

Further reading: Many of the stories in Pollack's debut collection, *The Rabbi in the Attic* (1991), also take place in the Catskills; a later story, "The Bris," was selected for the *Best American Short Stories 2007*. The starting point for explorations of the history of the Catskills and the Borsht Belt is the Catskills Institute, based at Brown University; the institute maintains a helpful website with links to relevant books and a number of interviews, including one with Pollack. Stanley Elkin's "Among the Witnesses" and Will Eisner's "Cookalein" are two stories set at resorts in the Catskills; but the most famous narrative to take on the milieu is the film *Dirty Dancing* (1987), starring Patrick Swayze and Jennifer Grey; see also Elinor Lippman's novel, *The Inn at Lake Devine* (1998).

· ·

107 – *The Jew of New York*
By Ben Katchor

PANTHEON, 1998. 98 PAGES.

For about their first 100 years of existence in the United States, comic books were regarded as simplistic, dumbed-down literature for the semiliterate—and the well-intentioned *Classics Illustrated* series, founded by a Jewish entrepreneur named Albert Kantor, did not help to dispel that misperception. The truth is that even a passing glance at a decent comic, or graphic novel, should inform the most skeptical reader that the genre requires about three times as much skill as writing a novel, which is difficult enough: to create a good comic, not only do you need to be able to write but also to draw and handle layout expertly. To create his masterful Jewish comics, Ben Katchor adds to all these skills a breathtaking sensitivity for Jewish culture and history and also what he has referred to as an "extensive background in book and print production." Nowhere is his virtuosity on display more than in his fantasia of the 1830s, *The Jew of New York*.

The plot of this novel is impossible to describe, but here goes nothing: Nathan Kishon, a butcher, is discredited through a scandal involving *treif* beef tongue and becomes a follower of Mordecai Manuel Noah—a real historical figure who wanted to establish a sovereign Jewish colony in upstate New York. After that falls through, Kishon meets a Jewish trapper, Ketzelbourd, who has been in the wild so long he has become animalistic and developed a bizarre sexual obsession. Among Kishon's adventures with Ketzelbourd is a brief sojourn at an air-worshiping commune that uses Hebrew script and practices the theories of Joseph Priestly, who discovered oxygen. Back in New York, an anti-Semitic satiric play about Noah is being put on by the New World Theater, whose crew includes a Jewish set designer. The book's climax, such as it is, takes place in the playhouse and involves Ketzelbourd attacking an actor, and an apparatus, designed to fill the theater with the aroma of pickled herring, burning the place down. But plot matters less than Katchor's gallery of perplexing characters on the most bewildering of missions, such as Yossl Feinbroyt, a kabbalistic-inclined scholar who transcribes, in English characters, the sounds people make while eating, and Francis Oriole, who plans to carbonate Lake Erie and pipe seltzer water to the masses.

Creating a fiction much stranger than truth, Katchor manages to evoke some critical themes from the weird old days of the early 19th century, including Noah's hopes for a Jewish state in America and the widely held belief that Native Americans might have been one of the lost tribes of Israel. (Katchor's cast includes an Indian, Elim-Min-Nopee, who has been trained to recite the Sabbath prayer *Lekhah Dodi* to dime-museum audiences.) Katchor's textual flourishes include a series of impossible period-replica handbills, such as a Yiddish transliteration of the introduction to the Declaration of Independence and a poster advocating restraint when it comes to "the practice of Onanism in private houses." Not always comprehensible—thankfully the book is short, as rereading seems almost inevitable if a reader wants to piece together much of the plot—Katchor's panels are nonetheless always meticulously produced and evocative, in a way that seems somehow vividly Jewish, of a time and place that never really was.

Further reading: Katchor's other strips, most of which have appeared in the *Forward* and in other newspapers, have been collected in the volumes *Cheap Novelties* (1991) and two others named for his famous character, Julius Knipl (1996 and 2000); his works have been translated into many languages, including French, Italian, and Japanese. Much of Katchor's fame owes to a sympathetic profile in the *New Yorker* in 1993; he was awarded a MacArthur Fellowship in 2000, and maintains a website at http://www.katchor.com. The list of worthwhile Jewish graphic novels of note has grown quickly and expands further every year. A few places to start would be Peter Kuper's adaptations of Kafka in *Give It Up!* (1995) and *The Metamorphosis* (2003), James Strum's *The Golem's Mighty Swing* (2001), J. T. Waldman's *Megillat Esther* (2005), Harvey Pekar's *The Quitter* (2005), Rutu Modan's *Exit Wounds* (2007), and Joann Sfar's *The Rabbi's Cat* (2005) and *Klezmer* (2006). Also see *The Jewish Graphic Novel* (2008), an academic study of the field.

· ·

108 – *For the Relief of Unbearable Urges*

By Nathan Englander

KNOPF, 1999. 205 PAGES.

Several of the stories in Nathan Englander's debut collection take place on the fringes of the world of ultra-Orthodox or *haredi* Jews, and each has a compelling hook: a Jerusalemite denied sexual intimacy by his wife obtains his rabbi's permission to visit a prostitute; a matchmaker tries to force a husband to grant a divorce to the wife he has abandoned; a rabbi moonlights as a department store Santa Claus to pay back his synagogue's debts; a female wig maker covets for herself the gorgeous locks of a lip-pierced, tattooed deliveryman she passes on a Manhattan sidewalk. Other stories traffic in magical occurrences: a Park Avenue gentile suddenly and inexplicably understands that he is "the bearer of a

Jewish soul"; the legendary foolish Wise Men of Chelm encounter the Holocaust; and an unpublished writer, famous to no one, is mysteriously selected to be purged along with the Yiddish greats in Stalin's Soviet Union.

What unites all of these tales is the author's probing for resonance, for intensity, for symbolic depth; Englander's narratives aim for, and at their best attain, that elusive and mystical meaningfulness that characterizes both exquisitely crafted short stories and religious experiences. Kafka and Malamud are Englander's obvious models in this regard, though those authors rarely drew upon actual Orthodox practice and mythology; in this sense, Isaac Bashevis Singer and Steve Stern may be better touchstones. Whatever the pedigree, Englander has made this mode his own, and with it earned himself the kind of publicity—as well as prizes, including the PEN/Malamud—that turned a small book of short fiction into a surprise bestseller. In retrospect, it makes good sense: while some Jews in the late 1990s turned to the Kabbalah Center for a convenient and digestible dose of the ineffable, others sought it out between the covers of books like this one.

Buoyed by reviews and a precedent-setting tour of Jewish community centers, Englander became something of a celebrity in the small world of Jewish publishing; as mentioned earlier, in "The Wig," the protagonist desires the hair of a horticulturalist—"a mane of curls the color of toasted bamboo that runs down to the middle of his back and ends in a deep, blunt ridge"—and this description uncannily echoes the author's well-known photo, in which curly hair tumbles down past his shoulders. As the star figure in a generation of young writers with Orthodox roots, including Pearl Abraham and Tova Mirvis, Englander's career will be followed closely to see if he can produce novels and more stories that deliver on the promise of this outstanding first collection.

Further reading: Englander's first novel, about a Jewish family in Buenos Aires during a wave of government terrorism, appeared eight years after his debut; it is called *The Ministry of Special Cases* (2007). Not much has yet been written on Englander, except for many celebratory book reviews. Ilan Stavans has a short essay on Englander's stories in *The Inveterate Dreamer* (2001), though, and given how regularly Englander's stories are taught at colleges, one can expect critical studies to follow as his oeuvre grows.

. . . .

109 – *The Ladies Auxiliary*

By Tova Mirvis

W. W. NORTON, 1999. 311 PAGES.

No one should be surprised that there are plenty of Jews in the American South—after all, more Jews lived in Charleston than in New York in the years before the Civil War—but it may be a revelation to some that a city like Memphis, Tennessee, contains a small but thriving Modern Orthodox community, complete with a religious high school and even a kosher restaurant or two. Tova Mirvis's debut novel, *The Ladies Auxiliary*, ushers readers into this charming, if parochial community.

Batsheva, who comes to the Orthodox precincts of Memphis via New York, stands out in that she is a convert to Judaism with a head of "white-blond hair," a tattoo left over from her wild adolescence, and a penchant for clothes just a little bit tighter and more flattering—though still technically modest—than are usually sported by patrons of Kahn's Kosher-Mart. Thanks to her endearing five-year-old daughter and the fact that her husband, a Memphis native, died in a car crash, she wins over the sympathies of most of the town's women, who narrate the novel in a chatty first-person plural. These gossipy ladies remain a little skeptical, though, of her artsy persona and her former allegiance to a Carlebach shul, especially when she invites them to a "women's only, Rosh Chodesh celebration in honor of the new moon," which sounds to them "like some feminist innovation." Tensions mount as Batsheva befriends the rabbi's only son, Yosef, and teaches art to the community's high school girls. As various parties tentatively rebel against the community's standards—eating at McDonald's, smoking pot, running away from home—the women blame it all on Batsheva's influence.

Mirvis's novel, a book group favorite, captures the kitschy details of culture in the "Jerusalem of the South," from a mikveh waiting room stocked with *Southern Living* and *Ladies Home Journal*, to the annual "Memphis-in-May Kosher Barbecue Contest," featuring teams called the "Alte-Cookers, the Memphis Mavens, and the Holy Smokers." At the same time, the story turns out to be more or less the universal story of modern Orthodoxy toward the turn of the millennium, as Batsheva's example encourages the faithful, and especially the women, to yearn for more spiritual meaning and social freedom in their Judaism. Mirvis knows about the controversies surrounding Orthodox feminism, even if her characters don't, but she approaches these explosive issues, as she does all of the novel's potential conflicts, with gentleness, sweetness, and subtlety.

Further reading: Mirvis's follow-up, *The Outside World* (2004), is a similarly breezy take on a modern Orthodox/ultra-Orthodox romance that begins in New York and winds up, lo and behold, in Tennessee. Other works set among Jews in the South include Louis Rubin's *The Golden Weather* (1961), the Oscar-winning film based on Alfred Uhry's play *Driving Miss Daisy* (1989), Judy Goldman's *The Slow Way Back* (2000), Roy Hoffman's novels of Jews in Alabama such as *Chicken Dreaming Corn* (2004), and Eli Evans's acclaimed "personal history," *The Provincials* (1973). Photographs and recipes of southern Jews can be found in *Shalom Y'All* (2002) and *Matzoh Ball Gumbo* (2005), respectively. For those interested in the issues of Orthodox feminism raised by Mirvis, Haviva Ner-David's *Life on the Fringes* (2000) is a fascinating account of the attempts of the author to bring together Orthodox practice with a resolutely egalitarian sensibility.

110 – *Moonlight on the Avenue of Faith*

By Gina Nahai

HARCOURT BRACE, 1999. 373 PAGES.

Call it what you will—*golus*, exile, dispersion—the Diaspora is a many-splendored thing: rather than a single leave-taking from one homeland, Jews have endured displacement after displacement throughout the centuries, meaning that there have been plenty of diasporas within the Diaspora. A century ago there were substantial communities of only Portuguese, German, and Russian Jews in the United States, but today there are thousands of former Bukharan Jews in Queens; former Syrian Jews on Long Island; and former South African, Latin American, Israeli, and Soviet Jews who have found their way to other parts of the so-called Promised Land. One of the largest and most vibrant of the expatriate groups is the Farsi-speaking Persian Jewish community centered in what has come to be called Tehrangeles. About 600,000 Iranian immigrants live in the Los Angeles area; not all of them are Jewish, certainly, but many are. Gina Nahai's *Moonlight on the Avenue of Faith* tells the story of how one such family arrived and where they came from.

Nahai's tale begins in Tehran's Jewish ghetto in 1938, with the birth of Roxanna the Angel. Ostensibly the novel is narrated by Roxanna's daughter, Lili, though frequently the narrative knows things Lili couldn't: not only all about her mother's magical dreams of flying and odd childhood in the home of an eccentric woman who poses as a Russian émigré but also Roxanna's later grim sojourn as a sex slave in a brothel just over the Turkish border. Lili's extended family suffers grotesque tortures, caused by their own pathetic desires, bad luck, and the corruptness of the shah's rule; the worst part, at least for Lili, is that Roxanna abandons her when she is just a kid. As the shah's regime implodes and life becomes harder for Jews and liberals in Iran, Lili's father ships her off to the United States, and she finds surrogate mothers—a dissolute and beautiful Iranian sex addict, and her aunt Miriam, who would in another context be called both a *balabusta* and a *yenta*—but the question that animates the novel, and explains Lili's apathy throughout her years at a Catholic school in Pasadena, is whether she will ever see her real mother again.

Nahai weaves into her story various historical developments—World War II, the Iranian Revolution, and the development of an Iranian Jewish enclave in Westwood, near UCLA, among others—but the regularity of miracles suggests she is after a magical, rather than realist, vision of our world. It is an approach with plenty of precedents, even in the American Jewish tradition (think of Steve Stern and Francine Prose); but it is not without problems. Nahai's details diverge occasionally from those of our world—a character in Tehran reads "a back issue of *Hustler*" in 1971 (though the magazine didn't start publishing until 1974), and another "sat shiva for thirty days" (though "shiva" literally means "seven," and that's how many days it lasts); in these moments, it is hard to tell whether Nahai is being playful or just plain sloppy. Readers don't seem to have minded these blips or Nahai's occasionally inelegant prose; the book spent 12 weeks on the *L.A. Times* bestseller list and has been translated into Dutch, Polish, French, Farsi, Hebrew, German, Greek, Norwegian, and Italian, among other languages.

Further reading: Nahai was born in Iran and educated at a Swiss boarding school and then at southern California universities; she holds an M.F.A. from the University of southern California, where she now teaches. Nahai's other novels so far about the Jews of Iran are *Cry of the Peacock* (1991) and *Caspian Rain* (2007). For those who want less magic and more facts, Daniel Tsadik's *Between Foreigners and Shi'is* (2007) is a concise scholarly history of Jews in 19th-century Iran; if you can find it, there is also a documentary film, *Jews of Iran* (2005), directed by Ramin Farahani that focuses on the 25,000 Jews who still live in the country. As Nahai has pointed out, interest in the Middle East since September 11, 2001, and more recently in Iran particularly, has spurred a wave of novels and memoirs by Iranians and Iranian Jews, including Marjane Satrapi's comic book memoir *Persepolis* (2003), Azar Nafisi's crowd-pleasing *Reading Lolita in Tehran* (2003) and, on the Jewish side, Dalia Sofer's *The Septembers of Shiraz* (2007). Meanwhile, the immigration narratives and tales of exotic Jews from far-flung locales just keep on coming: Lucette Lagnado's *The Man in the White Sharkskin Suit* (2007) details a modern exodus from Egypt, while Sophie Judah's *Dropped from Heaven* (2007) and Carmit Delman's *Burnt Bread and Chutney* (2003) focus on the Jews of India. It is probably just a matter of time until we see memoirs and novels about American Jews who hail from Ethiopia, Turkey, and anyplace else Jews have ever set foot.

. . . .

111 – *The Amazing Adventures of Kavalier & Clay*
By Michael Chabon

RANDOM HOUSE, 2000. 639 PAGES.

Jews invented the American comic book, and the superhero in particular. So, are Superman, Batman, and Spiderman all somehow Jewish, then? Well, not exactly. Fans, critics, and scholars might postulate about some essential Jewishness in each of these characters, but the truth is that their creators were unwilling to identify the heroes religiously, and, at the same time, were busy whitewashing their own Jewish origins. Thus finding what in Yiddish is called the *pintele Yid*—the nub of Jewish essence—in the history of comics, though hardly impossible, can pose quite a challenge.

In *The Amazing Adventures of Kavalier & Clay*, Michael Chabon achieves something different, and more astounding: he re-creates the history of comics around that *pintele Yid*. In his gorgeous prose and with an intricate, page-turning narrative, Chabon tells the story of Jews in comics more engagingly than anyone before or since, and the fact that this tale is fiction—that the two comics creators, Sam Clay and Joe Kavalier, and their signature creation, The Escapist, are all figments of Chabon's miraculous imagination—takes away nothing from its fundamental accuracy and makes it only that much more impressive.

The winner of many awards, including the Pulitzer Prize, Chabon's novel is full of delights, including the ways it links both the ancient legend of the golem and the horrors of World War II with the rise of the modern superhero; its sympathetic portraits of friendship and love, both gay and straight; its fresh and engrossing descriptions of New York in the 1930s; and its tour de force re-creations in prose of comic book issues. It is amazing that, in the years after the novel's enormous success, Chabon's invented comic book characters became real, as The Escapist was adapted into a comic book. Tremendous in its scope, exuberant in every way, and excitingly engaged with the history of Jews in America, Chabon's novel is as mythic and unforgettable as the best comics—and if you aren't a fan of comic books, it just might turn you into one.

Further reading: Chabon's earlier novels—*The Mysteries of Pittsburgh* (1988) and *Wonder Boys* (1995)—and his collections of short fiction, are all superb and deal with Jewish life; but *Kavalier & Clay* is his masterpiece so far. Of course, readers enamored of Chabon's story should immediately proceed to read the works of the great Jewish comic creators, including Will Eisner and Jack Kirby; and they might be interested in tracking down earlier comics with references to golems, such as an issue of *The Incredible Hulk*, *In the Shadow of the Golem* (#1:134, 1970), or a two-part Batman story, "The Golem of Gotham," in *Detective Comics* (#631–32, 1991). Nonfiction studies of comics and the Jews continue to proliferate; the bibliography at the back of Chabon's novel—documenting the prodigious research that went into it—is as good a place as any to find some preliminary reading suggestions in this field.

152

112 – *Bee Season*
By Myla Goldberg
DOUBLEDAY, 2000. 274 PAGES.

When reading Jewish fiction, it is surprisingly easy to forget about God. Fiction has traditionally been the domain of secularists, and, with a few salient exceptions, even novels dealing with Orthodox and Hasidic communities tend to focus on the behaviors of these groups as an anthropologist or sociologist might, devoting considerably less attention to theology and spirituality. Yet if 20th-century history teaches us anything, it is that no matter how thoroughly science and rationality have countered superstition, religious and spiritual beliefs continue to exert a tremendous influence on people all over the world. In America, the recent Kabbalah fad provides one powerful and bizarre example of the durability of spiritual thinking. The pop singer Madonna has been the most famous and ardent non-Jewish devotee of Kabbalah, but the confluence of new age culture and ancient Jewish mysticism also plays out in Myla Goldberg's book group favorite, *Bee Season.*

The novel's captivating conceit links Kabbalah with a traditional ritual of American elementary education, the spelling bee. Eliza Naumann, an otherwise undistinguished fifth grader, wows her classmates and family by spelling her way to the national finals on the basis of her supernatural ability to envision letters and words forming inside her head. Eliza's father, Saul, is a Reconstructionist hippie-style cantor who discovered "LSD and Jewish mysticism at the same time," in college, and though he has given up the drugs he has continued his pursuit of "*shefa,* the influx of the Divine." Believing that Eliza's spelling bee triumphs result not from a healthy vocabulary but from a kabbalistic gift, he sets out to train her in the practices of Abraham Abulafia, a 13th-century mystic whose works Saul has, conveniently enough, personally translated into English. Saul and Eliza aren't the only ones in the family with high aspirations, either. Eliza's brother, Aaron, seeks enlightenment in Eastern religions, finding his way to a Hare Krishna temple, while their overachieving mother, Miriam, pursues an illegal obsession that she, too, considers Jewish: she views her compulsive stealing as part of a project of *tikun olam,* repairing the world, in a mystical sense. Goldberg seems aware of the absurdity and potential perniciousness of blithely co-opting mystical ideas: when Saul describes Abulafia's rituals as "primarily a kind of Jewish yoga" it is hard not to cringe. Like Miriam, many synagogues and secular organizations have, in recent decades, embraced the term *tikun olam* for their social action committees and environmental programs with no connection whatsoever to kabbalistic eschatology. In general the seekers in *Bee Season* grope for spirituality out of desperation and pain, not a disinterested desire for cosmic truth. At the same time, though, Goldberg does not deny the possibility that a few of these wandering souls might find true transcendence.

Goldberg's execution isn't entirely consistent—the present-tense narration occasionally falters, and there are a couple of moments where the author's research seems to have stumbled—but *Bee Season* struck a chord with critics and readers. An emotional portrait of the dissolution of a grotesquely dysfunctional family, the novel exhibits the ways in which the promises of redemption and transcendence appeal even to those without a connection to the rituals and texts of traditional Judaism.

Further reading: A film version of the novel in 2005 featured Richard Gere as Saul, transforming him into an academic. Goldberg has since published a travel book about Prague and *Wickett's Remedy* (2005), a novel set during the influenza epidemic of 1918. Spelling bees have been featured in many recent films and books, including an excellent documentary, *Spellbound* (2002), and a Broadway musical, *The 25th Annual Putnam County Spelling Bee.* Those fascinated by Miriam's obsessive-compulsive behavior and its relation to Jewish life might be interested in Jennifer Traig's *Devil in the Details* (2004), a memoir of the author's struggle with

153

obsessive-compulsive disorder, or in *I Never Promised You a Rose Garden* (1964), a best-selling novel written by Joanne Greenberg under the pseudonym Hannah Green that links the experience of anti-Semitism with mental illness.

· ·

113 – *Days of Awe*
By Achy Obejas

BALLANTINE, 2001. 370 PAGES.

Traditional Passover seders always include the wish "Next year in Jerusalem," which expresses the Jewish desire to arrive not in the terrestrial, beleaguered, and too often deadly city we know, but in a sublime and peaceful, unearthly place that has been redeemed by the coming of the Messiah—which is why the formula is recited even at seders in Jerusalem itself. Achy Obejas's characters, Marranos and crypto-Jews, harbor similar messianic hopes, but instead of Zion they pine for Spain, Miami, and Havana, even if they already live in those places. Depending on their politics, they dream of a Cuba no longer under Fidel Castro's thumb, or one in which his socialist revolution has finally triumphed over its detractors; more broadly, they aspire to live in a world in which they can openly express their identities, be they religious, ethnic, political, or sexual.

A dense web of plotlines, histories, and family secrets, *Days of Awe* centers on a Cuban American woman, Alejandra San José, who was born in Havana on the same day as the Cuban Revolution. Having fled the island as an infant alongside her parents and a Holocaust survivor, Ale grows up in Chicago's Rogers Park neighborhood. Her father, Enrique, translates great works of Latin American literature into English, and she in turns becomes an oral interpreter; like many bilinguals, they share an interest in "words that refused to convert from one language to another." Though their relationship is an intimate one, Enrique never manages to communicate clearly with his daughter about their Jewish heritage and his own feelings about it. Ale learns that she is descended from Marranos—Jews who were converted to Christianity by the Spanish Inquisition but nonetheless maintained, in secret, Jewish rituals. The novel zigzags through Ale's past and future, treating a handful of her love affairs with men and women in Cuba and the United States, and flashing back to the experiences of her great-grandfather Ytzak, who grew up not far from the island's future dictator, and whose encounters with American Jews awakened a sense of profound Jewish affiliation within him.

Days of Awe's plot concerns Ale's trips back to Cuba and her slow discovery of her father's secrets, and it can be dizzying, not surprising, given the complexity of the connections she juggles: she is a Jew, a Cuban, an American, a lesbian, a daughter, a lover, and an individual. Obejas packs in historical information on the origins and experiences of Cuba's Jews—the novel comes complete with a

154

two-page bibliography—as well as quotations on exile, in her own translation, from Cuba's José Martí and Judah Halevi, the great poet of the Jewish Golden Age of Spain. At times a heartrending tale of love and loss, *Days of Awe* offers insight into the diverse and cosmopolitan Jewish experiences that have been folded into the American Jewish community.

Further reading: Obejas's two previous books deal with Cuban and Cuban American life, but not with Jews. A journalist, she was part of a *Chicago Tribune* team that won a Pulitzer Prize in explanatory reporting in 2001, and she maintains a website at http://achyobejas.com. A lively and occasionally acrimonious debate has sprung up in recent years about the claims of indigenous peoples in the American southwest to be crypto-Jews, with books published on the subject by scholars such as Stanley Hordes (2005) and Janet Leibman Jacobs (2002). Other novels that consider the crypto-Jewish legacy in the Americas or the legacy of the Inquisition include Katherine Alcalá's *Spirits of the Ordinary* (1997), Naomi Ragen's *The Ghost of Hannah Mendes* (1998), and the great Brazilian Jewish author Moacyr Scliar's *The Strange Nation of Rafael Mendes* (1983, translated 1988). Debra Spark's *The Ghosts of Bridgetown* (2001) explores the Jewish history of another island, Barbados.

. . . .

114 – *Paradise Park*
By Allegra Goodman

DIAL PRESS, 2001. 360 PAGES.

Allegra Goodman and the heroine of her delightful second novel, *Paradise Park*, are two sides of a coin. Goodman grew up in Honolulu and has lived much of her adult life in and around Boston, while the character, Sharon Spiegelman, raised in Boston, spends her 20s and 30s in Hawaii and returns to Boston only as she nears middle age. Running in similar circles, these two women couldn't be more different. To put it in the simplest terms, Goodman is brilliant and Sharon is a dimwit.

Sweet and optimistic, Sharon is a religious seeker. After being expelled from Boston University, where her father serves as a dean, she follows her environmentalist folk-dancing partner to Hawaii of all places. After he leaves her in the lurch, she obeys her unerringly terrible instincts and hooks up with one guy after another. All of them, from the native Hawaiian Christian to the military man to the married naturalist, are absolutely wrong for her. When these relationships fizzle out she seeks in religion what she hasn't found in romance, putting in time at a monastery, dabbling in evangelical Christianity, and decamping briefly for Jerusalem, all the while believing she has seen a vision of God on a touristy whale-watching excursion. Sharon's flakiness and tendency to apprehend meaning in everything make it seem perfectly natural when she falls in with a group of Hasidic Jews, whose fondness for ecstatic spirituality and mysticism resonate with her. Thanks to this connection, she drifts back to the mainland, and meets her *bashert*—that is, her fated lover—a Russian immigrant pianist who has also recently been drawn in by Hasidism.

A picaresque tale with a contemporary sense of humor, *Paradise Park* is enlivened by Goodman's cleverness and dramatic irony—we so often know what Sharon doesn't. At the same time, Goodman is not one to dally with trivialities. For one thing, she is interested in the alienation of Jews from Judaism; "Why is it," one of her characters asks, "that those of us who are born Jews look for answers in every single religion but our own?" In a broader sense, at stake in Sharon's journey are problems quite deep and philosophical, even if her narrative voice makes that hard to recognize. The title refers to an aviary in Honolulu where gorgeous tropical birds flit around, as if they were free, until they bump up against the wire fencing high in the sky. That's Sharon's metaphor, or at least one of her metaphors, for life. Is there such thing as true freedom? Is faith enough to provide it? That the novel manages to explore these questions without veering into preachiness or didacticism is just one more sign of Goodman's major talent.

Further reading: Goodman's résumé is astonishing: preternaturally mature, she sold her first short story to *Commentary* at the age of 17; her debut collection of fiction was published on the day she graduated Harvard; and she submitted her Ph.D. dissertation—about the notes John Keats wrote in the margins of his copy of Samuel Johnson's edition of Shakespeare—just a year after her second book, *The Family Markowitz* (1996), appeared to rave reviews. She has range, too: her first novel, *Kaaterskill Falls* (1998), which was nominated for the National Book Award, takes places in an Orthodox summer community, while a more recent book, *Intuition* (2006), deals with the world of science.

. . . .

115 – *Everything Is Illuminated*

By Jonathan Safran Foer

HOUGHTON MIFFLIN, 2002. 276 PAGES.

By the turn of the millennium, despite assertions of "Never Forget," it could not be denied that even the most searing memories of the mid-20th century had begun to fade. Though the Holocaust remained a prominent force in American political and cultural life—including Hollywood movies and New York publishing—a so-called third generation, the grandchildren of those who lived through the war, grew to maturity and discovered the horrors of World War II mostly through literature and pop culture. While a large trove of second-generation literature deals with the impact of the Holocaust on the children of survivors, Jonathan Safran Foer's acclaimed novel goes one inevitable step further and explores what the Holocaust means to those for whom it is associated with their *bubbes* and *zaydes*.

A publishing phenomenon, Foer's book began as his senior thesis at Princeton University and appeared to tremendous fanfare when he was all of 24. In the novel, a young man named Jonathan Safran Foer travels to Ukraine foolishly hoping to locate the woman who saved his grandfather during the Holocaust. That he knows almost nothing about the woman, or the town in which she supposedly lived half a century earlier, reflects the challenges facing the youngest generation of Jews in their attempts to recover their family histories; more than a few of them have embarked upon similar grim pilgrimages. What makes this sad story enticing is that it is narrated by Alexander Perchov, a young Ukrainian tour guide who cobbles it together with much too much help from a thesaurus. While he and his grandfather escort Jonathan around the Ukranian countryside, Alex mangles English with extraordinarily inappropriate synonyms; the title of his first chapter is "An Overture to the Commencement of a Very Rigid Journey."

Alex's hilarious chapters alternate with Jonathan's fanciful reconstructions of the history of his ancestors and their shtetl. These sections betray the overwhelming influence of South American magical realism on Foer's fertile imagination, and they tend to strike readers either as whimsical and delightful, or cloying and trite. In either case, the way they are assembled from Gabriel Garcia Marquez, *Alice in Wonderland,* and the shtetl tales of Isaac Bashevis Singer suggests the void opened up by the dying out of the generation of the survivors. The novel was adapted into an unremarkable movie and received a number of prizes, including the National Jewish Book Award and the Guardian First Book Prize, and it earned Foer enough money that he could devote himself full-time to a literary career. Whether he will capitalize on his early success to produce works of moral seriousness or whether he will indulge his worst tendencies toward sentimental shlock is anyone's guess; but his first novel is a testament to his incredible precocity and promise.

Further reading: Foer's second novel, *Extremely Loud and Incredibly Close* (2005), uses even more postmodern gimmicks, and it expands its focus to engage with tragedies including the firebombing of Dresden and the atomic destruction of Hiroshima. Some of Foer's readers preferred *The History of Love* (2005) by his wife, Nicole Krauss. Borat Sagdiyev, the fictional Kazakh journalist created by the British Jewish comedian Sasha Baron Cohen and featured in television and film skits, is a spiritual cousin to Alex Perchov—as was the stand-up comedian Yakov Smirnoff back in the 1980s. Judy Budnitz's *If I Told You Once* (1999) similarly depicts Jewish life in Eastern Europe with magical realist techniques, and Joseph Skibell's *A Blessing on the Moon* (1999) applies them to the Holocaust and its aftermath.

157

116 – *The Russian Debutante's Handbook*
By Gary Shteyngart
RIVERHEAD, 2002. 452 PAGES.

Already by the final years of the Cold War, and thanks in part to the lobbying efforts of Americans, Soviet Jews were flowing out of the Soviet Union and into America in large numbers. With the fall of the Berlin Wall, this steady stream swelled to a flood that was bound to remind observers of the immigration boom of the late 1880s. Some of the new arrivals were children who, having suffered plenty under a collapsing regime, now encountered fresh torments at synagogues, Jewish day schools, and other places where they stuck out as foreigners—that is, wherever the American Jewish community attempted clumsily to assimilate them. By the end of the millennium these kids had grown into adults and, in some cases, writers, and they began to produce a literary record of their bewildering experiences as refugees from communism.

The most successful of this young crop of writers is Gary Shteyngart, a native of Leningrad and a graduate of Oberlin College who has exploited his immigrant credentials for the sake of slapstick comedy and social satire, beginning with his debut novel, *The Russian Debutante's Handbook* in 2002. As the book opens on his 25th birthday, the author's autobiographical stand-in, Vladimir Gershkin, holds a liberal arts degree and earns eight dollars per hour clerking at a hapless immigrant aid society. Vlad, tangled up in a failing relationship with a matronly dominatrix, remembers fondly his days as a maladjusted high school geek bullied by his mother, and he has only one friend, a small-time drug dealer. After a brief tour of this excuse for a life, Shteyngart's plot chugs into motion, pushed forward by Vladimir's lust, boredom, and increasing greed. Vlad misadventures his way through several settings—Manhattan, Miami Beach, and, at greater length, a scantly fictionalized Prague—bumping into dozens of characters and ineptly gesturing at a life of crime. All of this picaresque fun is described in Shteyngart's humorous prose, which always seems to be winking bilingually at its own silly formal diction.

The book poses provocative questions about ethnicity, nationality, and so on, but Shteyngart refuses to hazard answers, opting instead for wacky car chases and broad satire. If there is a message here, it is that Vladimir's blithe selfishness is all we can expect from someone who has lived a short life and suffered the slights of both Communism and capitalism almost simultaneously. The novel's dark humor, in the tradition of Joseph Heller and Mordecai Richler, captures something of the smarmy tone of New York in the 1990s and the ex-pat scene in Prague, where thousands of young American Jews, Russian and otherwise, whiled away a few years. Shteyngart's prose is not mean-spirited, though: like the best satire, his novel delights in the settings and habits it skewers and in its hapless characters.

Further reading: Shteyngart's second novel, *Absurdistan* (2006), devotes some loving attention to New York, but most of its action takes place in the fictional, titular post-Soviet state. Shteyngart's peers in the first major wave of post-Soviet Jewish writing include Lara Vapnyar, whose *The Memoirs of a Muse* (2006) dramatizes the culture clash between Soviet and American Jews in the form of a doomed love affair, and David Bezmozgis, a Latvian Jewish filmmaker whose gorgeous short stories, collected in *Natasha* (2004), limn life in the post-Soviet community in Toronto. Ludmila Ulitskaya's *The Funeral Party* (2002), written and first published in Russian, concerns the final days of a Russian Jewish émigré in New York City.

117 – *Old School*

By Tobias Wolff

KNOPF, 2003. 195 PAGES.

In *Old School*, Tobias Wolff's protagonist, a scholarship student at an elite boarding school, has been raised Catholic and only recently discovered his father's Jewishness. "It was a fact," the boy remarks of his Jewish background, "but not a defining fact." He denies his heritage even when he could benefit from revealing it, despite claiming there is no anti-Semitism in the enlightened 1960s at the school. Admitting that "the Jewish boys, even the popular ones, even the athletes, had a subtly charged field around them, an air of apartness," he attempts first and foremost to fit in.

Wolff's primary concern is with the use of literary sources—books, poems, and what is known of the authors who create them—by young men in their processes of self-definition. The narrator and his buddies preside over the campus literary magazine, and they are thrilled when their school invites the master writers Robert Frost, Ayn Rand, and Ernest Hemingway to visit. The boys toil feverishly on stories and poems to impress the visitors, who, when they arrive, turn out to be confusing, disappointing, or both. Frost commands an earnest lad to quit school and flee to the Kamchatka Peninsula in Russia or to Brazil, while Rand's ranting deflates the magic of *The Fountainhead*. The climax arrives when the protagonist, inspired by Hemingway's impending arrival, tries to produce a story that will reveal the truth about who he is, both in terms of social class and religion. Searching for inspiration, he reads another student's story and suddenly feels "as if [his] inmost vault had been smashed open and looted and every hidden thing spread out across these pages."

To whom, ultimately, does such a story belong: to its author, or to the readers in whom it produces such startling effects? In the novel's late episodes, Wolff extends this question further, to wonder if the author's life and persona belong more to his readers, with whose lives he becomes inextricably entwined, than to himself. These heady issues emerge naturally from Wolff's skillful and simple

159

plot, which is narrated with the compression of a master of the short story form. The result is a brilliant novel about reading and writing informed by the experiences of a lifelong practitioner, but with none of the navel-gazing or preciousness typical of fiction about fiction. One can only hope that Wolff's extraordinary book will outlive the contemporaneous, and wholly unrelated, slapstick comedy movie of the same title.

Further reading: Somewhat like his protagonist, Wolff didn't discover he was half-Jewish until he was 19; in his autobiographies, his father's Jewishness and self-hatred surface only occasionally. *This Boy's Life* (1989), an award-winning memoir, was made into a film starring Robert De Niro and Leonardo DiCaprio (1993).

· ·

118 – *San Remo Drive*
By Leslie Epstein

HANDSEL BOOKS/OTHER PRESS, 2003. 238 PAGES.

Leslie Epstein's family has always been as interesting as his fiction, if not more so. Epstein is not shy about the fact that his father and uncle, two legendary Hollywood screenwriters, wrote *Casablanca*; these days, he is even more widely recognized as the father of Theo Epstein, who was, at 28, the youngest ever general manager of a Major League Baseball team, and who led the Red Sox to World Series victories in 2004 and 2007. While sensitive to issues of inheritance and posterity, Epstein's novels have distanced themselves from his own life and those of his famous relatives—as in the historical novels *Pinto and Sons* (1990), about a Jewish medical student in the American southwest in the mid-19th century, and especially *King of the Jews* (1979), which features a leader of the Judenrat in Poland during the Holocaust. In the more recent *San Remo Drive*, though—which bears the subtitle *A Novel from Memory*, as well as photographs of the author's family and home—Epstein plumbs his own childhood.

The novel first's four sections relate semiremembered, semi-imagined episodes from the author's boyhood, transposed onto a character named Richard Jacobi. Like Epstein, Richard grows up on the same street as the exiled Thomas Mann; like Epstein, he has a famous screenwriter father who dies young, a mentally unhinged younger brother, and an ever-present, glamorous, and warmly loving mother. (Responding to an interviewer's question as to whether his mother was his most significant influence, Epstein quipped, "Did you read *San Remo Drive*? . . . Well, there you have it.") These sections dramatize his father's persecution by McCarthyists and sudden death as well as the development of Richard's political consciousness and talent (in a departure from real life, he is a painter, not a writer). A wunderkind who goes to Yale and wins a Rhodes scholarship, Richard struggles to relate to his brother, Barton, a disturbed kid who embraces anti-Semitism, anti-communism, and Buddhism one after the other. Given that his parents aren't exactly interested in synagogues, Richard's sense of himself as a Jew arises largely as a reaction to Bartie's self-hatred and self-abnegation, which in turn are products of anti-Semitism; asked decades later why he chose to identify as a Jew, Richard says, "Because I found out . . . that some very bad people wanted to kill all the Jews" (as if to endorse Jean-Paul Sartre's assertion that anti-Semitism creates the Jew). In an outlandish but representative scene, Richard listens to firsthand testimony from an African American plumber and former World War II soldier about the dehumanization of Jews in Nazi concentration camps, while, at the same time, another plumber fondles Richard's penis. Such inexplicable confusions of sex, horror, and ethnic identity recur throughout the novel.

The novel's second half narrates Richard's return to his childhood home on San Remo Drive—apparently you *can* go home again—and his adoption of two Native American sons. On the eve of his departure for France, where his paintings are about to be celebrated, Richard confronts a crisis, reconnects with his muse and former mistress, and loses his mother. Epstein, as usual, can't resist slapstick humor or a lame pun—a tendency that some find delightful, and others find annoying, in much of his oeuvre—but in *San Remo Drive* these typical elements of Epstein's style are tempered by closer attention to verisimilitude, sincerity, and character development. The result is by turns touching, amusing, and confounding, and one of our finest novels about "movie people."

Further reading: In addition to the novels already mentioned, Epstein has published several fictions starring the irrepressible émigré Leib Goldkorn, which can be found in *Goldkorn Tales* (1985) and *Ice Fire Water* (1999). Bruce Wagner's novels, such as *I'm Losing You* (1996) and *I'll Let You Go* (2001), depict contemporary Hollywood life, while Neil Gabler's *An Empire of Their Own* (1989) is a historian's exploration of Jews' roles in the development of the film business. Sidney Meller's *Roots in the Sky* (1938), meanwhile, a somewhat hard-to-find novel about a rabbi's family in California, is a reminder that not all Jews on the West Coast have worked for the movies.

. . . .

119 – *The First Desire*

By Nancy Reisman

PANTHEON, 2004. 310 PAGES.

The city of Buffalo, New York, inspires thoughts of escape. This isn't just a reaction to the bitter winter storms, or to Niagara Falls, which reminds everyone who sees it of the fragility of human life. Buffalo happens also to be the only large American city that is less exciting than its Canadian neighbor; a current website describing itself as "Jewish Buffalo on the Web" answers the frequently asked question, "Where can I find single Jews in Buffalo?" definitively: "Toronto." Whatever causes this sense of nowhereness, the quality makes Buffalo an ideal setting for Nancy Reisman's startling debut novel, which is all about the need to get away and the impossibility of doing so. The reason, Reisman's characters discover, that you can't go home again is that you probably never left in the first place. Either that, or you were already gone the whole time you were there.

The First Desire begins with a shocking disappearance. One day in July 1929, Abe Cohen's eldest daughter, Goldie, vanishes. The siblings she has been taking care of since their mother's death—brassy Jo, flighty Celia, and ne'er-do-well Irving—were too busy or distracted to notice; Goldie's more responsible sister, Sadie, no longer lives at home and finds out only after Goldie has been gone for days. Goldie's absence weighs on the Cohens, mostly because they each yearn to put some distance between themselves and their family. Irving chases non-Jewish girls, pretends to be a slick non-Jew named Thomas West, and joins the army in World War II to escape some trouble he has stirred up. Jo, unable to articulate her sexual attraction to women, dreams of being stranded on a desert island with Amelia Earhart. Celia wanders the streets aimlessly. Sadie, meanwhile, isn't sure *what* she wants, but what she has is a marriage to an old-fashioned dentist whom she considers "the most familiar of strangers." Even Abe, supposedly the stable paterfamilias, pursues an affair with a not quite respectable woman, Lillian Schumacher, who indulges in "reefer" and "bootleg gin." Abe sits shiva for Goldie, despite never having found a trace of her, demonstrating how willing he is to wash his hands of his children when they fail to live up to his expectations. None of them, except maybe Sadie, really do. Yet they all remain linked to his legacy: in this sense, the book provides an apt metaphor for Jewishness in America, from which Jews rebel and wander, but find themselves drawn back to, again and again, often despite themselves.

Reisman weaves story lines together deftly, presenting the family's fortunes from the perspectives of Jo, Sadie, Goldie, Irving, and Lillian. The characters grow and change, and the theme of disappearing reverberates throughout the novel; "What compensations are there," Lillian wonders, "for the ways the living vanish?" Reisman manages to nail the historical details, too, without hammering her readers over the head with them. An honestly tragic book, *The First Desire* reflects the ways that Jewish families fall apart even as they endure.

Further reading: Reisman grew up in Buffalo in the 1960s and 1970s. Her first collection of stories, *House Fires* (1999), won the Iowa Short Fiction Award, and she has received many fellowships and prizes, including the 2005 Samuel Goldberg and Sons Foundation Prize for Jewish Fiction by Emerging Writers, for *The First Desire*.

120 – *Joy Comes in the Morning*
By Jonathan Rosen

FARRAR, STRAUS, AND GIROUX, 2004. 388 PAGES.

There have always been Jewish women with strong personal connections to God and with vast knowledge of Rabbinic texts—from the matriarch Sarah, said to be a greater prophet than her husband, Abraham, to the talmudic sage Bruriah to the Maiden of Ludmir, a Hasidic leader in 19th-century Ukraine. Until quite recently, however, there had never been a community in which women could be recognized as rabbis through a combination of piety and study, as their male counterparts could. In the United States, the first female rabbi was ordained in 1972; by 1983, the rabbinical seminaries of the Conservative, Reconstructionist, and Reform movements all had alumnae. Deborah Green, the heroine of Jonathan Rosen's *Joy Comes in the Morning*, is one such modern rabbi.

A gorgeous baseball fan with a dirty mouth and clothes a little more risqué than is appropriate for her profession, Rabbi Green has one serious problem: she is "thirty and single"—a situation made more painful for her by the fact that her job requires her to provide premarital counseling. After officiating at a wedding, she retreats to a bathroom stall and bursts into tears. Luckily, she meets Lev Friedman, an agnostic science writer and lost soul whose father, Henry, botches a suicide attempt and winds up at the hospital where Deborah provides chaplaincy services. As their inevitable courtship develops, Lev and Deborah bounce the tenets of faith and observance against those of science and rationalism. Meanwhile, through Deborah's job and personal struggles, the novel details the rituals and rhetoric of contemporary non-Orthodox Jews for whom spirituality and religiousness are meaningful and central. Although Deborah is a Reform rabbi, her actions suggest sympathies much more traditional than those of the Reform movement, historically; while the first class of Reform rabbis ordained in America dined on frog's legs and soft-shell crabs way back in 1883, Deborah not only keeps kosher, but also blesses her food and observes Passover, following what is accurately described as "an Orthodox impulse." Complementing this sense that Deborah cannot be pigeonholed by denomination, Rosen also calls into question the nature of religious authority, especially in a winning scene in which Lev illegitimately presides over a funeral, high on Xanax and cribbing from his girlfriend's "rabbi's manual."

Set in the year 2000 and textured with the real-life details of New York's Upper West Side, this gentle, mannered novel won a number of prizes (the Edward Lewis Wallant Award, the Chaim Potok Literary Award, and the Reform Judaism Prize for Jewish Fiction) and in many cases deliberately reflects the author's personal life—Rosen's wife is a Conservative rabbi, and that's not the only detail that matches. Though an interlude with a mentally unbalanced childhood friend of Lev's provides a touch of late suspense, and despite passing references to Lev's grandfather's Holocaust experience and to the coming trauma of September 11, 2001, the book's plot moves forward mostly on the basis of small conflicts—for example, will Lev's father let him use his father's prayer shawl for the wedding canopy?—and it isn't much of a page turner. Instead, this is a novel of ideas filled with translations and interpretations of religious texts (the title, for example, is drawn from Psalm 30), a useful jumping-off point for meditations on the nature of theology and belief in the contemporary world.

Further reading: Rosen, the son of the writer Norma Rosen, is the author of *Eve's Apple* (1997), a novel about a woman with an eating disorder, and is perhaps better known for *The Talmud and the Internet* (2000), a book-length essay and memoir. He has wielded influence as an editor of the English-language *Forward*'s Arts and Letters section, and of a series of short nonfiction studies under the Nextbook/Schocken imprint. Readers interested in the question of women on the pulpit should consult an admirable biography by Elisa Klapheck of the first woman rabbi, *Fraulein Rabbiner Jonas* (2004), who was ordained in Germany in the 1930s, which also includes the learned disquisition that pioneering woman wrote on the subject.

121 – *Collected Stories*
By Isaac Bashevis Singer

ENGLISH: VARIOUS TRANSLATORS. LIBRARY OF AMERICA, 2004. THREE VOLUMES.

The great critic Irving Howe once noted that fate "only allows one Yiddish writer at a time to be popular with American readers." As arbitrary as this sounds, it isn't far from the truth, and Isaac Bashevis Singer proves it. For the second half of the 20th century, and especially after he won the Nobel Prize in 1978, he rose to extraordinary fame as America's foremost Yiddish storyteller. Alongside his many novels and memoirs, over the course of a long career he published hundreds of short stories in Yiddish periodicals, especially the *Forverts*; many of these pieces were translated into English for prestigious publications such as the *Atlantic Monthly* and the *New Yorker*, which began to print fiction in translation in 1967 so that it could include Singer among its contributors.

What accounts for the appeal of Singer's stories? For one thing, he was prolific enough to satisfy many tastes, and in creating various literary personae he donned multitudinous hats, caps, yarmulkes, and *shtreimels*. When he writes about Eastern Europe before World War II, he invokes his aunt Yentl, who "told stories which had the scent of gossip," or he allows three idlers in the Radzymin study house to take over his narrative. For wartime and postwar tales, he purports to transcribe the monologues of exhibitionists who know his work—"I read you! I come from the towns you describe"—and look him up in the Manhattan phone book, desperate to submit their personal histories. In all cases, Singer has a taste for the sensational, the profane, and the fantastic: he favors shocking anecdotes of cross-dressing Hasids, daring escapes from Nazi Germany, touching descriptions of bizarrely loyal lovers, and supernatural tales of devils and demons. His best-known story, "Gimpel the Fool," which Saul Bellow translated in 1953, is a fitting representation of his oeuvre: set in a shtetl, it describes a pure-hearted simpleton who is abused by a sinful woman, and, rising above the temptation to revenge himself on the community, winds up a wandering Jew, waiting for the world to come. While it resonates with notions of Diaspora and destruction, the story takes seriously the needs, desires, and beliefs of one simple, even pathetic man. In a sense, the hundreds of other stories Singer wrote simply reproduce, across continents and decades, this remarkable attention and sympathy.

The wonderful 2004 edition of Singer's collected stories covers almost 3,000 pages, but even these three volumes cannot be called complete, because Singer published many short pieces under pseudonyms over the decades, and an absolute gathering of all his published works in translation seems unlikely. For many readers, a smaller grouping of stories, such as *The Collected Stories of Isaac Bashevis Singer* (1982), will be a sufficient introduction, and this three-volume set should fulfill even Singer's most ardent fans.

Further reading: As one of the most celebrated American Jewish writers and a master of Yiddish style, Singer has been the subject of innumerable biographies, studies, and profiles; a good place to start is Janet Hadda's contribution (1997). Singer's memoirs, published in volumes such as *In My Father's Court* (1966), are as entertaining as his fictional works. His first novel, *Satan in Goray* (1935), about a false messiah in the 17th century, should not be missed.

· ·

122 – *The World to Come*
By Dara Horn

W. W. NORTON, 2006. 315 PAGES.

Unlike most of her peers in the ranks of young, celebrated Jewish writers, who fret primarily about their ignorance and ambivalence about the textual and social traditions of their ancestors, Dara Horn knows her stuff cold. A Ph.D. in modern Jewish literature, Horn reads everything from the Torah to I. B. Singer in the original, and she brings her commitment to Jewish texts to bear in her novels. In fact, she admits to being less conscious of how English works in [her second book, *The World to Come,*] than how Hebrew or Yiddish work in it, since English is more medium than subject."

The result is an idiosyncratic book, part novel and part anthology, which reads at times as if it were being translated from a lost Jewish language. In fact, Horn interpolates into her narrative a series of stories in translation by Yiddish masters including Sholem Aleichem, Itzik Manger, Nachman of Bratslav,

Moyshe Nadir, Mani Leyb, and I. L. Peretz as well as providing condensed fictionalizations of the lives of the world-famous painter Marc Chagall and the neglected Soviet symbolist writer Der Nister ("The Hidden One"). To squeeze all of this in, Horn's imagination leaps through time and space, limning scenes on the outskirts of Moscow and in Vietnam as well as an otherworldly, fantastic place where people drink books like wine. The nub of this wildly expansive plot is the former child prodigy Ben Ziskind, who steals a painting by Chagall off the wall of the Jewish Museum in Manhattan, and it is in the course of explicating Ziskind's family history and the painting's provenance that Horn ranges so widely. Before she is done, she touches on terrorism in the aftermath of September 11, 2001, and the situation of Russian Jewish immigrants as well as on Ben's potential love life; and if not every strand of the story weaves seamlessly together, that is beside the point. The grand ambitions of *The World to Come* are themselves energizing.

Horn has been honored with just about every Jewish writing prize in the United States; more impressive, she also made Granta's prestigious *Best of Young American Novelists* list in 2007. As she was only 29 when her second novel appeared, and has all the credentials she'll need to settle into a comfortable academic post (if she wants to), there is reason to hope that Horn will have a long and productive career. Even more encouraging, she has an enormous, mostly unknown archive of Yiddish and Hebrew modernist writing from which to draw inspiration.

Further reading: Horn's first novel, *In the Image* (2002), won many Jewish book prizes and was a hit on the Jewish book fair circuit. In *The World to Come*, Horn herself includes a bibliography, recommending Der Nister's *The Family Mashber*, available in an English translation (1987), and other Yiddish favorites. Tamar Yellin's *The Genizah at the House of Sepher* (2005) is another recent novel of vast textual erudition.

. . . .

123 – *The Yiddish Policemen's Union*
By Michael Chabon

HARPERCOLLINS, 2007. 432 PAGES.

In the late 1990s, Michael Chabon published an essay about the book *Say It in Yiddish*, which seemed to him a handy guide to a fantasy land that has never existed, where one needs to know how to say "What is the flight number?" and "I will call a policeman" in *mameloshen*. The piece occasioned much chatter and protest among Yiddishists who thought that it disrespected their language, but Chabon's intentions were sweet and nostalgic, not destructive. Less than a decade later, Chabon proved this, applying his literary gifts to write a country into existence for which *Say It in Yiddish* would, indeed, be a useful guide.

In less capable hands, such an exercise might lapse into pure, far-fetched silliness, but Chabon did the legwork to translate his "What if?" of a Yiddish territory—in Alaska, of all places!—into a coherent fiction. In Chabon's version of history, the U.S. government designates a territory in Alaska as a temporary refuge for European Jews during World War II. (Such a proposal was actually considered, if quickly quashed, by Franklin Delano Roosevelt.) Fast-forward half a century, and the population of Sitka, Alaska, numbers 3.2 million—most of them Jews and all of them Yiddish speakers, including the Filipino maids and the tough-talking homicide detectives. The novel's hero, Meyer Landsman, is one of the latter—he is "the most decorated *shammes* in the District"—and he is in a bad way. He is recently divorced, his sister has died, and in two months, when the district reverts to U.S. sovereignty, Landsman and all of the other Alaskan Jews will be out of not only their jobs but also a homeland. If that isn't *tsuris* enough, a neighbor in the decrepit Esperanto-themed hotel where Landsman lives turns up with a bullet in the back of his head, execution-style. In short, as Chabon's characters frequently say, "These are strange times to be a Jew."

A primary pleasure of the novel is the tour it offers through Yiddish Sitka, a vigorously imagined urban locale with streets named for Yiddish culture heroes including Sh. Ansky, Sholem Asch, and Yankev Glatshteyn. Chabon, meanwhile, manages to make his English-language book read, at times, like an overly literal translation from a Yiddish original: it seems oddly old-fashioned, at first, when Landsman groans, "Woe is me," but what he is really saying is the familiar Yiddish expression, *"Vey iz mir."* And the mystery plot—which invokes a chess problem cadged from Vladimir Nabokov, a posse of vile Hasidic gangsters, and questions of Jewish international relations reflecting those of the real world— unfailingly drives the story forward, making this surely the most page-turning thriller about Yiddish nationalism ever published.

Further reading: There is a limited shelf of literary quality Jewish counterfactuals (historical novels about history that didn't, or didn't yet, happen): two important examples are Theodor Herzl's uncanny *Altneuland* (1902) and Philip Roth's *The Plot against America* (2004). Many other fictions, of drastically varying quality, imagine different outcomes of Nazism; Sinclair Lewis's *It Can't Happen Here* (1935) and Philip K. Dick's *The Man in the High Castle* (1962) are among the most famous; George Steiner's bizarre *The Portage to San Cristobal of A.H.* (1981) imagines that 30 years after Hitler's escape to South America, he is captured by Nazi hunters modeled after Simon Wiesenthal. Chabon followed up *The Yiddish Policemen's Union* with *Gentlemen of the Road* (2007), a swashbuckler set in the 10th century featuring Jews of Frankish, Abyssinian, and Khazar descent.

167

124 – *The Collected Stories*

By Leonard Michaels

FARRAR, STRAUS, AND GIROUX, 2007. 403 PAGES.

Among the most respected of American short story writers, Leonard Michaels didn't produce an enormous body of work. His oeuvre consists of a handful of collections of fiction, often fleshed out with reprints; a novel, *The Men's Club* (1981), which was turned into a movie; some memoirs, journals, and an autobiographical novella; and a smattering of academic publications—he was a Ph.D. in English, having written his dissertation on Byron. The relatively small extent of his published work doesn't capture Michaels's impact, though, as he was a master of compression who could tell quite a story with just a few words. There are a number of examples that begin and end in a single line. A characteristic one reads, in its entirety: "I phoned my mother. She said, 'You sound happy. What's the matter?'"

The Collected Stories includes the vast majority of Michaels's important short fiction, including all of his first two collections, *Going Places* (1969) and *I Would Have Saved Them If I Could* (1975). The first of these, containing a passel of award-winning pieces, got him nominated for the National Book Award. Reports from the trenches of the sexual revolution of the 1960s, these stories pair a thick poetic style with an audacity of content. "Manikin" describes the rape and suicide of a rabbi's daughter, "Making Changes" takes place at an orgy, "Murderers" features boys who spy on a rabbi's lovemaking with his wife from the roof of an apartment building, and in "Getting Lucky" a man is ejaculated by an unknown stranger's hand while riding the subway. Several stories in the latter collection, and the long piece "Journal" from 1990's *Shuffle*, are composed of a multitude of short narrative sections that don't obviously relate, relying instead on the subtler mechanics of a symphony—repetition, juxtaposition, counterpoint—to achieve their cumulative effects. It is surprising that, after finding success with this minimalist approach, toward the end of his career Michaels published a series of conventionally plotted, highly crafted fictions that lack the experimentalism of his earlier work but, perhaps for exactly that reason, have become audience favorites. Late stories such as "A Girl with a Monkey" and "Viva La Tropicana" offer all of the pleasures of mainstream fiction—setting, plot, conflict—that Michaels had studiously avoided for decades, as do the seven tales about Nachman, a mathematician at UCLA, which Michaels was revising for publication in book form at the time of his death in 2003.

Raised until the age of five in Yiddish, Michaels consistently impresses with verbal daring and startling images (for example, "The audience, submerged in silence, was like a many-eyed crocodile, the body suspended underwater, inert"). Though often and not unfairly thought of as a New York writer, he made fictional homes for himself in Ann Arbor and the Catskills, Los Angeles, Cuba, and Berkeley (where he taught for decades, mentoring such writers as David

Bezmozgis). His work, ranging from lyric flights to, improbably, gangster thrillers, offers something for every taste. If he wasn't consistent, so what? He could write sentences astounding in their elegance and honesty.

Further reading: Michaels's diaries were published as *Time Out of Mind* (1999), and much of his work is quite autobiographical, including *Shuffle* (1990). All of his fiction, meanwhile, is slated to be reissued soon by Farrar, Straus, and Giroux. Short story junkies should also seek out Richard Stern's career retrospective, *Almonds to Zhoof* (2005), or the collection of Harvey Swados's shorter fictions, *Nights in the Gardens of Brooklyn* (2004).

. . . .

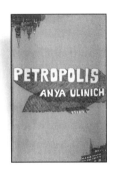

125 – *Petropolis*
By Anya Ulinich

VIKING, 2007. 325 PAGES.

The future of American Jewish literature looks a lot like the past, with a couple of major modifications. Like Mary Antin, David Levinsky, and Sholem Aleichem's Motl, Sasha Goldberg, the plucky heroine of Anya Ulinich's debut novel, wends her way from Eastern Europe to the United States, hoping to find the Promised Land there. While Sasha's predecessors escaped pogroms, though, her motivation to emigrate is much more mundane. Asked in an ESL class in Phoenix, Arizona, to explain why she came, she selects "(b) To seek a better life"—just like her Mexican classmates—because the other choices, including "(a) To escape religious oppression," "don't apply at all."

In fact, Sasha's Jewish grandfather, an engineer, had been "a media star" in Moscow in the 1960s and the winner of the Lenin Prize, having survived "Stalin's anti-Semitic campaign . . . more or less untouched." Sasha's father, Victor, a half-African orphan adopted by the Goldbergs, fared less well in Soviet society, and ended up having his daughter with a librarian in a hilariously desolate Siberian outpost called Asbestos 2 and then abandoning the two of them there. The desire to escape this hopeless backwater—where, in the first 14 years of her life, she studies art, suffers inevitable taunts at school, and gets herself impregnated by a charming nihilist whose family dwells in a concrete half-pipe in the garbage dump—spurs Sasha's westward trek through an arranged engagement to an American nerd. In the United States, Sasha escapes her potential husband, crashes with some Russians, and then briefly lodges with a grotesque and wealthy American Jewish family in a house outside Chicago seemingly based on Frank Lloyd Wright's Fallingwater. Never quite returning to art, Sasha nonetheless makes it to Brooklyn and achieves some approximation of the American dream: meeting her expenses as a cleaning woman, she saves enough not only to bring over the baby she left with her mother in Asbestos 2 but also to buy the kid a Hello Kitty music box, a Dora the Explorer backpack, and all the kitschy commercial children's spoils of capitalism. Meanwhile, Sasha's hometown on the margins of post-Soviet Russia, and her loving, assertive mother, wither and die.

Naive and precocious, an outsider's outsider, Sasha—and Ulinich, speaking through her—is perfectly positioned to critique contemporary American Jewish fiction and culture: when a friend in Phoenix tells her gory tales of her relatives' suffering in the Holocaust, Sasha objects, "Is your life so boring you need to dredge up dead babies that you've never even seen?" Elsewhere, Sasha's "intolerance for proper fairy tales" suggests a rejection of the ever-growing trend toward the fantastic in American Jewish fiction (in a promotional interview, Ulinich has said this explicitly: "I can't stand magical realism"). With an artist's eye for detail—the author, like her character, studied painting—Ulinich captures and deforms the absurdity of the contemporary immigrant experience and may one day write a comic epic of 21st-century Jewish life in the United States.

Further reading: Ulinich was born in 1973 and immigrated to the United States at the age of 17. Some of her peers in the most recent wave of post-Soviet writing include Ellen Littman, whose *The Last Chicken in America* (2007) is set among immigrants in a Pittsburgh neighborhood, Squirrel Hill; Sana Krasikov, whose first collection of stories is titled *One More Year* (2008); Irina Reyn, whose *What Happened to Anna K* (2008) rewrites Tolstoy's classic among Russian and Bukharan immigrants in Queens; and Keith Gessen, whose first novel is *All the Sad Young Literary Men* (2008). Ulinich's title derives from a poem by Osip Mandelstam, the great Russian Jewish poet who died in the gulag; his complete poems were published in English translation in 1973.

APPENDIXES

A. Jewish Characters in Modern American Fiction

As Louis Harap's *The Image of the Jew in American Literature: From Early Republic to Mass Immigration* (1974) makes clear, Jews have been appearing in American literature for centuries. There are few American masters who haven't mentioned a Jew here or there. Yet in the most widely read novels by the most celebrated American authors of the first decades of the 20th century, Jewish characters feature even more prominently. Ugly, unpleasant, or pathetic, they play pivotal roles and are always powerful.

Edith Wharton's *The House of Mirth* (1905), for example, turns on the speculations, both economic and romantic, of one Simon Rosedale, a "plump rosy man of the blond Jewish type." Jay Gatsby, the alluring center of F. Scott Fitzgerald's universally read *The Great Gatsby* (1925), wouldn't be quite so great, or so rich, if it weren't for his association with unscrupulous Meyer Wolfsheim, a "small, flat-nosed Jew." Willa Cather's *The Professor's House* (1925) features an entrepreneurial social climber named Louis Marsellus who exploits the legacy of a beloved young hero in a small university town. On the first page of his breakthrough novel, *The Sun Also Rises* (1926), meanwhile, Ernest Hemingway describes Robert Cohn as having taken up the sport of boxing "to counteract the feeling of inferiority and shyness he had felt on being treated as a Jew at Princeton"; though hapless, Cohn nonetheless manages to consummate his desire for the book's female lead while Hemingway's macho protagonist—injured in the war and consequently impotent—cannot. A few years later, buried amid the linguistic chaos of William Faulkner's *The Sound and the Fury* (1929), one discovers tirades against "dam eastern jews," while a "Jew lawyer from Memphis" makes a crucial appearance late in the great southern author's scandalous *Sanctuary* (1931).

This list represents only the tip of a disturbing iceberg. Other memorably unpleasant Jews appear in renowned works of American modernism by Djuna Barnes and Thomas Wolfe, as well as the more famously anti-Semitic prize-winning poetry of T. S. Eliot and Ezra Pound. Of course, the tradition of depicting the Jew as a villain stretches back much further in English literature: Chaucer's Jews murder an innocent Christian child, after all; Marlowe's Barabas and Shakespeare's Shylock lust after wealth and revenge; and Dickens's "villainous and repulsive" Fagin lures little boys into lives of crime.

It is no wonder, then, that Henry Roth—the author of perhaps the single greatest entry in the American Jewish literary tradition, *Call It Sleep* (1934)—has the highly autobiographical protagonist of his late novel *Mercy of a Rude Stream* (1994) recall that when he was a voracious reader, as a child, in the Harlem of the 1910s, "all he asked of a book was not to remind him too much that he was a Jew; the more he was taken with a book, the more he prayed that Jews would be overlooked." Similarly, decades later, the Canadian Jewish author Adele

Wiseman realized in her voracious childhood reading that "even in the middle of really good stories they lied about Jews and what we did and why we did it and how we lived and what we were like."

It would be a mistake to write off any of these writers as simple anti-Semites; they may have resented or even hated Jews, in some cases, but they weren't simpletons and their responses to and representations of Jews contain complications and surprises worthy of investigation. Many of these writers, it should be pointed out, depended on Jewish editors, agents, publishers, and critics for their livelihoods; Hemingway and Faulkner, for example, may never have seen print in the first place if a young Jewish publisher named Horace Liveright hadn't paid for *In Our Time* (1925) and *Soldier's Pay* (1926), their first books, respectively. For these writers—as for Shakespeare and Dickens as well as—for Henry James and Matthew Arnold—Jews served as windows onto the complex and vast landscapes of modern love, commerce, and community. To understand modern culture and America, these writers suggest, one needs to understand, or at least to consider, the Jews.

Similar motivations underlie the many English literary classics, American and European, in which Jews serve as exemplary figures of courage or humanity, in the vein of George Eliot's remarkable proto-Zionist *Daniel Deronda* (1876) and James Joyce's *Ulysses* (1934). Closer to home, late in Theodore Dreiser's *An American Tragedy* (1925), the protagonist, a non-Jewish murderer on death row, secures a glimmer of redemption while singing the Yom Kippur confession along with a fellow Jewish inmate. In Jean Toomer's pioneering *Cane* (1923), one story concerns a Southern girl of whom the narrator says, "At first sight of her I felt as if I heard a Jewish cantor sing." For later writers on the American left, Jews serve as model revolutionaries, as in James Farrell's *Studs Lonigan* trilogy (1938), John Dos Passos's *USA* trilogy (1930–36), Richard Wright's *Native Son* (1940), and Chester Himes's *The Lonely Crusade* (1947). For these writers, Jews represent the potential for political engagement and spiritual depth; for others, such as Sinclair Lewis, they represent the promise of capitalism, science, psychoanalysis, or skepticism.

If anything, the symbolic centrality of Jews in American literature only intensified after World War II. Jewish characters figure prominently in postmodern standards such as Walker Percy's *The Moviegoer* (1961), Thomas Pynchon's *The Crying of Lot 49* (1966), and Don DeLillo's *White Noise* (1985), representing victimhood, because of their connections to the Holocaust; urban intellectualism, because of the Jewishness of many of the major public thinkers of the 20th century, from the Frankfurt School to the New York Intellectuals; and popular culture, because of Hollywood.

B. Untranslated Yiddish and Hebrew Novels about America

The list of novels in Yiddish and Hebrew about America that have not been translated is considerable, and it contains works of genuine and lasting value, as well as, of course, some shlock. Readers literate in Yiddish should seek out the works of Morris Jonah Haimowitz, who wrote *Oyfn Veg* [On the way] (1914) in the Viennese style of Arthur Schnitzler and Stefan Zweig; David Ignatov, the hero of whose debut novel *In Keslgrub* [In whirlpool] (1918) dreams of a healthy rural alternative to the crushing atmosphere of New York City; B. Demblin, whose novels include *Vest-Said* [West side] (1938); Baruch Glasman, whose *Lender un Lebns* [Lands and lives] (1937), stars an immigrant shoemaker in the United States and the family he abandons in the Old Country; and S. Miller, whose short stories, many of which are set among Yiddish-speaking residents of Los Angeles, were gathered into numerous volumes. In a genuine miracle of modern technology, all of these long out-of-print works can be easily purchased online from the National Yiddish Book Center's digital archive.

A number of Yiddish writers whose works have been translated—Sholem Aleichem, Sholem Asch, David Pinski, Isaac Raboy, the Singer brothers, and Chaim Grade—are covered in this guide. Others who have been translated but penned only a few short stories about America are not included; it should be noted, though, that L. Shapiro's *The Cross* (2007), Abraham Reisen's *The Heart-Stirring Sermon* (1992), and Chaver Paver's *Clinton Street and Other Stories* (1974) each contain a handful of American stories, and a few anthologies have collected and translated Yiddish stories about America, including Max Rosenfeld's *Pushcarts and Dreamers: Stories of Jewish Life in America* (1967) and *New Yorkish and Other American Yiddish Stories* (1995), and Henry Goodman's *The New Country: Stories from the Yiddish about Life in America* (1961, 2001). Yiddish readers should consult *Amerike in Yiddishn Vort* (1955), a massive anthology of relevant texts.

There is an even more pervasive lack of translation into English of Hebrew fiction about America: distressingly, I could not find a single worthwhile Hebrew novel available in English translation, set in the United States, to cover in this guide. That doesn't mean worthwhile books on the subject don't exist, though. Simon Halkin published modernist narratives of immigrant life under the titles *Ye'hiel Ha-Hagri* [Yechiel the immigrant] (1928) and *Ad Mashber* [Until the crisis] (1929). Y. D. Berkowitz, Sholem Aleichem's son-in-law and Hebrew translator, wrote *Yemot Ha'Mashia* [In the days of the Messiah] (1937) in both Hebrew and Yiddish; it details the experiences of a group of American Jews traveling by sea to the Yishuv, the Jewish settlement in pre-independence Palestine. Reuben Wallenrod's Hebrew fiction about the American experience appeared in both novels—his first, *Ki Fanah Yom* [When day is set] (1946) takes place at a resort in the Catskills—and short stories, some of which are collected in *Bein Homot New York* [Inside the walls of New York] (1952). Samuel L. Blank also published relevant story collections, including *Bi'me'arbolet Ha'hayim* [In the whirlpool of life] (1954).

In addition to these mid-century works, younger Israeli authors have explored the close connections and frequency of relocation between their homeland and the United States, in more recent novels such as Razia Ben-Gurion's *Netishah* [Abandonment] (1987), Maya Arad's *Sheva Midot Ra'ot* [Seven moral failings] (2006), and Ayelet Ben-Ziv's *Ya'efet* [Jetlag] (2006). Assaf Gavron's *Moving* (2003), another contemporary example, features a few undocumented Israelis working as furniture movers in New York and is now being made into a film; its author has translated Jonathan Safran Foer's novels into Hebrew. David Ehrlich deals with life in the United States in a few of the stories in his *Ha-Bekarim shel Shelishi va Khamishi* [Tuesday and Thursday mornings] (1999) and *Kahol 18* [Blue 18] (2003), while the most popular of the younger generation of Israeli fiction writers, Etgar Keret, has also set a few of his stunning, imaginative short pieces in America. Some of these are available in English translation in his collections *The Bus Driver Who Wanted to Be God* (2004), *The Nimrod Flipout* (2006), and *The Girl on the Fridge* (2008).

C. Bibliographic Resources

The following bibliographies and historical surveys of American Jewish fiction and literature provide vast amounts of information on the subject. Some of them are specialized and expensive resources designed for librarians, and a few are nearly impossible to find these days; but they will be useful to readers searching for information on an author not discussed here, or for an alternatively organized overview of the field. Ask a local librarian if you are having trouble finding these works, which are listed here chronologically, oldest to newest.

David Philipson, *The Jew in English Fiction* (1918).

Joseph Mersand, *Tradition in American Literature: A Study of Jewish Characters and Authors* (1939).

Meyer Waxman, *A History of Jewish Literature* (volume 5, 1960).

Harold U. Ribalow, *120 American Jewish Novels* (1962).

Sol Liptzin, *The Jew in American Literature* (1966).

Sol Liptzin, *A History of Yiddish Literature* (1972).

Louis Harap, *The Image of the Jew in American Literature: From Early Republic to Mass Immigration* (1974).

Ira Nadel, *Jewish Writers of North America: A Guide to Information Sources* (1981).

Lewis Fried, Jules Chametzky, Gene Brown, and Louis Harap, *Handbook of American-Jewish Literature* (1988).

Gloria Cronin, *Jewish American Fiction Writers: An Annotated Bibliography* (1991).

Jules Chametzky, John Felstiner, Hilene Flanzbaum, and Kathryn Hellerstein, *Jewish American Literature: A Norton Anthology* (2001).

Hana Wirth-Nesher and Michael P. Kramer, *The Cambridge Companion to Jewish American Literature* (2003).

Rosalind Reisner, *Jewish American Literature: A Guide to Reading Interests* (2004).

Derek Parker Royal, "Contemporary Jewish American Narrative: A Selected Bibliography," *Shofar* 22:3 (spring 2004).

D. Anthologies

Give American Jews a printing press and, sooner or later, they'll give you back an anthology. It makes sense: Jews pray in a minyan, so why not publish 10—or 20, or 45—writers at once, too? Anthologies allow fields to be defined, authors to be celebrated, and readers to feel like they're getting a bargain, so they're a good deal for just about everybody involved. As it turns out, an interested reader can learn a lot about American Jewish fiction and its changing nature simply by sifting through anthologies from different decades—and by paying close, if skeptical, attention to the polemical statements that often serve as introductions to these collections. The following chronological list cannot claim to be completely comprehensive, but it offers a relatively large selection of American Jewish fiction anthologies, including some worthwhile anthologies that are more specialized as well as several that are broader in scope. Each includes at least a little American Jewish fiction.

Joseph Leftwich, *Yisroel: The First Jewish Omnibus* (1933).

Leo W. Schwarz, *The Jewish Caravan: Great Stories of Twenty-Five Centuries* (1935); reprinted with additions (1965).

Leo W. Schwarz, *A Golden Treasury of Jewish Literature* (1937).

Harold U. Ribalow, *This Land, These People* (1950).

Harold U. Ribalow, *These Your Children* (1952).

Leo W. Schwarz, *Feast of Leviathan: Tales of Adventure, Faith, and Love from Jewish Literature* (1956).

Harold U. Ribalow, *A Treasury of American Jewish Stories* (1958).

Harold U. Ribalow, *The Chosen* (1959).

Henry Goodman, *The New Country: Stories from the Yiddish about Life in America* (1961); abridged edition (2001).

Saul Bellow, *Great Jewish Short Stories* (1963).

Irving Malin and Irwin Stark, *Breakthrough: A Treasury of Contemporary American Jewish Literature* (1964).

Azriel Eisenberg, *The Golden Land: A Literary Portrait of American Jewry, 1654 to the Present* (1964).

Max Rosenfeld, *Pushcarts and Dreamers: Stories of Jewish Life in America* (1967).

Charles Angoff and Meyer Levin, *The Rise of American Jewish Literature: An Anthology of Selections from the Major Novels* (1970).

Irving Malin, *Contemporary American-Jewish Literature* (1973).

Abraham Chapman, *Jewish-American Literature: An Anthology of Fiction, Poetry, Autobiography, and Criticism* (1974).

Irving Howe, *Jewish American Stories* (1977).

Max Nadel, *Portraits of the American Jew: An Anthology of Short Stories by American Jewish Writers* (1977).

Julia Wolf Mazow, *The Woman Who Lost Her Names: Selected Writings by American Jewish Women* (1980).

Joyce Antler, *America and I: Short Stories by American Jewish Women Writers* (1991).

Ted Solotaroff and Nessa Rapoport, *Writing Our Way Home: Contemporary Stories by American Jewish Writers* (1992); reprinted as *The Schocken Book of Contemporary Jewish Fiction* (1996).

Gerald Shapiro, *American Jewish Fiction: A Century of Stories* (1998).

Hilda Raz, *The Prairie Schooner Anthology of Contemporary Jewish American Writing* (1998).

Ilan Stavans, *The Oxford Book of Jewish Stories* (1998).

Jules Chametzky, John Felstiner, Hilene Flanzbaum, and Kathryn Hellerstein, *Jewish American Literature: A Norton Anthology* (2001).

Paul Zakrzewski, *Lost Tribe: Jewish Fiction from the Edge* (2003).

Jerome Charyn, *Inside the Hornet's Head: An Anthology of Jewish American Writing* (2005).

Melvin Jules Bukiet and David Roskies, *Scribblers on the Roof* (2006).

E. American Jewish Literary Awards

Often ridiculous but usually well-intentioned, literary awards exist to promote and celebrate exceptional writing. At their best, these awards benefit just about everyone: authors receive a little cash and a plaque to hang in their studies; publishers paste a sticker on their paperbacks and garner extra sales for one of their books; readers discover a wonderful and deserving new work; and judges enjoy the exercise of their authority. Of course, even a cursory glance back at the winners of any of the world's most prestigious literary awards reveals that while they have sometimes gone to works of enduring value, the lists have also ignored the most deserving authors or books (Leo Tolstoy, for example, never received the Nobel Prize, even though he was eligible), and included winners who have quickly become obscure. Prizes can't be taken too seriously.

Still, American Jewish literary prizes—of which there have been many—offer us, at the very least, a list of books deemed by more or less qualified judges to be of interest. The lists here include all of the winners of the major prizes awarded by Jewish literary organizations based in the United States. Note that these prizes do not limit themselves to fiction by or about American Jews; they often include, for example, excellent works of Israeli literature in translation. (Note: Years in which awards were not given have been left off of the lists.)

National Jewish Book Award for Fiction

1949	Howard Fast	*My Glorious Brothers*
1950	John Hersey	*The Wall*
1951	Soma Morgenstern	*The Testament of the Lost Son*
1952	Zelda Popkin	*Quiet Street*
1953	Michael Blankfort	*The Juggler*
1954	Charles Angoff	*In the Morning Light*
1955	Louis Zara	*Blessed Is the Land*
1957	Leon Feuchtwanger	*Raquel: The Jewess of Toledo*
1958	Bernard Malamud	*The Assistant*
1959	Leon Uris	*Exodus*
1960	Philip Roth	*Goodbye, Columbus and Five Stories*
1961	Edward L. Wallant	*The Human Season*
1962	Samuel Yellen	*Wedding Band*
1963	Isaac Bashevis Singer	*The Slave*
1964	Joanne Greenberg	*The King's Persons*
1965	Elie Wiesel	*The Town beyond the Wall*
1966	Meyer Levin	*The Stronghold*
1967	Chaim Grade	*The Well*
1969	Charles Angoff	*Memory of Autumn*
1970	Leo Litwak	*Waiting for the News*
1972	Cynthia Ozick	*The Pagan Rabbi and Other Stories*
1973	Robert Kotlowitz	*Somewhere Else*

1974	Francine Prose	*Judah the Pious*
1975	Jean Karsavina	*White Eagle, Dark Skies*
1976	Johanna Kaplan	*Other People's Lives*
1977	Cynthia Ozick	*Bloodshed and Three Novellas*
1978	Chaim Grade	*The Yeshiva*
1979	Gloria Goldreich	*Leah's Journey*
1980	Daniel Fuchs	*The Apathetic Bookie Joint*
1981	Johanna Kaplan	*O My America!*
1982	Mark Helprin	*Ellis Island and Other Stories*
1983	Robert Greenfield	*The Temple*
1984	Arthur A. Cohen	*An Admirable Woman*
1985	Frederick Busch	*Invisible Mending*
1986	Arnost Luštig	*The Unloved: From the Diary of Perla S.*
1988	Philip Roth	*The Counterlife*
1989	Aharon Appelfeld	*The Immortal Barfuss*
1990	A. B. Yehoshua	*Five Seasons*
1991	Chaim Potok	*The Gift of Asher Lev*
1992	Nathan Shaham	*The Rosendorf Quartet*
1993	A. B. Yehoshua	*Mr. Mani*
1994	Alan Isler	*The Prince of West End Avenue*
1995	Rebecca Goldstein	*Mazel*
1996	Evan Zimroth	*Gangsters*
1997	Saul Bellow	*The Actual*
1998	Aharon Appelfeld	*The Iron Tracks*
1999	Steve Stern	*The Wedding Jester*
2000	Philip Roth	*The Human Stain*
2001	Jonathan Safran Foer	*Everything Is Illuminated*
2002–03	Gary Shteyngart	*The Russian Debutante's Handbook*
2002–03	Dara Horn	*In the Image*
2004	Marjorie Sandor	*Portrait of My Mother Who Posed Nude in Wartime*
2005	Michael Chabon	*The Final Solution*
2006	Dara Horn	*The World to Come*
2007	Meir Shalev	*A Boy and a Pigeon*

Edward Lewis Wallant Award

1963	Norman Fruchter	*Coat Upon a Stick*
1964	Seymour Epstein	*Leah*
1965	Hugh Nissenson	*A Pile of Stones*
1966	Gene Hurwitz	*Home Is Where You Start From*
1967	Chaim Potok	*The Chosen*
1969	Leo Litwak	*Waiting for the News*
1971	Cynthia Ozick	*The Pagan Rabbi and Other Stories*
1972	Robert Kotlowitz	*Somewhere Else*
1973	Arthur A. Cohen	*In the Days of Simon Stern*
1974	Susan Fromberg Schaeffer	*Anya*
1975	Anne Bernays	*Growing Up Rich*
1977	Curt Leviant	*The Yemenite Girl*
1980	Johanna Kaplan	*O My America!*
1981	Allen Hoffman	*Kagan's Superfecta*
1983	Francine Prose	*Hungry Hearts*
1985	Jay Neugeboren	*Before My Life Began*
1986	Daphne Merkin	*Enchantment*
1987	Steve Stern	*Lazar Malkin Enters Heaven*
1988	Tova Reich	*Master of the Return*
1989	Jerome Badanes	*The Final Opus of Leon Solomon*
1992	Melvin Jules Bukiet	*Stories of an Imaginary Childhood*
1993	Gerald Shapiro	*From Hunger*
1995	Rebecca Goldstein	*Mazel*
1996	Thane Rosenbaum	*Elijah Visible*
1997	Harvey Grossinger	*The Quarry*
1999	Allegra Goodman	*Kaaterskill Falls*
2000	Judy Budnitz	*If I Told You Once*
2001	Myla Goldberg	*Bee Season*
2003	Dara Horn	*In the Image*
2004	Joan Leegant	*An Hour in Paradise*
2005	Jonathan Rosen	*Joy Comes in the Morning*
2006	Nicole Krauss	*The History of Love*
2007	Ehud Havazelet	*Bearing the Body*

INDEX BY AUTHOR

INDEX BY TITLE

INDEX BY SUBJECT

201